Curriculum
THEORY

Curriculum
THEORY

Conflicting Visions and Enduring Concerns

Michael Stephen Schiro
Boston College

SAGE Publications
Los Angeles • London • New Delhi • Singapore

For information:

Sage Publications, Inc.
2455 Teller Road
Thousand Oaks, California 91320
E-mail: order@sagepub.com

Sage Publications Ltd.
1 Oliver's Yard
55 City Road
London EC1Y 1SP
United Kingdom

Sage Publications India Pvt. Ltd.
B 1/I 1 Mohan Cooperative Industrial Area
Mathura Road, New Delhi 110 044
India

Sage Publications Asia-Pacific Pte. Ltd.
33 Pekin Street #02-01
Far East Square
Singapore 048763

Printed in the United States of America

Library of Congress Cataloging-in-Publication Data

Schiro, Michael.
Curriculum theory: conflicting visions and enduring concerns/Michael S. Schiro.
    p. cm.
Includes bibliographical references and index.
ISBN 978-1-4129-5315-3 (cloth)
ISBN 978-1-4129-5316-0 (pbk.)

    1. Education—Curricula—Philosophy. 2. Education—Curricula—United States—Philosophy.
I. Title.

LB1570.S333 2008
375′.001—dc22   2007011265

This book is printed on acid-free paper.

07 08 09 10 11 10 9 8 7 6 5 4 3 2 1

Acquisitions Editor:	Diane McDaniel
Editorial Assistant:	Ashley Plummer
Production Editor:	Libby Larson
Copy Editor:	Rachel Keith
Typesetter:	C&M Digitals (P) Ltd.
Proofreader:	Theresa Kay
Indexer:	Michael Ferreira
Cover Designer:	Janet Foulger
Marketing Manager:	Nichole Angress

Contents

Extension Activities Available Online at www.sagepub.com/schiroextensionactivities

Additional Activities:

- Curriculum Ideologies Inventory
- Scope, Sequence, Integration, and Continuity Simulation
- Columbus and Knowledge Simulation
- Example of an Ideologies Play

Comments on Extension Activities for Faculty Teaching Courses on Curriculum

Preface

Intentions

Curriculum Theory: Conflicting Visions and Enduring Concerns is intended to help both experienced and pre-service educators understand the educational philosophies (or ideologies) they are likely to encounter in their everyday lives. To accomplish this, four visions of what curriculum should consist of are presented and analyzed in a way that will enable readers to reflect on their own educational beliefs.

Curriculum Theory goes beyond introducing educators to the conflicting visions of education that exist today. It considers those visions in the historical context in which they have developed over the last century—because concerns about education are not new, and we need to realize that many of today's new issues and "fads" are related to enduring educational concerns that have long been debated. This book also attempts to help educators understand how their own personal educational philosophies have been shaped during their lives and how their beliefs might evolve during the future span of their careers.

This book is not intended to introduce readers to advanced-level theoretical concerns of curriculum theorists, except as far as those concerns are embedded in the practical ideological viewpoints educators are likely to experience in their everyday lives.

Organization

Curriculum Theory: Conflicting Visions and Enduring Concerns is organized into an introductory chapter, four main chapters that examine each of the major curriculum ideologies, a chapter that compares the four ideologies, and a chapter that examines the ways in which debate over the ideologies influences the personal lives of individual educators over their life span. This organizational plan is illustrated in Figure 0.1.

Each of the four main chapters that examine a curriculum ideology is structured in the same way. Each chapter (1) opens with a brief overview of the ideology; (2) continues with a description of curricula that illustrate the ideology under discussion; (3) examines the ideology's educational vision, global assumptions, and conceptual framework while referencing descriptions of the curricula; (4) describes the historical evolution of the ideology over approximately the last hundred years; (5) examines in detail the ideology's aims, view of children, perspective on learning, concept of teaching, conception of knowledge, and beliefs about assessment; and (6) presents concluding perspectives on the ideology. This organizational plan is illustrated in Figure 0.2.

Ideologies are not compared in the chapters in which they are discussed. Each of the four main chapters provides readers with a sympathetic understanding of an

Figure 0.1   Organization of this book.

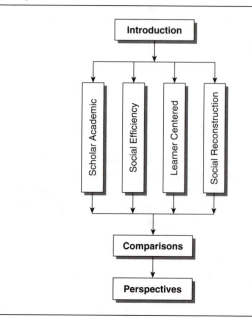

Figure 0.2   Typical organization of each main chapter.

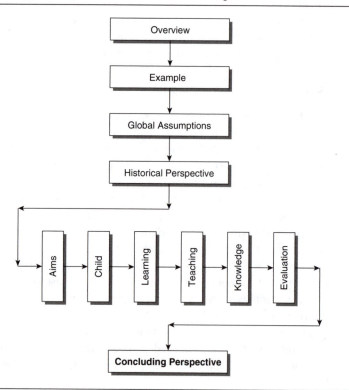

ideology from the perspective of educators who advocate that ideology, without reference to other ideologies. However, each ideology's underlying myths and assumptions are made clear, and the hidden meanings in its use of words such as *learning* and *knowledge* are closely examined—using critical analysis in the spirit of poststructuralism and postmodernism. The four ideologies are compared in a separate chapter designed to highlight their similarities and differences.

Readers are invited to visit www.sagepub.com/schiroextensionactivities, a Web site devoted to this book. There instructors will find ideas on how to use this book in teaching courses on curriculum. The extension activities on this site are designed to allow readers to personally confront, reflect on, and extend their knowledge of curriculum issues, as well as to experience current debates about education. These activities can be explored either alone or in the context of a class. For instance, debates require group participation, while examination of Web sites, movies, simulations, curriculum materials, and books and articles either can be pursued individually or can provide the substance for rich group discussions. There is no expectation that any reader will work through all of the extension activities related to a chapter, or that the activities must be done only at the time that a chapter is read.

Personal Perspective

I first encountered the four curriculum ideologies described in this book when I was teaching in public schools in the 1960s. I taught first in a high school, then in a middle school, and finally in an elementary school. I was under constant pressure in these schools to believe in and teach in accordance with several conflicting philosophical viewpoints. In addition, during the 1960s I saw curriculum developers create very different types of curricula and argue about which curriculum ideology should be the dominant one in schools.

Later, as a faculty member at Boston College during the 1970s, I witnessed faculty members' vigorous debate over whether we should orient our teacher education programs around the Scholar Academic or the Social Efficiency perspective. During the 1980s, the faculty argued over whether the Social Efficiency or the Learner Centered ideology should provide the underpinnings for our programs. During the 1990s, the debate was over whether the Learner Centered or the Social Reconstruction perspective should be our guiding light. Now, during the first years of the 21st century, we have "social justice" as our overarching educational theme at Boston College.

Over the last 40 years, I have observed that many educators either (a) hold the belief that their ideology is the only appropriate one for schools and that all other ideologies are enemies of education or (b) do not fully understand the nature of the debate over educational purposes and methods and as a result are buffeted about by each new educational issue and fad. Only rarely have I encountered educators who fully understand and appreciate the range of ideological perspectives available, the advantages and disadvantages of each, the implications of those perspectives for their teaching, and the possible impact of those ideologies on their own personal philosophies of education. Over the last 30 years I have attempted to help educators deal with these issues. This book is my attempt to help a larger audience struggle with philosophical issues I have seen many educators deal with on a daily basis.

Objectives of This Book

This book, like most books, is written with multiple goals in mind. Here are some of the major objectives of *Curriculum Theory: Conflicting Visions and Enduring Concerns*:

- To present readers with a clear, sympathetic, and unbiased perspective on the major curriculum philosophies (ideologies, viewpoints, or visions for schooling) that have influenced American educators and schooling over the last century. In so doing, this book will hopefully stimulate readers to better understand their own beliefs and also provide them with an understanding of alternate ways of thinking about the fundamental goals of education. Understanding one's own curriculum beliefs and the range of available ideological options can help educators more effectively clarify and shape their own curriculum goals and empower them to make themselves into the kinds of educators they want to be.

- To inform readers of the origins of these curriculum ideologies, the major advocates of these ideologies over the last century, the ways in which historical circumstances can influence educational thought, and the ways in which these ideologies have evolved over the last hundred years into their current form. In doing so, this book will place our current educational debates and issues in a historical context of enduring concerns.

- To provide readers with a model of how they can critically analyze educational movements (using a poststructuralist perspective) and the main currents of curriculum thought influencing American educational practice today. The model will demonstrate how to analyze and question one's thoughts and those of one's colleagues, official policies and agendas, and new curriculum fads promoted by politicians, textbook salesmen, school boards, curriculum consultants, and others attempting to influence schools. This should enable readers to more effectively contribute to the public debate about educational issues.

- To carefully examine the way educators use language based on their own frequently unspoken assumptions. For example, the word *knowledge* can mean understandings, skills, meanings, or values in different educational communities, and this book will highlight how these different meanings can profoundly influence educators' thought and instructional practice. It will also indicate the way in which language can influence how we think about educational issues, what roles we believe we are fulfilling when we instruct students or create curricula, and the power relationships we set in place among teachers and students. This should help readers better understand disagreements about curriculum that occur in schools, determine the ideologies and intentions of other educators, speak in the language of other educators while conveying their own meanings, and more effectively negotiate curriculum decisions with their colleagues, curriculum committees, school boards, and communities.

- To demonstrate how curriculum beliefs are related to instructional practice and to provide intellectual perspectives and tools that will facilitate translation of curriculum ideas into instructional practices.

- To highlight the complexities of curriculum work in a social context in which ideological struggles dominate current educational discourse and in which educators are constantly pressured to act in accordance with a variety of conflicting ideological perspectives. Having an understanding of the ideological pressures exerted by society and colleagues can help readers put those pressures in perspective and maintain their own values, beliefs, and practices.

- To illustrate how curriculum workers' philosophies can change over the span of their professional careers and how the communities they work in can influence their curriculum beliefs and practices. Hopefully this will enable readers to more easily accept changes in their own evolving curriculum beliefs and to pursue new curriculum initiatives.

Acknowledgments

I would like to thank the following people for reading the manuscript, providing me with valuable feedback, and helping me shape the book:

Rainy Cotti, Rhode Island College

Lawrence Lipsitz, Educational Technology Publications

Christina Wain, Boston College

I would also like to thank the following reviewers:

Alan Block, University of Wisconsin–Stout

Judith A. Boccia, University of Massachusetts Lowell

David N. Boote, University of Central Florida

Robert P. Green, Jr., Clemson University

Lars J. Helgeson, University of North Dakota

Lesia Lennex, Morehead State University

Corey R. Lock, University of North Carolina at Charlotte

Marc Mahlios, University of Kansas

J. Dan Marshall, Penn State University

R. D. Nordgren, Cleveland State University

Caroline R. Pryor, Southern Illinois University Edwardsville

William M. Reynolds, Georgia Southern University

C. Matt Seimears, Emporia State University

Ruth De C. Silva, University of North Texas

Introduction to the Curriculum Ideologies ❖

For almost a hundred years, educators have been at war with each other over what the nature of the American school curriculum should be. Underlying this war are four visions of what the school curriculum should look like. These visions are based on four curriculum ideologies—or curriculum philosophies—that advocate very different purposes for schooling and very different methods of achieving those respective purposes.

These four visions of schooling have both stimulated improvement in American schools and caused conflicts that have inhibited progress in the development of the school curriculum.

The competition between the four visions of education has stimulated advocates of each to develop increasingly powerful curricula, instructional methods, and research bases. The result is improved instruction for children.

The competition between the four visions of education has also made it difficult for educators and the general public to reach a consensus on the nature and purposes of the American school curriculum. Seemingly irresolvable disagreements include the reading controversies over whether it is more important to teach decoding (phonics) or comprehension (whole language), the mathematics disputes over whether it is more important to teach mathematical understanding or mathematics skills, and the history conflicts over whether it is more important to teach knowledge of the past or to build strategies for critically analyzing and reconstructing society in the future. These disputes have recently become so fierce that they have become known as the reading wars, the math wars, and the history wars. Inability to appreciate differences in vision for the school curriculum and reach a consensus about critical philosophical and pedagogical issues has made systematic improvement of the curriculum difficult.

Each of the four visions of curriculum embodies distinct beliefs about the type of knowledge that should be taught in schools, the inherent nature of children, what school learning consists of, how teachers should instruct children, and how children should be assessed. Each vision has its own value system, its own purposes of education, its own meanings for words (for example, does knowledge consist of understandings, skills, meanings, or values?), its own heroes whose beliefs it repeats, and its own villains whose beliefs it rails against.

Within this book, these visions are labeled the Scholar Academic ideology, the Social Efficiency ideology, the Learner Centered ideology, and the Social Reconstruction ideology. Each ideology has a long history and has been known by a variety of names. For example, at different times during the last hundred years the Learner Centered ideology has been called progressive education, open education, child-centered education, developmentally appropriate practice, and constructivism. These ideologies can influence people's ways of thinking about curriculum in the same powerful ways that their political beliefs can influence their stances on political issues.

The existence of these four ideologies causes difficulty for newcomers to the field, who are usually unaware of them and as a result often have difficulty determining how to philosophically orient themselves as subscribers to different ideologies pressure them for their allegiance. The existence of these four ideologies also causes concern among veteran teachers, who are frequently told by school administrators to embrace one curriculum fad after another—fads that often require major revision of the conceptual frameworks upon which teachers build their instruction. These curriculum philosophies frequently cause disagreement among curriculum workers, particularly curriculum developers, about what the nature of the curriculum they create and schools adopt should be. The competition among advocates of these four curriculum ideologies for influence on the school curriculum also causes concern—sometimes leading to the formation of political initiatives—among members of the general public who are interested in how their children and grandchildren are being educated, what goes on in our schools, and the ways in which schooling is influencing children's beliefs and social orientation. The best example of these political initiatives is perhaps the curriculum wars that took place in California between 1985 and 2000, during which two groups with competing ideologies had each other's favored curriculum programs removed from the list of state-funded curriculum materials and replaced by their own programs—after lengthy, well-publicized political battles (Becker & Jacob, 2000; Jackson, 1997a, 1997b; Pearson, 2004; Schoenfeld, 2004; Wilson, 2003).

The existence of these competing visions of what good education consists of and the corresponding lack of understanding regarding these visions among educators, curriculum workers, and the general public causes confusion and discomfort among Americans and within American education. As individuals, we are constantly disagreeing with each other—and with ourselves—about what we should be doing in our schools. As members of politically oriented groups, we lobby state departments of education over which textbooks or instructional programs should be used in our states. As a nation, we issue one prestigious report after another, many of them disagreeing with each other, about what the problems of American education are and how those problems should be solved.

As a country, we have enriched our school curriculum in many ways by drawing from the four ideologies. However, systematic improvement in our school curriculum has been difficult, for we have been unable to settle on a single ideological orientation or a negotiated compromise among ideological orientations, unable to set clear goals for our schools, and unable to pursue those goals with single-minded determination.

The confusion in American education that results from a lack of perspective on the four curriculum ideologies, ignorance about the nature of these four visions for education, and the continuing disagreement among educators and the general public over what the nature of the school curriculum should be disrupts the effectiveness of educators as individuals and our schools as organizations (of supposedly cohesive groups of people).

One purpose of this book is to provide readers a sympathetic perspective on these visions of schooling based on a comprehensive understanding of the four curriculum ideologies in the historical context in which they have existed over the last hundred years. Another purpose of this book is to give readers perspective on their own philosophies of education as they relate to the four curriculum ideologies that have had—and are currently having—a profound influence on American schools. This book first describes and analyzes each of the curriculum ideologies, then compares them, and finally discusses the complex ways in which they influence the lives of individual educators over the span of their careers.

Perspective on and understanding of these curriculum ideologies can have several benefits. First, when educators understand their own conceptual frameworks and the range of ideological options available to them, it can help them to more effectively clarify and accomplish their own curriculum and instructional goals. Second, when educators have perspective on and understand the range of philosophical beliefs that colleagues can hold, this can enable them to better understand the nature of curriculum disagreements that inevitably take place in schools, be more accepting of others, and more effectively work with people of differing opinions. Third, when educators understand the way in which language is used differently in each of the four ideologies, it can assist them in more effectively communicating and negotiating curriculum decisions with colleagues, curriculum committees, school boards, and their communities. Fourth, when educators have perspective on and understand the differences between the curriculum frameworks influencing the current public dialogue about education, it can facilitate their ability to more effectively contribute to the public debate about educational issues. Fifth, when educators have an understanding of the ideological pressures exerted on them by society and colleagues, this can help them put those pressures in perspective and minimize—as warranted—their influence (Cotti & Schiro, 2004).

Your Beliefs About Curriculum

This book is about both the nature of American education and the beliefs individuals have regarding the school curriculum. As a result, it is highly suggested that readers complete a short inventory that allows them to visually graph their curriculum beliefs. (The inventory and instructions for graphing its results are located in the Appendix.) I recommend that you complete the inventory now, before reading further, and again after you finish reading this book. The last chapter in this book discusses how and why educators change their curriculum ideologies over time. Seeing how your beliefs about curriculum change as you read this book will help you understand that chapter.

The Curriculum Ideologies

The Social Efficiency ideology, the Scholar Academic ideology, the Learner Centered ideology, and the Social Reconstruction ideology are the names given to the curriculum ideologies examined within this book.

The Scholar Academic Ideology

Scholar Academics believe that over the centuries our culture has accumulated important knowledge that has been organized into the academic disciplines found in universities. The purpose of education is to help children learn the accumulated knowledge of our culture: that of the academic disciplines. Acquiring an understanding of an academic discipline involves learning its content, conceptual frameworks, and ways of thinking. Teachers should be mini-scholars who have a deep understanding of their discipline and can clearly and accurately present it to children.

Scholar Academics assume that the academic disciplines, the world of the intellect, and the world of knowledge are loosely equivalent. The central task of education is taken to be the extension of the components of this equivalence, both on the cultural level, as reflected in the discovery of new truth, and on the individual level, as reflected in the enculturation of individuals into civilization's accumulated knowledge and ways of knowing.

An academic discipline is viewed as a hierarchical community of people in search of truth within one part of the universe of knowledge. The hierarchical communities consist of inquirers into the truth (the scholars at the top of the hierarchy), teachers of the truth (those who disseminate the truth that has been discovered by the scholars), and learners of the truth (students whose job it is to learn the truth so that they may become proficient members of the discipline).

The aim of education for Scholar Academics is the extension of their disciplines by introducing young people into them. This involves making youth members of a discipline by first moving them into it as students and then moving them from the bottom of the hierarchy toward its top. Extension of a discipline is accomplished through the transmission of its knowledge and ways of thinking to students. The curriculum provides the means of this transmission, and it derives both its meaning and its reason for existence from the academic disciplines. Scholar Academics' major concern is to construct a curriculum in such a way that it reflects the essence of their discipline.

The Social Efficiency Ideology

Social Efficiency advocates believe that the purpose of schooling is to efficiently meet the needs of society by training youth to function as future mature contributing members of society. Their goal is to train youth in the skills and procedures they will need in the workplace and at home to live productive lives and perpetuate the functioning of society.

Subscribers to the Social Efficiency ideology believe the essence of learners lies in their competencies and the activities they are capable of performing. Youth achieve an education by learning to perform the functions necessary for social productivity. Teachers manage instruction by selecting and using educational strategies designed to help learners acquire the behaviors prescribed by their curriculum. Instruction is guided by clearly defined behavioral objectives, and learners may require a lot of practice to gain and maintain mastery of skills.

Social Efficiency educators' first job is to determine the needs of society (or another more specialized client). The things that will fulfill these needs are called the terminal objectives of the curriculum. Educators must then find the most efficient way of producing a product—the educated person—who meets the terminal objectives of the curriculum and thus fulfills the needs of society (or the client).

Social Efficiency ideologists believe the most efficient achievement of a curriculum's terminal objectives results from applying the routines of scientific procedure to curriculum making. Central to Social Efficiency conceptions of scientific procedure is the assumption that change in human behavior (that is, learning) takes place within a fairly direct cause-effect, action-reaction, or stimulus-response context. This conception requires Social Efficiency educators to predetermine the relationships between cause and effect, action and reaction, and stimulus and response, and to predict the causes, actions, and stimuli (that is, the learning experiences) that will lead to the desired effects, reactions, and responses. Thus, three things that play an important role in the Social Efficiency ideology are the concept of learning (or change in human behavior), the creation and sequencing of learning experiences (the causes, actions, and stimuli which lead to the desired effects, reactions, and responses), and accountability to the client for whom educators work.

The Learner Centered Ideology

Learner Centered proponents focus not on the needs of society or the academic disciplines, but on the needs and concerns of individuals. They believe schools should be enjoyable places where people develop naturally according to their own innate natures. The goal of education is the growth of individuals, each in harmony with his or her own unique intellectual, social, emotional, and physical attributes.

Learner Centered educators believe people contain their own capabilities for growth, are the agents who must actualize their own capabilities, and are essentially good in nature. In addition, people are viewed as the source of content for the curriculum; their ends are considered to be the appropriate ends for the curriculum.

This leads Learner Centered advocates to treat the concept of growth as the central theme of their endeavors. Growth of learners in terms of their unfolding in conformity with the laws of their being becomes educators' objective. As a result, education involves drawing out the inherent capabilities of people. It is a facilitator of healthy, virtuous, and beneficial growth if what is drawn out is naturally coaxed out of people's innate abilities.

The potential for growth lies within people. However, people are stimulated to grow and construct meaning as a result of interacting with their physical, intellectual, and social environments. Learning is thus considered a function of the interaction between a person and his or her environment. Because individuals' interactions with their environment are assumed to be unique to the individual involved in the interaction, it is further assumed that the result of learning (the construction of meaning) is also unique to the individual.

Learner Centered curricula are thus thought of as contexts, environments, or units of work in which students can make meaning for themselves by interacting with other students, teachers, ideas, and things. It is the job of educators to carefully create those contexts, environments, or units of work, which will stimulate growth in people as they construct meaning (and thus learning and knowledge) for themselves.

The Social Reconstruction Ideology

Social Reconstructionists are conscious of the problems of our society and the injustices done to its members, such as those originating from racial, gender, social, and economic inequalities. They assume that the purpose of education is to facilitate the construction of a new and more just society that offers maximum satisfaction to all of its members.

Social Reconstructionists view curriculum from a social perspective. First, they assume that our current society is unhealthy. They believe its very survival is threatened. Second, they assume that something can be done to keep society from destroying itself. This involves developing a vision of a society that is better than the existing one, a society in which its problems and conflicts are resolved. Third, they assume that action must be directed toward reconstructing society along the lines suggested by the vision.

Social Reconstructionists assume that education is the social process through which society is reconstructed. They have faith in the ability of education, through the medium of curriculum, to teach people to understand their society in such a way that they can develop a vision of a better society and act to bring that vision into existence.

Because Social Reconstructionists view education from a social perspective, the nature of society as it *is* and as it *should be* become the determinants of most of their assumptions. They consider human experience to be shaped most powerfully by cultural factors—and assume that meaning in people's lives is determined by their social experiences. They believe that truth and knowledge are based in and defined by cultural assumptions.

As a result, Social Reconstructionists believe that there is no good individual, good education, truth, or knowledge apart from some conception of the nature of the good society. Since society is undergoing a crisis, it follows that the good person, the good education, truth, and knowledge are also undergoing a crisis. The aim of Social Reconstructionists is to rectify this situation by eliminating from their culture aspects that they consider undesirable, substituting in their place social values that they consider desirable, and by doing so to reconstruct their culture so that its members will attain maximum satisfaction of their material, spiritual, and intellectual wants.

Historical Perspective on the Ideologies

Each of the curriculum ideologies has a history. Recognition of the traditions out of which each grew gives an important sense of perspective. Although the origin and evolution of each ideology provides a fascinating study in itself, this book will concern itself with the ideologies only as they have existed since 1880. The Scholar Academic ideology will be examined by exploring the period of curriculum development that resulted from the work of Charles Eliot and the Committee of Ten in the 1890s, the "new curriculum" movement of the 1960s, and E. D. Hirsch's cultural literacy movement at the end of the 20th century. The nature of the Social Efficiency ideology will be explored by examining the tradition linking Franklin Bobbitt, Ralph Tyler, and the No Child Left Behind Act. Tracing the evolution of the Learner Centered ideology will lead us to an examination of the continuity of belief uniting the work of Francis Parker in the 19th century, the progressive education movement in the first half of the 20th century, and the open education, developmentally appropriate practice, and constructivist movements of the last 40 years. Examination of the Social Reconstruction ideology will include an investigation of the tradition, publicly initiated by George Counts, that has evolved into the present social justice movement. My intent is to help readers understand the ideologies within the richness of the traditions out of which they grew rather than view them solely as they are presently manifested.

Curriculum Workers

People who work on curriculum engage in many different types of endeavors. The ideologies elaborated in this book are relevant to the endeavors of the following curriculum workers.

Curriculum practitioners use curricula within the instructional arena and supervise its use in schools. Classroom teachers who plan instruction using social studies textbooks, implement a reading program, or derive a science program from curriculum ideas offered on a Web site are curriculum practitioners. School administrators who make curriculum adjustments to meet state or national curriculum standards, implement team teaching, encourage teachers to utilize a particular instructional methodology, or insist on the use of a particular textbook series are also curriculum practitioners.

Curriculum disseminators make known to curriculum practitioners the existence of curricula and the proper methods of using them. A curriculum disseminator might be a textbook salesperson, a school district subject matter specialist, a college professor offering a methods course, or a workshop leader for a publishing company or professional organization (such as the National Council of Teachers of Mathematics).

Curriculum evaluators collect, examine, and assess data for the purpose of reporting on the effectiveness, efficiency, and worth of the endeavors and creations of other curriculum workers. Curriculum evaluators might be employed by a private testing service, the central administration of a school district, a government-monitoring agency, a publishing company, or a curriculum development group. Their reports are meant to aid in decision making concerning curriculum materials, student achievement, teacher effectiveness, and school accountability.

Curriculum advocates are educators and members of the general public who are concerned about and attempt to influence what is taught in schools and how it is taught. A curriculum advocate might be a parent attempting to influence the curriculum decisions of his child's school, a citizen trying to influence the curriculum decisions of the state department of education, or a politician (perhaps a president, governor, or legislator) attempting to implement her curriculum ideas through the political process.

Curriculum developers intentionally create curriculum materials and strategies for others to use in the instructional arena. The important ideas here are "for others to use" and "instructional." Curriculum developers can be textbook writers, teachers who work on school curriculum committees, curriculum specialists who work for private educational organizations, or concerned citizens who design instructional materials for homeschooling.

Curriculum theorists examine the philosophical and ideological underpinnings of existing curricula; study how curricula are used, disseminated, created, and evaluated; study the endeavors and intents of other curriculum workers; speculate on what curricula should accomplish; probe the "whys" of their own examinations; and write books such as this one, all for the purpose of contributing to the general body of knowledge about effective curriculum practice, dissemination, advocacy, development, and evaluation.

This book is about the ideological stances of all of these types of curriculum workers. However, the curriculum ideologies described in this book can often be best observed in the programmatic intents and endeavors of people as they engage in the process of curriculum creation (or the planning of instruction). As a result, this book will frequently focus on the endeavors of curriculum developers as though they typify and represent the curriculum ideologies of a much broader spectrum of curriculum workers. Thus, discussion of the beliefs of curriculum workers in general will often be intertwined with descriptions of the particular endeavors of curriculum developers.

The Nature of the Curriculum Ideologies

In this book, the curriculum visions, philosophies, doctrines, opinions, conceptual frameworks, and belief systems of educators are called *curriculum ideologies.*

An *ideology* is a collection of ideas, a comprehensive vision, a way of looking at things, or a worldview that embodies the way a person or a group of people believes the world should be organized and function. It is "a certain ethical set of ideals, principles, doctrines, myths or symbols of a social movement, institution, class, or large group that explains how society should work, and offer some political and cultural blueprint for a certain social order" (Wikipedia, n.d., ¶ 1). The word is also used to describe

> how cultures [or subcultures] are structured in ways that enable the group holding power to have the maximum control with the minimum of conflict. This is not a matter of groups deliberately planning to oppress people or alter their consciousness . . . , but rather a matter of how . . . institutions in society work through values, conceptions of the world, and symbol systems, in order to legitimize the current order. Briefly, this legitimization is managed through the widespread teaching . . . of ideas about the way things are, how the world "really" works and should work. These ideas (often embedded in symbols and cultural practices) orient people's thinking in such a way that they accept the current way of doing things, the current sense of what is "natural," and the current understanding of their roles in society. This socialization process, the shaping of our cognitive and affective interpretations of our social world . . . is carried out . . . by the churches, the schools, the family, and through cultural forms. (Lye, 1997, ¶ 1)

Note, from this description, that ideologies carry cultural impulses to dominate rival ideologies and control aspects of their culture (in our case, education). Note also that they replicate themselves by educating (socializing, indoctrinating, acculturating) people to their beliefs by subtly attempting to "orient people's thinking in such a way that they accept" the ideology's view of the way things should be done, the ideology's sense of what is natural, and the ideology's position on roles in society.

The consequence of this in our culture, in which adherents of four curriculum ideologies vie for control over our educational system, is that proponents of each ideology attempt to convert other people to their viewpoint as they assert that their educational perspective is the only proper, natural, and acceptable way of viewing the field. These attempts result in constant pressure on teachers, educators, and members of the general public to accept one ideology and reject the others. It is as though four great magnets tug on all of us who are interested in education, pulling us in four different directions. This has led to an ideological war in the U.S. that is being fought on two fronts: the educational establishment and the minds and spirits of every American concerned with what is happening in our educational system. This is not the way things have to be. Certain cultures have allowed one ideology to completely dominate the others, and other cultures have found a way to get the ideologies to cooperate rather than compete with each other. But in America, at the beginning of the 21st century, believers in each ideology view every person as a fellow member, a possible convert, or an enemy. Therefore, educators and members of the general public who have committed to one ideology feel comfortable and secure that their worldview is the best one, while those who have not committed to one ideology feel constantly torn between rival viewpoints. For those who do not have an understanding of the available alternatives, this frequently leads to feelings of either self-righteousness or insecurity and confusion.

There are two major reasons I use the phrase *curriculum ideology* in this book. One relates to my choice of the word *ideology* rather than the more common term *philosophy*. *Ideology* is used to distinguish between motives that underlie behavior and articulated beliefs. This book is concerned about the former and not the latter. The problem addressed by this distinction is that expressed intent (or philosophy) is frequently contradicted by actual behavior. Educators dealing with curriculum are often not conscious of the major assumptions underlying their actions, just as adherents of many political groups are often not conscious of the motives and impulses that drive them to act within the approved modes of behavior sanctioned by their political group. A distinction needs to be made between the visions, myths, doctrines, opinions, worldviews, and belief systems motivating curriculum workers to behave as they do and the *verbalizations* that curriculum workers make. Thus, I use the word *ideology*.

The other reason behind my use of the phrase *curriculum ideology* relates to my choice of the word *curriculum*. It is necessary to distinguish between the curriculum domain, the instructional domain, the epistemological domain, the learning theory domain, the psychoanalytic domain, the developmental domain, and so on, when discussing the endeavors of persons interested in curriculum. This is because people often behave differently when working within these different areas of discourse, just as teachers often relate differently to their own children and to their students. A person often behaves differently when acting on (or thinking about) curriculum issues from how he or she acts (or thinks) as a psychologist, parent, philosopher, or epistemologist. The conceptual systems people use are often tied to the role in which they see themselves functioning. For example, educators often behave differently and use different conceptual frameworks when they plan instruction and deal with curriculum issues versus when they execute instruction and interact with children. Thus, *curriculum ideologies* refer to people's endeavors while they engage in curriculum activity or think about curriculum issues. Curriculum ideologies do not refer to all belief systems of people, or even to all belief systems related to education.

The description of the ideologies presented in this book emerged from an analysis of the actions and beliefs of American educators (particularly curriculum developers) regarding curriculum during the 20th century. This framework for examining teacher beliefs is supported by the professional literature on curriculum positions in the U.S. Table 1.1 shows the alignment of the classification schemes of nine recent curriculum theorists. Almost all theorists have identified positions similar to the Scholar Academic, Social Efficiency, Learner Centered, and Social Reconstruction positions. Two schemes do not identify the Social Reconstruction position; however, this is not surprising, because Social Reconstruction just reemerged as a distinct position in about 1990. For example, in 1986 and 1987, Schubert distinguished only three positions, while in 1996 he revised his classification scheme to include four positions. Only one scheme does not identify the Social Efficiency position. Four schemes distinguish two positions where other schemes identify only one position. Note also that even though the terms used to label positions may differ, the underlying positions are the

❖ **Table 1.1**   Comparison of curriculum classification schemes.

Schiro (2008)	Eisner (1974)	McNeil (1977)	Schubert (1996)	Fenstermacher & Soltis (1992)	Posner (1992)	Zeichner (1993)	Joseph et al. (2000)	Ellis (2004)	Kliebard (2004)
scholar academic	academic rationalism	academic	intellectual traditionalist	liberationist	traditional & structure of the disciplines	academic	constructing understanding & connecting to the cannon	knowledge centered	humanist
social efficiency	technology & cognitive processes	technological	social behaviorist	executive	behavioral	social efficiency	training for work and survival		social efficiency
learner centered	self actualization	humanist	experientialist	therapist	experiential & cognitive	developmentalist	developing self and spirit	progressive & learner centered	child study
social reconstruction	social reconstructionism	social reconstructionist	critical reconstructionist			social reconstructionist	confronting the dominant order & deliberating democracy	society centered	social-meliorist

same. Terminology has frequently changed over the last century. For example, different labels for the Learner Centered ideology in the U.S. have included child study (1890s), progressive education (1910–1950), open education (1965–1980), developmentalist (1970–1990), and constructivist (1990–present).

Two kinds of classificatory systems are useful in illuminating the differences among educators (and members of the general public) who are interested in curriculum. These systems are depicted in Figure 1.1. One classificatory system is designed to map out the entire population of educators into a finite set of disjoint categories into which any person can be uniquely classified. Figure 1.1a portrays this kind of classificatory system, in which the entire population of educators is divided into four separate categories—SE, SA, LC, and SR. Here, it is assumed that there is a great deal of uniformity within each category as well as a great amount of difference between categories. This kind of classificatory system is not useful in distinguishing between curriculum ideologies. A classificatory system of ideal types that portrays a finite number of positions representing the range of practices utilized by educators is more useful. Figure 1.1b portrays this kind of classificatory system, which consists of four ideal types—the four curriculum ideologies—that provide exemplars of the essence of the four distinct curriculum worldviews of educators. Each ideal type is an archetype that portrays an idealized model of a particular view of curriculum, with the individual practices and beliefs engaged in by educators being approximations of the ideal types. In Figure 1.1b, educators (and members of the general public) interested in curriculum cluster around the ideal types without having to behave exactly in accordance with them—their distance from an ideal type in a particular direction being an indicator of both how and how much they differ from that ideal type.

The four ideologies presented in this book—the ideal types—have been chosen because they represent the current range of beliefs among those interested in curriculum, because each has clearly identifiable roots in and influences on American education,

❖ **Figure 1.1**   Classificatory systems.

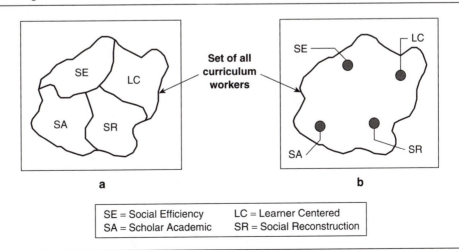

SE = Social Efficiency   LC = Learner Centered
SA = Scholar Academic   SR = Social Reconstruction

because they offer dramatic alternatives to each other, and because they seem to be prototypes around which educators cluster—the density of the set of all educators in Figure 1.1b being highest around ideal types SE, SA, LC, and SR. Because the curriculum ideologies represent ideal types abstracted from reality, and not reality itself, even though educators will be spoken of as believing or behaving in accordance with certain beliefs, it is difficult to find educators who exactly fit the characterizations; and even though the expressed thoughts and observable behavior of most educators approximate the characteristics of only one of the ideal types, many educators exist whose behavior is a combination of the characteristics of more than one ideal type.

Activities that extend the ideas in this chapter and book are located on the Sage Web site at www.sagepub.com/schiroextensionactivities.

2

Scholar Academic Ideology

❖

Curriculum workers who use the Scholar Academic ideology view the formal education that takes place in schools as a process of acculturating children into society in such a way that they become good citizens. This involves teaching children "the basic information needed to thrive in the modern world" as a culturally literate adult (Hirsch, 1987, p. xiii). This "basic information" consists of the shared knowledge acquired by educated adults within society. This shared knowledge includes the background knowledge that literate adults use to understand each other and events within their world, as well as "the shared attitudes and conventions that color" their understanding of human interactions and events (pp. 14–15). This shared knowledge of culturally literate adults is viewed as having been collected by and residing within the academic disciplines found within colleges and universities. The academic disciplines have names like history, physics, and mathematics. They represent the different areas of study found in most institutions of higher education and include the knowledge base associated with each area of study. It is the knowledge—"the information, attitudes, and assumptions"—of the academic disciplines that forms the content of the school curriculum (p. 127). In addition, when creating curriculum, Scholar Academic workers assume the perspective of those who are knowledgeable about the discipline and act as though they are members of a discipline.

Scholar Academic Curricula

Two curriculum development endeavors that flourished between 1950 and 1975 provide examples of the essence of the Scholar Academic ideology.

UICSM and SMSG School Mathematics

In 1951, Max Beberman formed the University of Illinois Committee on School Mathematics (UICSM). UICSM was formed for a number of reasons: because it was discovered during World War II that many Americans had a very poor understanding of mathematics; because university faculty felt that incoming college freshmen were poorly prepared to study college mathematics, engineering, and science; because the content of school mathematics was outdated and included little mathematics developed after 1800; and because the content of school mathematics seldom focused on mathematical ideas that university academicians considered important. The last two reasons need to be viewed from the perspective that mathematicians redeveloped the field of mathematics between 1800 and 1950, and that they were excited about and proud of their "new math" that contained both new foundational content (such as set theory) and new ways of thinking about mathematics (such as rigorous proof based on a few underlying assumptions that relate a large number of associated ideas).

Max Beberman was a mathematics educator who was excited about the new math and wanted to give schoolchildren a chance to learn what mathematicians had recently discovered. He wanted the school mathematics curriculum to reflect the essence of modern day mathematics. He was sure children could learn the foundational content of the new math, such as set theory. He was also sure children could learn to rigorously prove mathematical statements the same way mathematicians did—they would just have to prove easier things.

Beberman went to professional academic mathematics to find out what the content of the new-math curriculum should be. Mathematicians told educators what mathematics the curriculum should contain. Educators then figured out how to make that mathematics teachable and learnable.

UICSM developed secondary school textbooks that both (a) included new mathematical ideas that mathematicians thought were important and (b) required high school students to prove mathematical statements in the ways university-based academic mathematicians did.

Beginning in 1958, the work of UICSM was carried down to the elementary school level when Edward Begle started the School Mathematics Study Group (SMSG). After the USSR launched the first space satellite (Sputnik) in 1957, the National Science Foundation (NSF) generously funded SMSG, because Americans became terrified that Russian space superiority might threaten the national security, prosperity, and international influence of the U.S. (The terror resulting from the launch of Sputnik and the federal government's response of increasing spending on education and beginning new educational initiatives was similar to what happened after the terrorist attacks of September 11, 2001.)

SMSG developed textbook prototypes that included ideas mathematicians thought important. For example, set theory became one of the major ideas introduced to primary school children in the new SMSG curriculum. Previously, set theory had been taught only to mathematics university students. The new SMSG mathematics curriculum also required elementary school students to prove mathematical statements in the same way mathematicians might. For example, elementary school students now used the associative, distributive, and commutative principles to prove mathematical statements.

The phrase "the new math" was coined to describe the mathematical content and thinking processes UICSM and SMSG included in their curricula as well as the ideas and ways of thinking mathematicians had developed over the previous 150 years.

If we were to look into a fourth-grade classroom to see how this new math was being taught in 1965, this is what we might see. We might see a teacher at the front of the room presenting students with a lecture on "if-then" thinking, after which she has her students, sitting at their seats, do a set of problems from their textbook, such as "If n + 6 = 17, then n =   ." A few days later, this lesson is followed by a lecture on sets, unions, and intersections. Then students do a page of exercises in which they use the concepts of set, union, and intersection to complete problems involving hypothetical (if-then) thinking (SMSG, 1962, pp. 327–339). While presenting her lectures on hypothetical thinking and set theory, the teacher emphasizes that students should be very excited, because they are studying in the fourth grade topics that she did not understand until just recently and that prior to a few years before only mathematics majors at universities studied.

A few days later, in this same fourth-grade class, we would see the teacher giving a lecture on the distributive property of multiplication to her students, in which she presents a proof for why 7 x 20 = 140. The proof looks like this:

$$7 \times 20 = 7 \times (10 + 10) \qquad \text{Rename 20 as (10+10)}$$
$$= (7 \times 10) + (7 \times 10) \qquad \text{Distribute 7 over } (10 + 10)$$
$$= 70 + 70 \qquad \text{Multiply 7 and 10}$$
$$= 140 \qquad \text{Add 70 and 70 (SMSG, 1962, p. 346)}$$

During her lecture, the teacher excitedly emphasizes that in doing proofs like this students are learning to think like mathematicians, and that they should feel privileged to have the chance to learn to think like mathematicians in the fourth grade, because when she went through school she was not given a chance to think like this until much later in her education. After the teacher's presentation, the fourth-graders complete exercises in their textbook in which they do problems similar to the one the teacher provided as an example and write out each step in the manner she demonstrated (SMSG, 1962, p. 347).

Man: A Course of Study

Man: A Course of Study (MACOS) is a social studies curriculum project that was funded by the NSF between 1963 and 1970. Its intent was to revitalize the teaching of social studies in Grades 5 and 6 by introducing children to the essence of the social science disciplines of anthropology, ethnography, and social psychology (Education Development Center, 1968).

Major social science scholars, including Jerome Bruner, Irven DeVore, Nickolass Tinbergen, and Asen Balikci, helped create MACOS, designing their curriculum to reflect the knowledge base, research findings, and styles of intellectual inquiry of anthropology, ethnography, and social psychology. They constructed their curriculum so that children could explore the same questions scholars in these fields ask, using the same research methods scholars use. The major question MACOS explores is, what is human about human beings?

Children explore human nature by studying salmon, herring gulls (Tinbergen), baboons (DeVore), and Netsilik Eskimos (Balikci). MACOS did not produce a textbook. Instead, it produced a wide array of exciting instructional materials, including films, booklets, sound recordings, and instructional games.

MACOS contained many unnarrated films that presented raw data about salmon, herring gulls, baboons, and Netsilik Eskimos. Children did not just passively watch these movies, but they were to actively engage in observation, constructing hypotheses, and discussing what they observed. Many films were dramatic and showed such things as a Netsilik Eskimo child stoning a seagull to death and his family celebrating his first kill that contributed to his family's food supply (which raised questions of how we get our food and the types of initiation rituals different cultures contain).

MACOS produced many small student booklets that presented knowledge about such things as innate versus learned behavior, natural selection, life cycles, and communication. Children read the booklets as though they were research reports so they could talk in the way that social scientists might about the films they watched. For example, children read and discussed the booklet *Selections From Field Notes, 1959, March-August, Irven DeVore, Anthropologist,* which presented actual field notes recorded by DeVore as he observed baboons' behavior in their natural environment. They read *Field Notes* so that they could both discuss topics and think in ways similar to DeVore when he used field notes, and take notes about films they watched on baboon behavior in the same way that an anthropologist might.

The program contained academic games so that children could put themselves in the roles of people they studied and ask questions that compared the experiences of those people to their own experiences. (For instance, children played a seal hunting game while studying movies of Eskimos hunting, killing, and eating seals.) The program also contained sound recordings, such as those of baboons, which raised questions about communication among baboons and humans. And MACOS contained many stories, plays, and songs of the Netsilik (such as *The True Play of How Itimagnart Got Kingnak: The Girl He Really Wanted*) so that children could compare the messages of Netsilik culture about such things as love and death to the teachings of their own culture.

Since most elementary school teachers during the 1960s and 1970s had not studied anthropology, ethnography, and social psychology in any depth during college, MACOS contained a teacher education program designed to help elementary school teachers understand the knowledge base, research findings, and styles of intellectual inquiry of these academic disciplines. The teacher training program consisted of intensive summer workshops, in-service workshops, and a telephone hotline (which teachers could call to ask questions of scholars about anthropology, ethnography, or social psychology and of educators about how to handle difficult pedagogical issues that arose as they were teaching).

If we were to look into a sixth-grade class to see how MACOS was being taught in 1970, this is what we might see. We might see a teacher leading a discussion with her class about a booklet they are reading that contains DeVore's field notes. The discussion centers on how an anthropologist observes animal behavior, records it, and then learns from his observations and recordings, and by inference how the students in the class are to observe baboon behavior, record what they observe, and learn from their observations by following DeVore's model. Later the class reads a booklet called *The Baboon Troop,* in which issues related to the ideas of living in groups, dominance, and affectional bonds are introduced. The class then watches a film called *The Baboon Troop,* which contains only the sounds of nature without any voice overlays, during which students take "field notes" in the same way DeVore did. The teacher then leads a class discussion in which the following types of questions are raised and in which students answer based on their observations from the film and the "field notes" they took during the film: "What is the advantage to baboons of living in troops?" (Education Development Center, 1968, p. 32). "What problems would a lone baboon have?" (p. 66). "If baboons are aggressive animals, what keeps them from fighting each other?" (p. 35). What types of "affectional bonds" exist between the baboons? (p. 32). After each question is discussed with respect to baboons, the teacher raises related questions about humans: "What would you find hardest about living alone? What advantages are there for humans living in groups? . . . What kinds of things do children argue about? Why do some arguments not turn into fights?" (p. 66). How do people show affection toward each other? What are some of the advantages of having friends?

We will now examine why these curricula are examples of Scholar Academic endeavors and how they relate to current day educational activities.

Curriculum and the Disciplines

Curriculum workers who use the Scholar Academic ideology view curriculum creation from the perspective of the academic disciplines. The induction of the child into an academic discipline—each discipline representing one component of literate culture—is the goal of each of their curricula. Scholar Academics create curricula by working within the domains of their academic disciplines as though they are functionaries of their disciplines. They attempt to make each curriculum an epitome of its parent discipline. The following statement by Whitefield gives the flavor of the way in which Scholar Academics, and the creators of UICSM, SMSG, and MACOS, see the world through the eyes of an academic discipline:

> Initiation into the disciplines of knowledge, our vehicle for becoming fully human, is the worthwhile activity for the curriculum of general education. It provides the base upon which the person as a person can develop to realize his full stature as a free mind and as a citizen. All this is not to imply that the individual and society are not important, but they become, temporarily at least, secondary, as we endeavor to establish a framework . . . for selecting kinds of learning experiences which will inculcate knowledge and abilities of most worth. The curriculum must therefore draw upon analyses of the nature of knowledge and the inherent human abilities it develops in order to determine its nature, prior to analyses of society, the learner, and the learning process. The last three will at least add very useful glosses to the framework, but should not determine it. . . . We should therefore ground our curricular objectives in the distinctive disciplines of knowledge, rather than in social needs, theories of personality, or in a national base knowledge for "living in the modern world." For it is the disciplines themselves which predetermine these important factors, as well as our underlying ethical conception of what is good and what is worthwhile. (1971, p. 12)

The meaning of some of the phrases within this statement will now be examined.

Initiation Into the Disciplines

Initiation of children into the disciplines of knowledge is the underlying motive of educators working within the Scholar Academic ideology. This entails introducing children into both the knowledge base of a discipline and the ways in which academicians within the discipline think, feel, and communicate. On one hand, this involves, as Whitefield says, *initiating* children into an academic discipline at the level at which it is being taught—for example, helping 10-year-old children understand and behave as 10-year-old novice mathematicians (SMSG) or anthropologists (MACOS). On the other hand, it involves acculturating (or inducting) children into an academic discipline in such a way that when they grow up they will (if they have the potential and desire) become active members of that discipline—for example, preparing a 10-year-old child to become a chemist, linguist, or historian.

What is crucial here is that Scholar Academic developers create curriculum so that children who encounter it will learn to think and behave the same way university academicians do. This involves more than simply creating an educational program designed to inform children about an academic discipline. The curriculum is intended to initiate and acculturate children *into* a discipline, not merely to inform them *about* a discipline. Scholar Academics try to create curriculum in such a way that, for example, "the schoolboy learning physics *is* a physicist," performing the same types of intellectual activity the professional physicist performs (Bruner, 1960, p. 14). This means that the curriculum must convey more than just the knowledge of an academic discipline. It must also convey such things as the academician's ways of thinking and feeling. This was crucial to the curricula described at the beginning of this chapter, as Jerome Bruner hinted in 1966 when he wrote about projects such as SMSG and MACOS:

> A body of knowledge, enshrined in a university faculty and embodied in a series of authoritative volumes, is the result of much prior intellectual activity. To instruct someone in these disciplines is not a matter of getting him to commit results to mind. Rather, it is to teach him to participate in the process that makes possible the establishment of knowledge. We teach a subject not to produce little living libraries on that subject, but, rather, to get a student to think mathematically for himself, to consider matters as an historian does, to take part in the process of knowledge-getting. (p. 72)

Curricula created by Scholar Academics do not embody just a back-to-the-basics, get-tough, content-oriented approach to education. To think of them as such is to misunderstand the educators' endeavors, which are directed toward translating a discipline into experiences that acculturate children into the discipline by both teaching them the discipline's knowledge and enabling them to think, behave, and feel as members of the discipline.

Grounding Curriculum in a Discipline

In grounding curriculum in a distinct academic discipline, Scholar Academics attempt to construct curriculum so that it becomes a reflection of, or epitome of, the academic discipline. The following description of the efforts of Scholar Academic curriculum developers, such as those presented earlier in this chapter, illustrates this:

> When one talks with the initiators of such projects, particularly at the beginning of their efforts, one finds that they do not begin by talking about the manner in which they would

like to change pupils' behavior. Rather they are dissatisfied with existing curricula in their respective subject fields, and they want to build something new. If pressed, they might indicate that existing programs stress concepts considered trivial by those who practice the discipline. They might also say that the curriculum poorly reflects styles of intellectual inquiry in the various fields. Press them further, and they might say that they want to build a new program that more accurately displays the "essence" of history, or physics, or economics or whatever. Or a program that better transmits a comprehension of the elaborate and elegant interconnections among various concepts within the discipline. (Atkin, 1968, pp. 28–29)

Developers conceive of their curricula as embodying a portion of a discipline. They construct curricula so that they will reflect the nature of a discipline in such a way that students coming in contact with the curricula will be exposed to the essence of the disciplines themselves.

Drawing Upon the Discipline's Knowledge

In formulating the substance of their curricula, Scholar Academics "draw upon analyses of the nature of knowledge" within a discipline (as Whitefield says). In doing so, they focus solely on what they perceive to be the intrinsic nature of the discipline. King and Brownell, in *The Curriculum and the Disciplines of Knowledge*, emphasized this in 1966 when describing programs such as SMSG and MACOS:

> We can summarize the first task of any curriculum planning group, committee, or person as the definition of the nature of the discipline of which the course or courses is a part. The task can be accomplished by (1) establishing the most characteristic view and the range of views of man and nature held by the members of the discipline; (2) describing the mode of inquiry, skills, and rules for truth used by the discoursers; (3) identifying the domain of the discipline and the aspect or perspective characteristic of it; (4) determining the key concepts of the discipline; (5) characterizing the substratum languages and the particular terminology and notation of the discipline; (6) noting the linguistic heritage and communications network of the discipline; (7) setting forth the tradition and history of the idea of the discipline; and (8) explicating the instructive character of the discipline. (pp. 187–188)*

As such, the initial endeavors during curriculum construction are grounded in an academic discipline. The intent is for curricula to become re-presentations of what is already known and accepted as authoritative within their disciplines. In designing curricula, "one of the first jobs of the curriculum maker, [is] namely to study the discipline in a detail and manner which will allow him to characterize the variety of forms of knowledge of the discipline" (Connelly, 1964, p. 111). Many educators working in schools have neither the resources nor the training to do this. Instead, in designing their curricula, they consult textbooks, memories of courses taken during their academic training, or other artifacts of an academic discipline accessible to them. For example, Harvard Project Physics began when

---

*From *The Curriculum and the Disciplines of Knowledge* by King, A. R., & Brownell, J. A., copyright © 1966. Reprinted with permission from Arthur R. King, Jr.

Dr. F. James Rutherford, an experienced high school science teacher and administrator in California, undertook the preparation of a trial draft of a new course text, based on a widely used college textbook, *Introduction to Concepts and Theories in Physical Science,* by Gerald Holton, Professor of Physics at Harvard University. (Harvard Project Physics, 1969, p. 5)

Whether a curriculum is designed by a scholar who has firsthand knowledge of a discipline or by an educator who must rely on secondary resources, its origins lie outside the curriculum development process. The origins of Scholar Academic curricula lie within their respective academic disciplines, and the developer's first task is to consult and gain an understanding of the discipline that the curriculum is to elaborate. It is not the job of a developer to generate new academic knowledge for use in a curriculum. The goal of the developer, as curriculum developer, is not to engage in basic research. Rather, the developer's job is to consult existing knowledge that has been sanctioned by an academic discipline. Knowledge must be accepted by a discipline before it can be used as curriculum content.

Priorities

Focusing solely on existing elaborations of an academic discipline while formulating the essence of a curriculum means that curriculum concerns other than those embodied within the discipline itself are excluded from contributing to the development of the essence of the curriculum. It means that the essence of the curriculum is formulated (as Whitefield says) "prior to analyses of society, the learner, and the learning process." In other words:

My thesis, briefly, is that *all* curriculum content should be drawn from the disciplines, or, to put it another way, that *only* knowledge contained in the disciplines is appropriate to the curriculum. . . . This means that psychological needs, social problems, and any of a variety of patterns of material based on other than discipline content are not appropriate to the determination of what is taught. (Phenix, 1962, pp. 57–58)

Scholar Academics make "subject matter," which they conceive to be the essence of the academic disciplines, their central concern while creating curricula. In doing so, other concerns about society, the learner, and the learning process become of secondary importance. These other concerns, however, do have a role to play once the essence of the curriculum is formulated—helping to put the essence of the curriculum into a form suitable for use during instruction. But the priorities are clear: subject matter comes first, and "the choice of curriculum content [subject matter] can be made independent of instructional methods [the effect of applying concerns about student, teacher, and milieu], but the choice of instructional method is dependent upon the nature of the curriculum content" and becomes a concern of the developer only after curriculum content is delineated (Beauchamp & Beauchamp, 1967, p. 80).

Two implications of this must be understood. First, Scholar Academics assume that the *subjects* that are taught within the schools must be selected from among the academic disciplines—that for every school subject there must be a corresponding academic discipline (although for every academic discipline there need not be a school subject). It is also believed that the *specific subject matter* taught within schools must be drawn from among the academic disciplines and only from among them—that the content taught within the schools must be selected from the knowledge bases of academic disciplines.

Second, Scholar Academics believe that the only demand that should be allowed to influence the school program is the one that (as Whitefield says) "provides the base upon which the person as a person can develop to realize his full stature as a free *mind* [italics added]"—that is, the intellectual demands embodied within the academic disciplines that are concerned solely with the development of the intellect through the pursuit of knowledge. Specifically, the immediate demands of physical, social, economic, and political life are not to influence what occurs in schools. This means that the school must protect itself from allowing its program to be influenced by special-interest pressures that insist that people, in addition to being intellectual creatures, are also *occupational* creatures who work to support themselves, their family, and their society, *physical* creatures who require good health to lead constructive lives, *political* creatures who live within a family, community, nation, and world, *social* creatures whose meanings are defined by their society and who must live within a society, and *religious* creatures who are sustained through their lives by a faith and hope in something beyond themselves (King & Brownell, 1966, chap. 1). The school is to have as its highest priority the cultivation of the human mind as expressed within the academic disciplines, and the only demands that should be allowed to influence the school program are those that support this priority. This means that schools are not to include occupational, professional, vocational, technical, commercial, agricultural, business, industrial, or homemaking training for children.

Disciplines, Intellect, Knowledge

Underlying the Scholar Academic ideology is a belief that man's essence is summed up by his ability to think, to understand, to know, to reason, to reflect, to remember, to question, to ponder—in short, to exercise the intellectual capabilities of his mind in his endeavor to understand his world. It is believed that the fundamental human motivation that raises man above the lower animals is his search for knowledge and his ability to use his intellect in that search. This intellectual perspective on man is assumed to provide the basic motive underlying all educational endeavors: that education's rightful purpose is, as Whitefield says, to "provide the base upon which the person as a person can develop to realize his full stature as a free mind."

Scholar Academics do not stop here. They make a further critical assumption. They assume that there exists a loose equivalence between the world of the intellect, the world of knowledge, and the academic disciplines.

The world of the intellect contains those ways of thinking, reasoning, understanding, and reflecting that allow individuals to comprehend their world. It also contains the institutionalized ways of knowing, remembering, questioning, and deliberating that are passed from one generation to the next. For both the individual and the culture, "intellect has become, through its organization of all that is known and its search for the unknown, that best and perhaps only bridge to meaning" (King

& Brownell, 1966, pp. 22–23). In addition, the "intellect is man's schooled power of knowing, of understanding" (p. 20). It grows and develops only "according to the forms of the disciplines" (Phenix, 1964, p. 50).

The world of knowledge contains everything the individual has come to understand and know about his world. It also contains all of the meanings that the culture as a whole has accumulated over the centuries and preserved in its traditions. The world of knowledge contains not only that which is known, but also such things as the ways of knowing and postures toward knowledge that have been developed, codified, and preserved by the culture. And knowledge is the very substance of the academic disciplines. It is the embodiment of man's intellectual achievements.

The academic disciplines are the consequences of the direct pursuit of knowledge by individuals within the culture and the culture as a whole. They are the organizations that gather, define, sanction, store, organize, and disseminate the culture's existing knowledge and ways of knowing. They encompass the organized accumulation of civilization's knowledge, the ways in which man generates knowledge using his intellect, and the intellect's systems of symbols and thoughts. The academic disciplines are "the means by which men's minds master nature and grasp ideas" (King & Brownell, 1966, p. 24). In general, academic disciplines consist of communities of scholars who reside within institutions of higher learning. They bear names such as mathematics, physics, history, anthropology, philosophy, and psychology.

In assuming that there is a loose equivalence between the world of the intellect, the world of knowledge, and the academic disciplines, Scholar Academics also accept the belief that the contents of these three areas are identical. In addition, and this is crucial, they assume that *those things not included in the academic disciplines are not worthy of being contained in the world of the intellect or the world of knowledge*, and vice versa. Thus, the worlds of intellect, knowledge, and the academic disciplines are viewed as roughly equivalent in terms of both what they *include* and what they *exclude*.

The consequences for schools and the school curriculum follow directly. The primary concern for schooling should be the development of the child's intellect, which involves the acquisition of knowledge, which in turn entails learning the content of the academic disciplines. In addition, any "information" not sanctioned by an academic discipline is not worthy of being called knowledge or worthwhile for the intellect to consider, and thus not worthy of inclusion in school curricula or worthy of being taught within schools. As King and Brownell phrase it, "The prime claim of the intellect [on the schools], then, is best met in the schools when the disciplines of knowledge are the fundamental content of the curriculum—its resources and its responsibility" (1966, p. 37).

Education as an Extension of Disciplines, Intellect, Knowledge

The central task of school education is thus taken to be the extension of the components of the equivalence class containing the academic disciplines, the world of the intellect, and the world of knowledge. They are to be extended both on the individual level, through acculturation of individuals into civilization's accumulated knowledge and ways of knowing, and on the cultural level, through the discovery of new knowledge.

The school curriculum provides the means of acculturating the young into the worlds of knowledge, the intellect, and the academic disciplines. The central concern of the curriculum developer is the extension of these worlds by introducing the young into them—for Scholar Academics believe these worlds are enlarged when new minds acquire the knowledge they contain.

In addition, the theory of the nature of the equivalence becomes "the model for a theory of curriculum" and curriculum creation (King & Brownell, 1966, p. 67). That is, Scholar Academics' conception of the nature of an academic discipline (and its associated knowledge base and intellectual achievements) determines their conception of what curriculum is, the subject matter it is to contain, and how it should be created. This occurs on two levels: the global level, where the equivalence between knowledge, intellect, and the disciplines ranges over the whole universe of knowledge; and the local level, where the equivalence between knowledge, intellect, and the disciplines takes on its particular meaning within each academic discipline.

Disciplines, Knowledge, Intellect: Global Considerations

One of the striking characteristics of the modern view of the world of the disciplines, knowledge, and intellect is that there exist, as Whitefield puts it, "*distinctive* [italics added] disciplines of knowledge." There is not just one academic discipline. There is not just one type of knowledge. There is not just one way of knowing.

Many separate, distinct academic disciplines exist, bearing such names as mathematics, philosophy, history, anthropology, English, and biology. Each discipline is autonomous, determining the nature of its own knowledge and ways of knowing. It can be judged only according to its own criteria. Each is self-governing, and none is responsible to any authority outside or beyond itself. There is no superior body of knowledge or common way of knowing to which the disciplines are subordinate. The academic disciplines reside more in a multiversity than a university.

The world of knowledge is viewed as consisting of a variety of distinct and discontinuous clusters of locally organized knowledge and ways of knowing. It is not viewed as homogeneous and uniform. Each of the diverse clusters of knowledge is uniquely and intrinsically organized, and each is identifiable as an academic discipline. The plurality within the world of knowledge thus parallels the plurality among the disciplines.

There are many different ways of constructing knowledge within the world of the intellect. There are many distinct traditions of thinking and knowing in which a person's mind can be educated. The ways of understanding characteristic of axiomatic mathematics, analytic philosophy, interpretative history, experimental psychology, observational anthropology, and statistical economics are viewed as different. Each of the many ways of knowing within the world of the intellect has been developed to its highest level of refinement by an academic discipline, and each academic discipline has its characteristic modes of reasoning that it teaches to its members. The plurality within the world of the intellect thus parallels the plurality of the disciplines.

These beliefs in the autonomy of the disciplines and the plurality of disciplines, knowledge, and intellect are supported by the theory of equivalence among the academic disciplines, the world of knowledge, and the world of the intellect. They are in sharp contrast to pre-20th-century assumptions of the hegemony of philosophy over the disciplines and the reliance on philosophy for the meaning of knowledge, and they provide unique guidelines for curriculum making.

First, curriculum is viewed as consisting of separate subjects, each of which represents and reflects a single partition of the world of knowledge as represented by an academic discipline. Second, responsibility for curriculum creation within each subject belongs solely to representatives of the corresponding discipline who are acquainted with its portion of the world of knowledge and the world of the intellect. No extradisciplinary authority legislates behaviors appropriate for representatives of the disciplines to engage in while creating curricula.

Disciplines, Knowledge, Intellect: Local Considerations

At the local level, curriculum development is an intradisciplinary affair. The nature of each discipline dictates how educators are to create curricula that reflect the essence of that discipline. That is, the nature of each discipline "can be used to reflect back on each discipline in search of its clues for curriculum" (King & Brownell, 1966, p. 95) in order to make the curriculum a reflection of the discipline "as the scholar himself regards that discipline" (Cambridge Conference on School Mathematics [CCSM], 1963, p. vii), as was attempted with UICSM, SMSG, and MACOS.

The members of each discipline have sole responsibility for that part of the school curriculum that corresponds to their discipline. As members of their disciplines, they create curriculum so that it reflects their conception of the nature of the discipline. As a result, curriculum development at the local level becomes a provincial affair in which the developer's prime concern is the individual discipline his curriculum is to reflect:

> The focus of attention in each of these [curriculum] projects is an individual discipline. Little or no attention is given to the relationships of the individual fields to each other or to the program of studies within which they must find their place. National committees in the fields of chemistry, physics, and biology have proceeded independently of each other, the projects in economics, geography, and anthropology are unrelated to one another. (Bellack, 1964, p. 27)

The Academic Disciplines

Let us now examine how educators working within the Scholar Academic ideology view the nature of their disciplines. To convey the spirit of the conceptual framework being described, the discussion is somewhat allegorical.

The Discipline as a Community

One of three basic descriptions has generally been used to define an academic discipline: (1) a defined area of study; (2) the collection of facts, writings, and other works of scholars associated with a well-defined area of study; and (3) a "community of individuals whose ultimate task is the gaining of meaning" in one domain of the world of knowledge (King & Brownell, 1966, p. 68). We will view an academic discipline as a community of people in search of truth within one partition of the universe of knowledge. As a community, each discipline has a tradition and a history; a heritage of literature and artifacts; a specialized language, grammar, and logic for expression of ideas; a communications network; a valuational and affective stance; and "territorial possession" of a particular set of concepts, beliefs, and knowledge.

The primary reason for the existence of a discipline, the motivation drawing people to participate in a discipline, and the cohesive force holding people together within a discipline is the discipline's search for truth. At the very core of each discipline is the problem of self-extension through the pursuit of knowledge and truth. The central concern of each discipline is its own growth, both in terms of the discovery of new knowledge and thus the enlargement of its domain of inquiry (epistemic development) and in terms of passing on to others that which is already known—thereby enlarging both the amount and level of knowledge within the community making up the discipline (community development). Academic disciplines are not static communities concerned only with preservation of "what was." They are dynamic communities concerned with their own extension into "what will be." This was very much the case with the discipline of mathematics that supported UICSM and SMSG.

The Discipline as a Hierarchical Community

Disciplines are viewed as hierarchical communities consisting of inquirers into new knowledge, teachers of knowledge, and learners of knowledge (see Figure 2.1.). At the top of the hierarchy are scholars, who rule over the discipline as scholar-kings much as Plato's philosopher-kings were to rule over the Republic. It is their function to search for knowledge that is yet unknown. At the next level of the hierarchy are teachers, who disseminate knowledge that has been discovered by scholars and sanctioned by the discipline. At the bottom of the hierarchy are students, who are neophytes in their encounters with the discipline. It is their job to learn the discipline's knowledge so they may become proficient members of the discipline. The broken horizontal lines separating the major hierarchical levels in Figure 2.1 indicate that the boundaries between the levels of the hierarchy are not clear and precise and that there is overlap between the categories of scholar, teacher, and student.

❖ **Figure 2.1**   The hierarchical organization of a discipline.

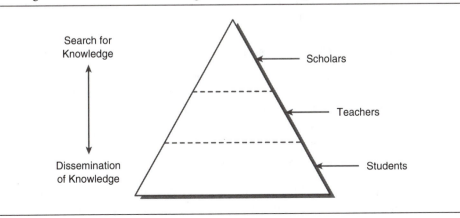

Within each category are many gradations of placement: from research scholars to instructors, from university professors to preschool teachers, and from doctoral candidates to nursery schoolers. The criteria ranking members of the discipline within the hierarchy are intellectual ones involving the member's ability to contribute to the extension of the discipline and how much of the discipline's knowledge the member has acquired. Members' rankings are directly proportional to their prestige, which is in turn directly proportional to how close they are to the hierarchy's apex. Note that there are fewer members of the discipline close to the hierarchy's apex than to its base. Note also that scholars, teachers, and students are all viewed as members of the discipline—all of them engaged at their own level and in their own way in their discipline's extension. As Bruner says,

> intellectual activity anywhere is the same, whether at the frontier of knowledge or in a third-grade classroom. What a scientist does at his desk or in his laboratory, what a literary critic does in reading a poem, are of the same order as what anybody else does when he is engaged in like activities—if he is to achieve understanding. The difference is in degree, not in kind. The schoolboy learning physics is a physicist, and it is easier for him to learn physics behaving like a physicist than doing something else. (1960, p. 14)

The Learning ↔ Teaching Dynamic of the Discipline

The dynamic of the discipline is inherent in the dual activity of "search for knowledge" ↔ "dissemination of knowledge" present at all levels of the intellectual hierarchy, as portrayed in Figure 2.1. The discipline as a whole and the members of the discipline as individuals are constantly motivated in an upward direction in search of the unknown, be they scholars in search of as yet unknown knowledge or students in search of knowledge unknown to them but known to the discipline. And the discipline as a whole and the members of the discipline as individuals are constantly motivated in a downward direction to disseminate the known, be they scholars reporting to others what they have discovered or teachers conveying what they have learned. The knowledge of the discipline is viewed as having two characteristics: it can be learned, and, once learned, it can be taught. "The distinguishing mark of any discipline is that the knowledge which comprises it is instructive—that it is peculiarly suited for teaching and learning" (Phenix, 1962, p. 57). Active members of the discipline—be they scholars, teachers, or students—are viewed as constantly engaged in the dual activity of learning ↔ teaching.

The Educative Process Within the Academic Community

Scholar Academics view education as a process of acculturating students into a discipline, and thus into one portion of their culture's knowledge base. They are concerned with students' acquisition of the discipline's knowledge, ways of knowing, attitudes toward itself, and traditions. They want to make students members of their discipline by first moving students into the discipline and then moving them from a lower to a higher level in its hierarchy.

The aim is to induct students into an academic discipline by giving them a participant's knowledge of the discipline rather than an observer's knowledge about the discipline, as was the case in the curricula described earlier in this chapter. Membership in a discipline is the result of education within a discipline: One becomes a member of a discipline by learning to participate in the discipline. *The Curriculum and the Disciplines of Knowledge* hints at this when it proclaims, "The view of knowledge used as the basis of this book places the increasing ability to participate in the discourse or characteristic activity of the several disciplines of the curriculum as the focal point for instruction" (King & Brownell, 1966, p. 79). Bruner suggests this when he writes,

> To instruct someone in these disciplines is . . . to teach him to participate in the process that makes possible the establishment of knowledge. We teach a subject . . . to get a student . . . to take part in the process of knowledge getting. (1966, p. 72)

Because the disciplines are viewed as communities with lives of their own and because education is thought of as acculturation into the academic communities, it is assumed that "education for the discipline" is the same as "education for life" (Sizer, 1964, p. 132). Elementary school curricula within a discipline are developed with the intent of preparing students for high school work in that discipline, and high school curricula within a discipline are developed to prepare students for university work within the discipline, and university study within a discipline is intended to prepare the student for a life of study and work within the discipline.

Education in a discipline involves entering the discipline at a low level of the discipline's hierarchy and working one's way toward the top of the hierarchy. It involves learning the knowledge of the discipline and teaching what one has learned to others. And it involves dropping out of the discipline when one can no longer function as a constructive member of the discipline.

A "territorial imperative" is constantly at work in two ways. First, education outside of the discipline is discouraged and frowned on. Potential members of the discipline are not to be lost to "technical education" or "vocational education." Educators within the disciplines have no desire to share the domain of schooling with rivals. All students are viewed as potential property of the disciplines and encouraged to pursue a life dedicated to the search for knowledge within them.

Second, education within the disciplines involves the special cultivation of those members of the discipline most likely to spend their lives within the discipline and most likely to make contributions to the discipline. After a certain level of schooling, students who show lack of interest in the discipline or who lack the ability to contribute to the discipline are largely ignored by Scholar Academics and encouraged either to "drop out" of the academic community or to stabilize themselves at a particular level within the hierarchy (perhaps by becoming elementary or secondary school teachers). Curricula are designed to preserve the hierarchical nature of the academic community by producing an intellectual elite through the selective promotion of students in such a manner that increasingly more members of the discipline will exist at the bottom of the hierarchy portrayed in Figure 2.1 than at the top of it.

Curriculum Issues

Thus far this chapter has described several characteristics of the Scholar Academic ideology. It has shown how educators view curriculum from the perspectives of the academic disciplines, how they view education as initiation into the disciplines and curriculum creation as elaboration on a discipline. It has also discussed the equivalence between the academic disciplines, the world of the intellect, and the world of knowledge and has portrayed the nature of the equivalence at the local level by such phrases as "hierarchical community," "community with a tradition," "extension through a search for and dissemination of knowledge," "domain of inquiry within one partition of the world of knowledge," "education through acculturation," and "acculturation into a hierarchical community." Three issues raised by this conceptual framework will now be examined: classification and selection of disciplines (a global issue), having the curriculum reflect the discipline (a local issue), and curriculum improvement.

Classification and Selection of Disciplines

The world of knowledge is not homogeneous and uniform but pluralistic. Paralleling this pluralism is the multiplicity of disciplines, each autonomous unto itself. There is no superior discipline governing all other disciplines. As a result, the problem arises of identifying the separate disciplines, determining the nature of each, and deciding on the relationship among them. This is called the problem of the classification of the disciplines. Paralleling this problem is that of the classification of the world of knowledge: determining how the world of knowledge is to be broken up into clusters, what the essence and value of each cluster is, and how the different clusters are related to each other.

From the Scholar Academic viewpoint, it is impossible to determine what knowledge should be taught in the schools until the world of knowledge is classified. Similarly, until the problem of the classification of the disciplines is resolved, one cannot determine which disciplines should be taught in the schools. Determination of the school program is thus dependent on answers given to these problems. "The significance of this set of problems to education is obvious enough. To identify the disciplines which constitute contemporary knowledge is to identify the various materials which constitute the resources of education and its obligations" (Schwab, 1964a, p. 7).

The issue of classification arises (a) because there exist different ways of classifying the disciplines and the world of knowledge, (b) because within any classification there exist more disciplines and knowledge than there is room for in the schools, (c) because inherent in different classifications are different conceptions of the nature of the well-educated man, and (d) because within different classifications there are different assumptions about which knowledge and which disciplines have the greatest value. Solution of the problems of classification is crucial in determining the proportional representation (including omission) of the different disciplines and knowledges within the school program.

Classifications can be radically different. For example, Comte's classification is based on dependency relationships among disciplines (biology is dependent on chemistry, which is dependent on physics, which is dependent on mathematics, etc.), while Aristotle's classification is based on the distinction between theoretical (to intellectualize), practical (to do), and productive (to make) types of knowledge.

Significantly different types of educational problems arise from different classifications. For example, under Comte's classification, the issue of vocational education is easily dismissed, while under Aristotle's classification, it is difficult not to include vocational education within the schools. Today the issue of vocational education can be easily dismissed within the Scholar Academic ideology because the scheme utilized for classifying the world of knowledge into disciplines is a hierarchical one that takes into account primarily "theoretical" types of knowledge (in the Aristotelian sense of the word) and that considers "practical" types of knowledge as dependent on and derivative from theoretical types of knowledge (in the sense of the Comtian interpretation).

Different classifications suggest significantly different solutions to considerations such as what disciplines should be included in the curriculum, how much time should be given to each discipline, and what disciplines "may be joined together for purposes of instruction, what should be held apart, and in what sequence they may best be taught" (Schwab, 1964a, p. 7).

Most educators, of course, do not bother themselves with questions about the classification of the disciplines or the world of knowledge. They unknowingly accept the assumptions taught them by their disciplines, then argue the case for the representation of their discipline within the schools and design their curricula based on assumptions that they have not rigorously thought out, assumptions derived from the impulse of their individual academic communities to preserve themselves and extend themselves (both with respect to community development and epistemological development). However, conflicts often arise among disciplines as they compete for representation within the school program. And these conflicts are often dependent on assumptions about the classification of knowledge and are often argued, unknowingly, around such assumptions. This was the case when more than 40 different subjects taught in high school at the end of the 19th century were replaced by five subjects, each representing academic disciplines, and the high school curriculum was standardized as a result of the endeavors or the Committee of Ten, the many lectures of Charles Eliot, and the first school reform movement within the Scholar Academic ideology that took place between about 1880 and 1910. This was the case when Latin and Greek were replaced in the schools by social studies, civics, and English language study between 1880 and 1950.

Curriculum as a Reflection of the Discipline

At the local level, educators work solely in their own disciplines. The major concern of Scholar Academic developers at this level is to construct curricula that reflect the essence of their discipline, for it is believed that curricula that accurately reflect their respective disciplines facilitate acculturation of students into them. This was the case with UICSM, SMSG, and MACOS.

Having the curriculum reflect the essence of the discipline it represents means that the curriculum "(1) must be an epitome of the discipline; (2) must have an approach and sequence in conformance with and in support of the discipline; and (3) must be alike in fundamental concepts and mode of inquiry" (King & Brownell, 1966, p. 190).

Accompanying the concern that a curriculum should reflect the discipline it represents are assumptions such as the following: that the developer's attention while creating curriculum should be focused solely on the discipline (King & Brownell, 1966, pp. 187–188); that the only source for curriculum content is the discipline itself (Phenix, 1964, p. 51); that the sole criterion for selection of curriculum content is that such content reflect the authentic structure of "the discipline in question as the scholar himself regards that discipline" (CCSM, 1963, p. iii); that the curriculum "should be determined by the most fundamental understanding that can be achieved of the underlying principles that give structure to" or are inherent in the discipline (Bruner, 1960, p. 31); that questions about the relationship of curriculum to existing educational resources, teachability, and learnability are to be dealt with after the scope and sequence of the curriculum are detailed (CCSM, 1963, pp. 2–5); that the needs of children and society have little place in determining the content of the curriculum (Fraser, 1962, p. 23); and that advice from social sciences such as psychology and sociology on how to teach a discipline is to be sought only after the essence of the curriculum is determined (King & Brownell, 1966, pp. 105–110).

Two problems that must be dealt with in determining the essence of an academic discipline are deciding what the essence of the discipline actually is and coping with the changing nature of the structure of any discipline.

Determining the essence of an academic discipline is not always easy. Frequently, different perspectives exist. For example, is ecology summed up by the phrase "set of antecedent-consequent events," "structures and functions," or "homeostatic mechanism"? Perhaps each phrase provides a different view of the nature of ecology. Deciding which position to take can pose a problem for curriculum developers, especially if they create curricula as a team. The Biological Science Curriculum Study (BSCS), another of the curriculum projects active during the 1960s, resolved its disagreements by fragmenting into three commissions, each of which developed its own curriculum: the green version (ecological), the blue version (molecular), and the yellow version (cellular). Another example of choosing among different perspectives is deciding which of the following best reflects a discipline's essence: the discipline's collection of ideas; collection of facts; collection of concepts; collection of principles; collection of relations among facts, concepts, and principles; collection of patterns organizing facts, concepts, principles, and relations among such; or collection of generalizations from which the facts, concepts, principles, ideas, relations, and patterns of the discipline can be generated.

In identifying the essence of a discipline, Scholar Academic developers must also determine such things as how the discipline discovers new knowledge and how students should learn the discipline, because "the structure, or logic, of each of the scholarly disciplines offers a way of learning the discipline itself" (Foshay, 1970, p. 349) and because "the disciplines themselves, understood as ways of making knowledge, not merely as knowledge already made, offer suggestions about how they may themselves be learned" (Schwab, 1962, p. 197). Note two assumptions here: that each of the many disciplines has its own inherent learning theory and that there is thus not "a simple theory of learning leading to one best learning-teaching structure for our schools . . . but . . . a number of different . . . [learning theories] each appropriate or 'best' for a discipline" (Schwab, 1962, p. 197), and that children should learn the discipline in a manner that parallels the way in which the discipline obtains new knowledge and new ways of knowing (that is, children learning the discipline should engage in the same type of activity as the scholar doing research; Phenix, 1962, pp. 64–65).

Scholar Academics must also deal with concerns such as making sure that the medium used in delivering the curriculum reflects the medium used for inquiry and the reporting of inquiry within the discipline and that the learning experiences constituting the curriculum are consonant with those experienced by practicing members of the discipline.

A second problem faced by Scholar Academics is the refusal of the disciplines—as vital evolving communities—to remain static. The disciplines are constantly growing, and thus their natures are constantly changing. Unknown knowledge is discovered and reorganized in ever more sophisticated paradigms. For example, in the 1890s the substantive structures of the scientific disciplines could be described as taxonomic, morphological, classificatory, macroscopic, and static, while in the 1960s their substantive structures were best described as microscopic, dynamic, structural, relational, and functional. It is quite appropriate that 1890 curricula were different from 1960 curricula (such as SMSG math), and that 1960 curricula are different from 2000 curricula, for the disciplines themselves are evolving.

Curriculum Improvement

Scholar Academic curriculum workers view curriculum improvement as taking place within the existing socio-administrative structure of the educational establishment. Their concern is with the knowledge structure of the school—primarily with the scope and sequence of what is taught, and secondarily with the methodology used in teaching—and not with the nature of the school as a social institution. Thus, Scholar Academics may speak frequently of out-of-date content or poor teachers but seldom of corrupt lay control or the complex power structure inside and outside the schools that influences them. They see the school as an "ideal" institution whose primary purpose is the acculturation of students into the world of knowledge and not as a social institution functioning within the sociopsychological, socioeconomic, eco-environmental, and politico-administrative structure of its society.

The two primary media used to stimulate curriculum improvement are the conference and the textbook. The conference is a meeting between scholars, teachers, or a combination of scholars and teachers that results in reports that make recommendations about what should be taught in schools. The intent of curriculum conferences (whether intradisciplinary or interdisciplinary) is to bring about curriculum improvement by producing prestigious reports that affect the knowledge structure of the curriculum by pressuring either schools or textbook preparers to implement the recommendations of the report. As Harold Rugg wrote in 1927 about the Committee of Ten, the Committee of Fifteen, and other national committees of the 1890s, they

> have exerted a tremendous influence in shaping the school curriculum. The prestige of their reports was so great that, once published, their recommendations were copied into entrance requirements of universities and they constituted the outline to which textbooks had to correspond if the authors and publishers expected widespread adoption. Both state and local, town and city systems came to base their syllabi definitely upon the recommendations of the committee. (p. 64)

Such influence over the school curriculum was the hope of those who wrote more recent reports, such as *A Nation at Risk* (National Commission on Excellence in Education [NCEE], 1983) and *Teaching at Risk* (The Teaching Commission, 2004). Such influence over the school curriculum was also the hope of those who wrote the new mathematics, science, and history standards of professional organizations and state departments of education.

The textbook is a daily program prepared by members of a discipline (including teachers) that prescribes what is to be taught in schools. Textbook writing is an intradisciplinary endeavor. It can result in a text for students, a curriculum guide for teachers, or both. Laboratory activities, movies, or field trips can accompany textbooks. Textbook writing and school district curriculum guide writing are viewed as improving education by affecting what is taught within a course on a day-by-day, month-by-month, and year-by-year basis.

Note that these mechanisms for curriculum improvement closely parallel two modes of communication utilized by members of the academic disciplines: the scholarly conference and the research report or textbook.

Historical Context

Scholar Academics see themselves as having been given a hard time in the past. First, other educators associate their endeavors with traditional education and with an "imaginary traditional classroom" that is a composite of everything that is wrong with our schools. This is not accurate, for Scholar Academics do not want education to be sterile, regimented, and boring. They want to revitalize and enrich the education that children receive in schools. Second, members of other ideologies have constantly attacked and tried to change some of the things Scholar Academics hold most sacred about our educational system. For example, proponents of vocational and commercial education have attacked the Scholar Academic belief that all children should have access to the academic curriculum because it is the best way for them to acquire the knowledge our culture has accumulated over the centuries. The result is that many children have been deprived of an academic education—of the education Scholar Academics view as the great equalizer of democracy and that allows children from all socioeconomic classes to compete for success in our society.

For many years, Scholar Academics quietly endured attacks on their educational agendas, but in the last quarter century they have begun to strike back and vehemently participate in the power struggle over who will control our schools and what will occur in them. We are in a time of math wars, history wars, and reading wars. To judge the energy underlying the current curriculum wars, one need only do an Internet search using phrases such as "reading wars" or "math wars" and see the number of items posted and the angry tone of many of them.

Let us look back a little over a century, to see—from the Scholar Academic perspective—some of the roots of the current curriculum wars, some of the advocates of the ideology, and how the ideology has changed over the last hundred years until now.

Lester Frank Ward (1841–1913), a founder of the field of sociology, argued vehemently against the popular belief of Herbert Spencer that the purpose of education should be utilitarian and vocational. In the 1880s, he argued that the purpose of education should be to transmit to all members of society knowledge of their cultural heritage, and that access to such knowledge is the key to individual betterment, equalization of men's position in society, maintenance of a democratic society, and social progress (Ravitch, 2000a, pp. 26–29).

Charles W. Eliot (1834–1926), president of Harvard University and chairman of the Committee of Ten, was a proponent of academic education under the belief that the way to improve society is by improving the "intelligence" of individuals, which he believed could be accomplished by developing people's mental power: their power to think and reason by studying their cultural heritage (Ravitch, 2000a, pp. 30–31). (At the end of the 19th century, faculty psychology was popular, and one trained the "thinking muscles of the mind" by exercising them on the content of different disciplines.) As president of Harvard, Eliot represented university academicians who had within the last hundred years reorganized their way of viewing the nature of knowledge. The new organization emphasized the plurality and autonomy of academic disciplines (and their associated knowledge), as compared to the old organization that was based on hierarchical dependency relationships among disciplines (and their knowledge). Eliot wanted two things. He wanted to impose this new view of the nature of knowledge embraced by the university on high schools (so their curricula would reflect the structure of knowledge at universities). He also wanted to standardize the high school curriculum so that students from different high schools would arrive at college with similar academic preparation. (It was difficult for universities when students came from high schools with different types of curricula, curricula that differentially emphasized Greek, Latin, surveying, English literature, seamanship, etc.)

William Torrey Harris (1835–1909), U.S. commissioner of education from 1889 to 1906 and a member of the Committee of Ten as well as the Committee of Fifteen (which reported on elementary education in 1895), was a proponent of academic education who believed that the purpose of education is to provide individuals with the accumulated knowledge of the human race by having them study certain academic subjects. He argued that all children should have access to an excellent education, not just the children of the wealthy (Ravitch, 2000a, pp. 32–38).

In 1892, the National Education Association (NEA) created the first blue ribbon panel on education: the Committee of Ten, on which Eliot and Harris were prominent members. The committee was formed to solve the problem of the diverse requirements that existed for college admissions and the broad range of high school curricula and graduation requirements (which were as likely to include surveying, Greek, and bookkeeping as history, mathematics, and Latin). The Committee issued its report in 1893. Its recommendations resulted in the standardization of the high school academic curriculum, which remains largely intact to this day: 4 years of English, history, mathematics, and foreign language and 3 years of science (NEA, 1893). The Committee merged Harris's concern that students acquire rich academic content with Eliot's concern that students develop their thinking ability, asserting that students should acquire the accumulated knowledge of our culture and its ways of thinking as represented in the academic disciplines of English, history, mathematics, science, and foreign languages. (The report did not say that all subjects were of equal value and it made no decisions about the curriculum of vocational, manual, and commercial education.) In addition, the Committee recommended that

> every subject which is taught at all in a secondary school should be taught in the same way and to the same extent to every pupil so long as he pursues it, no matter what the probable destination of the pupil may be, or at what point his education is to cease. (NEA, 1893)

In other words, all children were to have equal access to an excellent education. These remained important goals of the Scholar Academic ideology throughout the 20th century and are reflected in such reports and acts as *A Nation at Risk* (NCEE, 1983), *Teaching at Risk* (The Teaching Commission, 2004), the Goals 2000: Education America Act (1994), and the No Child Left Behind Act (2002). Many Scholar Academic endeavors during the 20th century involved defending these goals and attacking those who challenged them.

William C. Bagley (1872–1946), a professor of education at the University of Illinois, founder of the *Journal of Educational Psychology*, president of the National Society for the Study of Education, and head of the department of teacher education at Teachers College, Columbia University, beginning in 1918, was a major proponent of the Scholar Academic ideology during the first half of the 20th century and defended its assumptions against the attempts of other ideologies to control what young people studied in schools. He fought against Learner Centered attempts to make schools more responsive to the needs and interests of students by substituting interesting activity for thoughtful study of significant cultural traditions; against Social Efficiency attempts to promote industrial education, vocational education, commercial education, domestic science, agricultural studies, manual training, and other utilitarian studies instead of the development of the intellect; against the intelligence testing movement's attempt to classify and sort children for different types of education rather than provide them all with the best intellectual education possible; and against Social Reconstruction attempts to make schools into social change agencies critical of American traditions rather than to provide children with a common language of cultural knowledge with which they could communicate. He believed that the cultural knowledge accumulated by humanity over the ages was an invaluable heritage that needed to be taught to each succeeding generation for social progress to continue. He believed that schools should provide a common curriculum for all students that was grounded in the academic disciplines of the liberal arts. He argued against curriculum differentiation—against the tracking of students in schools into manual labor, vocational education, general education, and college-bound groups, each receiving a different type of education suited to their future occupations. He believed that all children should have the same academic education, independent of their intelligence or future occupation. In addition, he argued that what schools needed were better instructional methods, better teaching materials, and more-qualified teachers (Ravitch, 2000a, chaps. 5–8).

Like Bagley, W. E. B. DuBois (1868–1963) fought against forces that opposed Scholar Academic ideals. He was an outspoken opponent of Booker T. Washington's advocacy of manual education and vocational education for African Americans. He argued for an academic and equal education for everyone, independent of race, and suggested that "The Talented Tenth of the Negro race must be made leaders" for the rest of the race through college education so that they could provide leadership to others (Ravitch, 2000b, pp. 373–378). DuBois also argued against the view that education was to build a new social order and eradicate social problems. Education, he proclaimed in 1935, was to teach academic content such as reading, writing, and counting, which he refers to in this passage from a speech to African American teachers in Georgia:

Whenever a teachers' convention meets and tried to find out how it can cure the ills of society, there is simply one answer; the school has but one way to cure the ills of society and that is by making men intelligent. To make men intelligent, the school has again but one way, and that is, first and last, to teach them to read, write and count. And if the school fails to do that, and tries beyond that to do something for which a school is not adapted, it not only fails in its own function, but it fails in all other attempted functions. Because no school as such can organize industry, or settle the matter of wage and income, can found homes or furnish parents, can establish justice or make a civilized world. (Null & Ravitch, 2006, pp. xiv–xv)

Other proponents of the Scholar Academic ideology who defended its assumptions in the 1930s and 1940s include Robert Maynard Hutchings (who promoted the Great Books curriculum and believed that the aim of education was "the cultivation of the intellect for its own sake" [Hutchins, 1936, p. 301]) and Isaac L. Kandel. Kandel's beliefs, which are typical of others who promoted the Scholar Academic ideology during this period, may be summarized this way: Society creates schools "to perpetuate themselves." The function of schools is to perpetuate society by acculturating children into our society's cultural traditions and way of life by teaching them its "common understandings, common knowledge, common values, and a common language of discourse, all of which are necessary for participation of equals in a democratic society." Children, as well as society, have much to gain by acquiring the accumulated knowledge and wisdom of humankind that has been created over the centuries and preserved and organized in the academic disciplines. Teachers should transmit this "priceless heritage to their students"; help "children understand [their culture and] society and gain access to its tools—its books, techniques, customs, mores, and institutions"; and help them acquire the "intellectual and moral discipline" necessary to effectively function in a democratic society (Ravitch, 2000a, pp. 320–321).

What these educators were fighting for becomes clear when we note that between 1900 and 1955 the enrollment of students in academic tracks of high schools dropped as new tracks in vocational education and general education multiplied and students entered them. For example, between 1900 and 1955 enrollments in geometry dropped from about 27% to 11% and enrollments in physics dropped from about 19% to 5%, while between 1920 and 1955 enrollments in ancient and medieval history dropped from more than 30% to less than 2% and enrollments in foreign languages dropped from about 83% to 21% (Ravitch, 2000a, p. 350). If college entrance requirements had not demanded that applicants to college complete the academic curriculum required by the Committee of Ten, there might not have been any students left studying our "priceless cultural heritage."

During World War II, the U.S. Armed Forces and educators associated with it noted the high level of illiteracy and lack of mathematical skills among the U.S. population. Over the next 10 years, many educators and scholars began to worry about this and to act to rectify it, including those who worked on UICSM mathematics. Then in 1957, when Russia launched Sputnik, the American public became terrified that we would lose the cold war. Their terror resulted in demands that schools promote greater participation among students in science, mathematics, and other academic subjects. The president and Congress responded by authorizing and funding the National Science Foundation and other branches of the government to develop new academic curricula in the basic subject areas of elementary and secondary schools (starting with science and mathematics)—curricula that reflected the essence of these subjects as viewed by practicing scientists and mathematicians. It is out of these initiatives that SMSG mathematics was funded, as well as curricula in physics, biology, and other areas of science. For the next 15 years, scholars from academic disciplines ranging from mathematics and science to history and the arts developed curricula that reflected what was then the current view of the accumulated knowledge of their disciplines and the ways of thinking about the world embraced by their disciplines. Their curricula reflected both the content and ways of thinking that they assumed represented the highest levels of our priceless cultural heritage (both Harris's emphasis on rich academic content and Eliot's emphasis on thinking ability). During this period, however, the styles of thought taught to children reflected the academic disciplines' modes of inquiry rather than the intellectual muscles of children's minds. This was a time in which new exciting instructional methods and new more powerful teaching materials were incorporated into school curricula. In addition, teacher education programs began to place increased emphasis on intellectual excellence, as masters of arts (and science) in teaching programs were begun that required not only that students have an undergraduate major in an arts and sciences discipline but also that they do significant graduate work in that discipline. From 1955 to 1970, Scholar Academics pursued Bagley's desire for better instructional methods, better teaching materials, and more-qualified teachers for our schools.

From the mid 1960s to the mid 1980s, Scholar Academic initiatives were overtaken by efforts of other ideologies.

Then the American public was aroused to again perceive the nation and education to be in a state of crisis as international comparisons of children's educational achievements showed the U.S. to be behind many other nations, as the National Assessment of Educational Progress (NAEP, the federally funded program that periodically assesses student academic achievement in the U.S.) showed declines in student achievement in academic subjects, and as our "once unchallenged preeminence in commerce, industry, science, and technological innovation [was reported to have been] overtaken by competitors throughout the world" (NCEE, 1983, p. 1). The National Commission on Excellence in Education published *A Nation at Risk* to highlight the dangers facing the U.S. and to insist that

> all, regardless of race or class or economic status, are entitled to a fair chance [to succeed in life] and to the tools for developing their individual powers of mind and spirit to the utmost . . . thereby serving not only their own interests but also the progress of society itself. (NCEE, 1983, p. 1)

The report also recommended

> that State and local high school graduation requirements be strengthened and that, at a minimum, all student seeking a diploma be required to . . . [take] the following curriculum during their fours years of high school: (a) 4 years of English; (b) 3 years of mathematics; (c) 3 years of science; (d) 3 years of social studies; and (e) one-half year of

computer science. For the college-bound, 2 years of foreign language in high school are strongly recommended. (NCEE, 1983, p. 9)

Notice that these recommendations are almost identical to those the Committee of Ten made 90 years earlier, both in the areas of required study in high school and in the emphasis that all students be given "a fair chance" to study these subjects. News media reported on *A Nation at Risk* and stirred up considerable public concern that led to new initiatives in the curriculum wars. Many of these initiatives promoted Scholar Academic agendas.

Three examples illustrate different ways in which educators promoted the Scholar Academic ideology at the end of the 20th and beginning of the 21st centuries: Hirsch's curriculum endeavors, Quirk's Internet efforts, and the standards movement. Note in these examples, which are described below, that they attempt to use political processes to influence the school curriculum by appealing to the general public, as "lay policy-makers," to take action, often by "revolutionizing education from the outside in" (Finn, 1991, p. 46). Many of their writings are, in fact, addressed to parents, suggesting that they take action through their local schools, school districts, state governments, or national initiatives (Bennett, Finn, & Cribb, 1999). In general, the argument begins with assumptions found in *A Nation at Risk*: that the future of our nation is "still at risk" (Finn, 1991, p. 1) because our schools are failing (not because society, government, or industry are not doing what they should). Evidence for this claim is gathered primarily from standardized test scores, such as those of NAEP and the Trends in International Mathematics and Science Study (TIMSS; Yecke, 2003), for it is believed that standardized "testing and assessment results are our greatest single source of information on academic performance" (Finn, 1991, p. 159). They proceed to argue that the problem stems from "progressive education" forces having corrupted our schools over the last century (Jacobs, 2006). As Finn asserts, "This mind-set is characteristic of the child-centered philosophy that has dominated the education profession since the early twentieth century. But it is a philosophy that has brought the nation to the brink of ruin" (1991, p. 172). These forces have supposedly corrupted our schools by promoting such things as "Multiculturalism," "Discovery Learning," "Teachers as Facilitators," "Developmentalism," "Multiple Intelligences," "Cooperative Learning," "Self-Esteem," and "Bilingual Education" (Bennett et al., 1999, pp. 584–626). The solution to the problem, it is argued, is to pay more attention to the "academic curriculum . . . the basics . . . the academic core in five subjects: English; history and geography; the arts; math; and science" (p. 91). As Bennett, Finn, and Cribb continue, this is because

> some things are more important to know than others. . . . The [desired elementary and middle school] curriculum puts academics first. It sets high but attainable standards. It teaches fundamental . . . knowledge . . . knowledge that becomes a foundation for deeper, more sophisticated studies in high school and college. (pp. 92–93)

E. D. Hirsch wrote the book *Cultural Literacy*, in which he asserted that education should be a process of acculturating children into society in such a way that they become good citizens by learning the shared accumulated knowledge of their culture, which includes the background knowledge that literate adults use to understand each other and events in their world as well as "the shared attitudes and conventions that color" their understanding of human interactions and events (1987, p. xiii). He also insisted that all children—regardless of social class, economic status, and family and cultural background—should have a chance to receive a stimulating intellectual education, and he compiled long lists of the specific knowledge he thought children should learn at each grade level.

Bill Quirk has fought the math wars for the Scholar Academic ideology through the Internet. He has used his Web site, www.wgquirk.com, to attack those who do not agree with the Scholar Academic position—"constructivists" in particular. His following statement illustrates his views of the mission of education, teaching, and assessment, as well as his belief that all children should have a rigorous academic education:

> [The math wars are] about the primary mission of American public education. . . . The ongoing strength of any society depends on the quality of the shared tradition of knowledge that is passed on from generation to generation. American schools need to teach children the core content associated with the foundational knowledge domains of English, mathematics, science, history, and geography. But our self-described "reformers" reject the very concept of knowledge transmission, refusing to recognize a common core of knowledge that all kids should learn . . . reformers have been forced to redefine the meaning of "teacher" and "test." "Teachers" are now to "guide" and "create rich enabling environments for student discovery," not impart knowledge. . . . They have redefined "test" to mean "find out what each child has personally discovered," not what the child has failed to learn. (Quirk, 2005, ¶ 1, 2, 4)

Other Web sites that promote the Scholar Academic ideology include http://coreknowledge.org, http://www.edexcellence.net, and http://www.mathematically correct.com.

Other educators who have fought for the Scholar Academic ideology have contributed to the debate over what should be taught in schools by promoting their ideas through the curriculum standards that many states and national organizations develop. The standards delineate in each content area and at each grade level what children should learn. From coast to coast, debates have raged over what should and should not be included in the standards of specific content areas, such as history. In many cases, public debate related to the math wars, history wars, and reading wars has influenced state departments of education to favor particular ideological positions in their state standards, as occurred in California and Massachusetts. Continuing pressure is exerted on states by many Scholar Academic advocacy groups to make state standards conform to the group's conceptions of what the content of standards should be, with passing and failing marks for standards being handed out frequently (Finn, Julian, & Petrilli, 2006).

Partially as a result of Scholar Academic endeavors such as these, the percentage of high school graduates enrolled in academic tracks versus vocational or general education tracks rose from 42% in 1982 to 69% in 1994 (Ravitch, 2000a, p. 451).

We now shift from examining the context within which Scholar Academics work to examining their conception of their professional aims, the nature of knowledge, the nature of the child, the nature of learning, the nature of teaching, and the nature of evaluation.

Aims

The aim of Scholar Academics is to extend the academic disciplines (the world of knowledge and the world of the intellect) by transmitting their essence to students. The extension of disciplines by acculturating new members into them serves the long-range purposes of (a) preserving the existence of the disciplines by guaranteeing that there exist members of the disciplines who will carry on their traditions and further their epistemic development and (b) building literacy of the disciplines' knowledge within the general population so that its members will benefit from the knowledge discovered by the disciplines and so that they will support the endeavors of the disciplines (as representatives of the accumulated knowledge of our culture). Doing so both (a) preserves and extends essential components of our culture and (b) acculturates children into an important dimension of its cultural knowledge base.

These long-range aims are rather vague and intangible. They do not specify why a particular item is included in a curriculum. As a result, Scholar Academics are often charged with being overly concerned about the means of accomplishing an unspecified and vague end to the exclusion of being concerned about the ends of the educational endeavor in which they are engaged. In essence, this charge reduces to the claim that Scholar Academics have neither aims for their curricula nor justification for the existence of the substantive aspects of their curricula. These claims are not justifiable. If people do not verbally specify their aims and clarify their justifications, this does not mean that they do not exist. Scholar Academics assume a priori that the benefits of being acculturated into the world of the intellect need no pragmatic defense—that the benefits of preserving the culture's ways of knowing by extending the disciplines are central to the preservation of civilization and that the extension of the world of knowledge within the minds of students is the defined mission of the school.

The means of extending a discipline is by transmitting its knowledge to students. Because transmission of knowledge is the immediate task Scholar Academics continuously face, it is often taken to be equivalent to acculturating students into a discipline. Thus, it is often mistaken to be the primary aim (end) rather than recognized as the secondary aim (means).

Knowledge

The Nature of Knowledge

The primary characteristic of the knowledge that Scholar Academics consider to be potential curriculum content is that it is claimed by one of the academic disciplines as belonging to its domain. For these educators, "the only really useful knowledge is that which conforms to the structures revealed in the cognitive disciplines" (Phenix, 1964, p. 51). The knowledge of most worth is that on which the epistemic development of a discipline depends and which contributes most to community development within the discipline. Knowledge thus derives its value and its claim to being knowledge from its ability to contribute to the extension of an academic discipline.

The Form of Knowledge

There are several characteristics of the knowledge valued most by Scholar Academics.

First, knowledge gives people the ability to understand their world. This is in contrast to giving people, for example, the ability to do things, construct meaning, or act in accordance with a set of values.

Second, knowledge takes the form of both "content" and "process" (Schwab, 1964a, p. 72). When the word *knowledge* is used, it means both "that which is known" and "the way in which something is known." A bit of knowledge is viewed as implicitly carrying both substantive and methodological aspects of a discipline.

Third, knowledge has a form that is called instructive, or didactic. As such, it is capable of being transmitted from one human to another, retained in the mind of the person to whom it is transmitted, and used by the person to whom it is transmitted to give meaning to yet unknown knowledge. Didactic knowledge is repeatable and impersonal. It can be repeated without losing its point, the occasions for delivering it are not fixed, and special circumstances are not needed for its transmission. Any suitably trained teacher can transmit knowledge to any suitably trained student. This means that information tied to particular nonrecurring circumstances, such as a particular item of conversational, bargaining, reassuring, or prosecuting information, is not considered to be worthwhile knowledge for the school curriculum. It also means that personal information that cannot be communicated without losing its point, such as feelings of competence, power, self-esteem, or love, is not considered to be worthwhile curriculum knowledge.

Finally, knowledge is a representation of reality and not reality itself. Whether reality is taken to be an idea (as Plato believed) or a physical occurrence (as Aristotle believed), knowledge is a representation of reality and not reality itself. Students learn about reality; they do not learn reality. Teachers transmit knowledge of reality; they do not transmit reality. People possess knowledge of reality; they do not possess reality.

The Origin of Curriculum Knowledge

The process of obtaining curriculum knowledge requires that (a) something exist in objective reality, (b) the academic discipline discover it and sanction its existence by including it in the discipline, and (c) the developer select it for inclusion in the curriculum from the discipline, and then (d) it can be transmitted into the student's mind. Having collected curriculum knowledge, the developer can then imbed it within a curriculum and transmit it to students. This is represented in Figure 2.2. Note that the source for curriculum content is the discipline and that the test for the worth of

❖ **Figure 2.2**   The Scholar Academic process of obtaining curriculum knowledge.

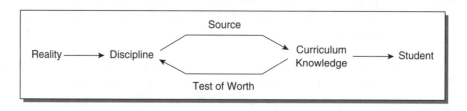

knowledge depends on how well it reflects the essence of the discipline. The creators of UICSM, SMSG, and MACOS obtained the knowledge they embedded in their curricula in this way.

Knowledge and Objective Reality

What is implicit in the above comments needs to be stated explicitly. Scholar Academics accept the duality between the subjective reality within each individual's mind and the objective reality outside each person's mind. Knowledge can originate within either subjective reality or objective reality. However, only knowledge that can be externalized, objectified, and impersonalized within objective reality is of worth. Knowledge suitable for curriculum content must be observable within objective reality. That which is known only within the mind of an individual and incapable of being presented, observed, scrutinized, and acquired by the members of the discipline as a community is not worthy of inclusion in the curriculum.

The Child

The Child as Mind

Scholar Academics are less concerned with the child than with curriculum content. When they do speak of the child, they speak of the child's mind. In particular, they speak of the rational or intellectual aspects of the child's mind. Man—the child and the student—is viewed as a creature of intellect. Other aspects of man's nature are of little concern to these developers.

> Man is the symbolizing animal. He reasons. He remembers. He reflects. He meditates. He imagines. He cultivates his mind by acquiring, retaining, and extending knowledge. He struggles to control his emotions and actions with reason. He makes knowledge a virtue and ignorance an evil. He questions appearances in search of reality. . . . These aspects of intellect distinguish man from other creatures. The intellect is man's schooled power of knowing, of understanding. (King & Brownell, 1966, p. 20)

The child is thus viewed as a mind, the important aspects of mind being those "powers" that are capable of being "schooled" within the academic disciplines.

The Child as Memory and Reason

The mind of man is viewed as consisting of two facilities: one is for storage and the other for performing mental operations on that which is stored. The former is often called memory and the latter reason. The former is capable of being filled and the latter is capable of being shaped to conform to an academic discipline's ways of thinking.

The Incomplete Child

Scholar Academics view students as neophytes in the disciplines of knowledge:

> The student is a neophyte in the encounters with the [academic] community of discourse; he is, nevertheless to be considered a member of the community, immature to be sure, but

capable of virtually unlimited development. He is learning the ways of gaining knowledge in the discipline . . . seeking always to gain meaning through the ensemble of fundamental principles that characterize the discipline. (King & Brownell, 1966, p. 121)

Scholar Academics view the student as an immature member of an academic discipline who is capable of acculturation within that discipline as a result of learning its content and ways of thinking. They see students as minds at the bottom of the academic hierarchy who are capable of being raised to a higher level within the hierarchy.

Scholar Academics regard students to be capable of learning because students' minds are missing something they are capable of acquiring. Whether these educators view the mind as empty and capable of being filled, blank and capable of being written upon, untrained and capable of being trained, naive and capable of being made sophisticated, or unexercised and capable of being exercised, they perceive students to be missing something that exists outside their minds and is capable of being transmitted into their minds. (As Locke said in 1690, "Let us then suppose the mind to be, as we say, white paper, void of all characters, without any ideas" [Locke, 1690/1995, Book II, chap. 1, section 2]). Scholar Academics often speak of students as sponges (Keynes, 1995, p. 64) capable of absorbing the ideas and ways of thinking of an academic discipline (Bennett et al., 1999, p. 280). Both their memory and reason are considered incomplete but capable of being made less incomplete as a result of their learning an academic discipline.

Learning

The Learning ↔ Teaching Dynamic

The learning ↔ teaching dynamic is at the very core of both civilization and the academic disciplines. Civilization is viewed as an organization of communal intelligence whose central socialization process centers on its formal learning ↔ teaching function, and academic disciplines are viewed as communities of intellects whose central dynamic is that of their learning ↔ teaching function. As a result, a learning ↔ teaching atmosphere pervades all activity within the Scholar Academic ideology. Man is viewed as an animal designed both to learn and to teach. Similarly, society is viewed as a community whose major function is one of communal extension through teaching.

Direction Within the Learning ↔ Teaching Dynamic

Scholar Academics view learning as a function of teaching. Learning results from teaching, and how a person learns is a consequence of how a person is taught. In its starkest simplicity, learning is viewed from the perspective of "x teaches y to z" rather than from the perspective of "z learns y from x." Here the process "teaches y" determines the process "learns y," and the phrase "teaches y to z" comprises the experiences encountered by and learned by the student. Learning is thus viewed from the perspective of the transmitter rather than from the perspective of the receiver of learning.

Transmitting and Receiving
Agents of the Learning ↔ Teaching Dynamic

Within the learning ↔ teaching relationship, the teacher is viewed as a transmitter and the learner is viewed as a receiver of the discipline's knowledge. Students are viewed as being drawn into the discipline. Disciplines "take . . . hold on the minds of pupils" (NEA, 1893). Here it is assumed that "students have an enormous capacity to learn and will absorb ideas like sponges if properly [taught,] motivated and encouraged" (Keynes, 1995, p. 64).

Whether the view is of students' memory being filled or of students filling their memory, students are on the receiving end of the learning ↔ teaching relationship. Whether students' disciplined reasoning ability is trained or students develop their reasoning ability in correspondence with the thinking styles of a discipline, students are shaped by the intellectual structures of the discipline. Whether the major emphasis is on knowledge being impressed upon mind or on mind giving meaning to knowledge presented to it, the source of knowledge lies outside the student and is actively transmitted to the student by a teacher.

Within the Scholar Academic ideology, learning is the result of an intentional activity initiated by the teacher and deliberately aimed at the student. That which is learned is primarily a result of activity on the part of the teacher and secondarily a result of activity on the part of the learner.

Learning Theory as Reflection of the Discipline

One of the central hypotheses of the Scholar Academic ideology is that the theory of learning appropriate for use in an academic discipline's curriculum is (a) unique to the discipline and (b) to be a reflection of the structure of the discipline and derived from the nature of the discipline itself. The belief is that the discipline carries inherent within itself a methodology for teaching and learning.

Lack of Concern With Formal Learning Theory

Although Scholar Academics profess an interest in the writings on learning theory produced by philosophers and social scientists, they tend to ignore such writings while working on curricula. As developers at the Cambridge Conference on School Mathematics (which supported the endeavors of UICSM and SMSG) wrote, "The conference should deal primarily with the goals of school mathematics, leaving aside the relationship of these goals of existing educational resources," and thus "we made no attempt to take account of recent research in cognitive psychology" (1963, pp. 2–3). There is no need for a learning theory separate from the discipline, for it is believed that the very nature of the discipline dictates the way in which it is to be learned and taught. When educators engage in inquiry into the nature of learning, it is usually with respect to a particular discipline and its curricula.

Many Theories of Learning

One of the implications of the belief that every discipline carries inherent within itself a unique theory of learning ↔ teaching particularly suited to itself is the assumption that there exist many different theories of learning rather than one generalizable learning theory (Schwab, 1962, p. 19). Each of the many disciplines has its own unique theory of learning ↔ teaching that reflects its nature, and each of these unique theories of learning ↔ teaching is to be used in curricula corresponding to the discipline (Phenix, 1966, p. 31).

Learning to Parallel Inquiry

Another implication of the belief that each discipline carries inherent within itself its own theories of learning ↔ teaching is the assumption that children should learn the discipline in a manner that parallels the way in which the discipline obtains new knowledge and new ways of knowing, that is, that children learning the discipline should engage in the same type of activity as the scholar doing research. "Education should be conceived as a guided recapitulation of the processes of inquiry which gave rise to the fruitful bodies of organized knowledge comprising the established disciplines" (Phenix, 1962, p. 63).

Readiness

Readiness issues are generally dealt with from the perspective of Bruner's statement "that any subject can be taught effectively in some intellectually honest form to any child at any stage of development" (1963, p. 529). A variety of elaborate interpretations of what this means have been offered (Shulman, 1968, p. 38). It is possible that Bruner meant exactly what he said: that readiness is to be dealt with through the simplification of topics initially too difficult for children to understand. When coordinated with the concept of "a spiral curriculum, in which the same subject arises at different times with increasing degrees of complexity and rigor" (CCSM, 1963, p. 13), the Scholar Academic approach to readiness becomes more clearly defined. It becomes even clearer when they appeal to Adler's statement that "the best education for the best is the best education for all" (1982, pp. 6–7) and Keynes's statement that "the content, teaching styles, and support activities available to the students are designed to enable virtually *all* students . . . to be highly successful" (1995, p. 59).

Scholar Academics do, however, differentiate between students. They do not regard them as all the same, and as a result they see tracking as a useful practice. As Bennett, Finn, and Cribb elaborate,

> the kind of tracking that can be useful is the type that treats all children to serious academic content, regardless of the group they are in or the speed with which they're mastering the curriculum. Schools must deal with the reality that different children do learn at different speeds and can handle subjects in varying degrees of depth. Grouping by ability and achievement makes it easier for teachers to tailor instruction so that everyone is suitably challenged. (1999, p. 613)

Note here that while students can be grouped according to "ability and achievement" so that they can "learn at different speeds and . . . degrees of depth," it is still emphasized that tracking must treat "all children to serious academic content."

Teaching

Teaching is a function of academic disciplines that enables students to learn them. Its aims are to acculturate students into a discipline and to transmit the discipline to students in such a way that its knowledge ends up in their minds.

Teaching is viewed within the context of the discipline. Its functions are functions of the discipline. Its functionaries are functionaries of the disciplines. Its methods are methods inherent in the discipline's communications system. And its successes and failures are the strengths and weaknesses of the discipline. Particularly important here is the belief that

> the teacher's qualification as a member of one or more disciplines is basic. The teacher is ideally an exemplar of the discipline to his students and to his colleagues; he is the embodiment of its values, its language, its skills, its ways of finding meaning. (King & Brownell, 1966, p. 157)

> Most importantly he is a continuing member of the discipline who has reflected on the nature of that discipline, its traditions, its ways of gaining knowledge, its assumptions about what can be known and how it can be known. (King & Brownell, 1966, p. 121)

Three of the major teaching methods are didactic discourse, supervised practice, and Socratic discussion. These are also the major communication media of most academic disciplines.

Didactic discourse is used during instruction to help students acquire organized knowledge sanctioned by a discipline. It primarily takes the form of spoken language utilized in either formal or informal lectures and written language utilized in textbooks (or digital replacements of such; Adler, 1982, pp. 22–25). The descriptions of classroom instruction using UICSM, SMSG, and MACOS at the beginning of this chapter provide examples of how didactic discourse is used. Didactic discourse has the following characteristics: (a) it is intended to be kept in mind (rather than responded to or acted on); (b) it is intended to better the mind of the recipient (through strengthening its power or improving its storage rather than simply interesting, soothing, or stimulating the recipient); (c) it is intended to help students acquire greater understanding; and (d) it is impersonal and nonsituational in that it can be transmitted to any suitably prepared student in any situation (rather than needing a special recipient and a specially prepared environment, as in the case of making love; Ryle, 1949, p. 310).

Didactic discourse can be accompanied by such things as pictures, illustrations, diagrams, equations, and demonstrations. It is also the primary mode of communication used by the academic disciplines to report their findings in journals and reports.

Supervised practice involves helping students acquire intellectual skills associated with a discipline (Adler, 1982, pp. 25–28). For example, under supervised practice, one might learn how to "do" the multiplication associated with the understanding of multiplication one acquires through didactic discourse, as illustrated in the SMSG classroom example. Or, during supervised practice, one might learn how to use the "anthropological methods of research" associated with the understanding of anthropology that one acquires from didactic discourse, as illustrated in the MACOS classroom example. Within the Scholar Academic ideology, supervised practice is always connected to knowledge of a discipline and always refers to intellectual skills. It does not refer to learning such things as how to drive a car, fix a flat tire, swim using the sidestroke, or make a bed.

Socratic discussion is a form of

> teaching by asking questions, by leading discussions, by helping students to raise their minds up from a state of understanding less to a state of understanding or appreciating more. . . . In no other way can children's understanding of what they know be improved, and their appreciation of cultural objects be enhanced. (Adler, 1982, p. 29)

This "interrogative or discussion method of teaching" (Adler, 1982, p. 29) requires students to reflect on previously learned knowledge (acquired through reading or didactic instruction) by testing their understanding against the understanding of teachers or peers through disciplined conversation in order to acquire a greater depth of understanding of the knowledge being discussed. This instructional method can be used to sharpen children's "ability to think clearly, critically, and reflectively" as a member of an academic discipline might, using previously acquired intellectual skills (acquired through supervised practice or didactic instruction; p. 30). Socratic discussion "teaches participants how to analyze their own minds as well as the thought of others, which is to say it engages students in disciplined conversation about ideas" (p. 30) in the same way in which scholars might converse about ideas during an academic colloquium or discussion. Socratic discussion is always associated with knowledge of a discipline or a discipline's way of thinking or knowing, is used to enable students to reflect on previously acquired understandings or skills, serves the purpose of increasing students' previously acquired understanding or skills, and takes place as a result of testing such understanding or skills during a conversation, carefully orchestrated by a teacher, with either a teacher or peers. It was illustrated during the discussion of MACOS classroom instruction.

Note that didactic discourse, supervised practice, and Socratic discussion are methods of instruction that complement each other, and that other instructional methods can be used in coordination with them.

Note also that the instructional methods (and thus the manner in which the student learns) embedded in a curriculum are to reflect the essence of a discipline:

> For example, the primary *method* of teaching history at any level is that of historiography, or the *method* of the mature professional [working within the discipline]. . . . Each material, reading, and lesson sequence [making up the curriculum] should be consistent with a warranted interpretation . . . of the characteristic elements of the discipline. . . . Therefore every [aspect of the curriculum] plan must have *an approach* and *a system* or *sequence* in conformance with the discipline. (King & Brownell, 1966, pp. 160, 189)

Within the Scholar Academic ideology, teachers are primarily mediators between the curriculum and the student. They are transmitters of the discipline.

Teachers are mini-scholars who devote themselves to interpreting and presenting a discipline to students rather than to the creation of new knowledge (King & Brownell, 1966, pp. 121, 197). As such, teachers must have a thorough understanding of the discipline that they teach. At the middle and secondary school levels, this means that they should have majored in college in the content area that they teach.

Evaluation

Scholar Academics believe that worthwhile curriculum knowledge is objective rather than subjective in nature. Similarly, they believe that evaluation should be objective in nature—both in terms of what types of knowledge are assessed and in terms of how one goes about assessing children, teachers, schools, and curriculum materials.

Scholar Academics are not shy or hesitant about giving tests, collecting data from tests, or using the data they collect to make comparisons. As Finn says, "Testing and assessment results are our greatest single source of information on academic performance" (1991, p. 159).

There are different purposes for evaluation. Some types of evaluation rank scores from best to worst. Other types of evaluation are criterion based and simply indicate whether a child, teacher, school, or piece of curriculum material is or is not adequate. Consistent with their hierarchical view of academic communities, Scholar Academics use evaluation measures that rank children, teachers, schools, and curriculum materials—rather than simply indicating whether they pass or fail according to some criterion. As Finn writes,

> we're accustomed to league standings in the world of baseball, price-earnings ratios in the stock market, and circulation figures in the newspaper business. Comparisons of precisely this kind in the field of education have been propelling the contemporary excellence movement. (1991, p. 172)

Given their belief in the value of objective evaluation that ranks the things being evaluated, Scholar Academics are supporters of high-stakes testing, such as the "objective" national exams mandated by the No Child Left Behind Act. As Bennett, Finn, and Cribb say, "High-stakes tests—the kind whose results really do count toward important decisions like promotion and graduation . . . are necessary" (1999, p. 587). Scholar Academics believe that high-stakes testing of children should be used for grading, promotion, and school graduation. They also advocate high-stakes testing for teacher licensure. They believe in aggregating student scores on high-stakes testing and using the results to compare schools and school districts, both to determine which schools and school districts are failing (so that they can be taken over by their state governments and improved) and to stimulate competition between school systems and thereby improve their rankings (and thus the education of their students). As Finn says,

> the exams will appraise individual achievement but will be designed so that their results can be aggregated, analyzed, and compared at all the other levels we care about: the classroom, the school, the local system, the state, and the nation as a whole. (1991, p. 265)

Scholar Academics believe in the use of aggregated student scores on high-stakes national exams at the state level and the publication of the ranked performance of each state for a number of reasons, including the stimulation of competition between states as a way of getting them to improve their educational systems and the pressuring of states to take curriculum initiatives, such as the implementation of specific types of state academic content standards, which is one way of persuading teachers and schools to teach to the tests and thereby influencing the content of the school curriculum (Finn et al., 2006). As Finn emphasizes,

the exams will differ from today's familiar standardized testing programs, too, in that teachers and schools will be encouraged to "teach to" them; indeed, preparing students for these exams will comprise a sizable portion of what schools do. . . . Working in league with the curriculum, these exams are meant to *alter* behavior in millions of individual instances. (1991, p. 264)

Two types of evaluation need discussion: student evaluation and curriculum evaluation.

Student Evaluation

Evaluation of students attempts to measure students' ability to re-present to members of the discipline that which has been transmitted to them through the curriculum. This evaluation rests on a correspondence theory of knowledge: the extent to which what is in one's mind reflects the discipline is the extent to which one possesses knowledge. The purpose of student evaluation is to certify those students who are rising within the occupational hierarchy of the discipline. Evaluation has as its intent the ranking of evaluees—assigning evaluees a sequential ordering from best to worst within the test group. The ranking is determined a posteriori through norm-referenced tests, the results of which are determined after students have been evaluated. It is not used to separate students according to what they know, but according to who knows it best.

Curriculum Evaluation

Scholar Academics use both summative and formative evaluation. Summative evaluation takes place after a curriculum is created or implemented and serves the purpose of informing the public of its effectiveness. Formative evaluation takes place while a curriculum is being developed or implemented and serves the purpose of providing information that allows the curriculum to be revised and improved.

Summative evaluation measures how well the curriculum reflects the discipline and prepares the student for further work in the discipline. Scholars (or persons behaving as they believe scholars would) determine how well the curriculum reflects the discipline. Ferris gives the flavor of this type of assessment when he writes, "Because of the *eminence* of the scientists who have been involved in the development of each of these new high school science courses, it can be *presumed* that the course content is accurate and authoritative" (Ferris, 1962, p. 162). Standardized achievement tests determine how well a curriculum prepares students for further work in the discipline.

There are two aspects of formative evaluation: one pertains to curriculum content and the other to the learning experiences used during instruction. Scholars (or persons behaving as they believe scholars would) assess curriculum content through the use of logical analysis to determine how well it reflects the discipline.

Evaluation of a curriculum's learning experiences is carried out both through logical analysis—to determine how well they embody the essence of the curriculum—and through field-testing—to determine their effectiveness in helping teachers teach and students learn the discipline. During field testing, learning experiences are assessed primarily in terms of the teacher's ability to use the curriculum with students (through informal reports from teachers of what does or does not work in the classroom) and secondarily in terms of the student's ability to learn from the curriculum (using achievement tests). In both cases, formative evaluation focuses on the overall effect of a learning experience and provides feedback such as "more refinement needed" or "things are fine" rather than details of the particular successes and failures of a learning experience.

Concluding Perspective

The Scholar Academic ideology is often assumed to represent traditional education. This is an unfair assessment. The ideology has done much to give intellectual vitality, excitement, depth, rigor, and currency to the school curriculum. Its intent of teaching children our shared cultural traditions as they are codified in the academic disciplines and stimulating children to explore the exciting world of knowledge and intellect in the same manner as scholars goes far beyond traditional educational practice. Scholar Academics' insistence that children understand the knowledge they acquire, that teachers be mini-scholars who expertly transmit that which is known to those who do not know it, and that education promote intellectual excellence has done much to improve our schools.

Through the endeavors of the Committee of Ten, the Scholar Academic ideology exerted enormous influence on the school curriculum at the end of the 19th century, when its advocates standardized the school curriculum with the academic disciplines of English, mathematics, science, history, and foreign languages at its core. Its influence then declined as other ideologies flourished. It regained its influence in the 1950s and 1960s, when, after the Sputnik scare and with the infusion of federal funds into education, advocates of the ideology updated and revitalized the content of school curriculum so that it reflected scholars' most current understanding and ways of thinking. By 1970, its influence had again declined as other ideologies became prominent, although its advocates continued their criticism of other ideologies through such media as the back-to-the-basics movement. With the rise of the standards movement at the end of the 20th century, this ideology again asserted its influence on updating the knowledge of the school curriculum, redirecting students to take college preparatory academic classes in high school, insisting that teachers be mini-scholars and have academic degrees in the subjects they taught, and promoting academic excellence. The recurring terrorist threats and fear that American education is not providing children with an adequate education to maintain the country's premier economic

❖ **Figure 2.3**   Times of relative high and low activity of the Scholar Academic ideology.

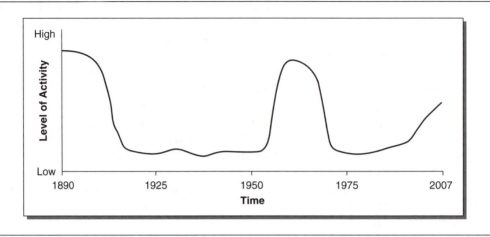

status provides a natural political and social stimulus for the Scholar Academic ideology to continue to assert its influence on American schools. Figure 2.3 provides a rough estimation of when advocates of this ideology have been most active, with respect to their own norms, in attempting to influence American education.

Activities designed to extend what is written here and provide additional insight into the ideology are located on the Sage Web site at www.sagepub .com/schiroextensionactivities.

Social Efficiency Ideology

A Scientific Technique of Curriculum Making

In 1913, Franklin Bobbitt launched the Social Efficiency ideology by demanding that educators learn to use the scientific techniques of production developed by industry (Bobbitt, 1913). In 1918, Bobbitt published *The Curriculum*—the book that marks the birth of the field of curriculum. In it he declared that the educational "task preceding all others is the determination of . . . a scientific technique" of curriculum design (Bobbitt, 1918). He described the underpinning of his scientific technique this way:

> The central theory is simple. Human life, however varied, consists in the performance of specific activities. Education that prepares for life is one that prepares . . . for these specific activities. However numerous and diverse they may be . . . they can be discovered. This requires only that one go out into the world of affairs and discover the particulars of which these affairs consist. These will show the abilities, attitudes, habits, appreciations, and forms of knowledge that men need. These will be the objectives of the curriculum. They will be numerous, definite, and particularized. The curriculum will then be that series of experiences which children and youth must have by way of attaining those objectives . . . that *series of things which children and youth must do and experience* by way of developing abilities to do the things well that make up the affairs of adult life; and to be in all respects what adults should be. (p. 42)

Note here that the "objectives" of education are assumed to be the "numerous, definite, and particularized" "performances" needed "to do the things well that make up the affairs of adult life," and that the curriculum should be the "series of things which children and youth must do and experience" to obtain those performances.

In 1949, Ralph Tyler presented Bobbitt's scientific technique in its broadest form in *Basic Principles of Curriculum and Instruction* by introducing four basic questions every educator must answer when creating curriculum or instructional programs:

1. What educational purposes should the school seek to attain?

2. What educational experiences can be provided that are likely to attain these purposes?

51

3. How can these educational experiences be effectively organized?

4. How can we determine whether these purposes are being attained? (p. 1)

Let us briefly examine each of Tyler's questions.

The first question is "What educational purposes should the school seek to attain?" In other words, what educational purposes should a curriculum or instructional program have as its goal? These "educational purposes" are what Bobbitt called the "objectives of the curriculum." Determination of curriculum objectives is the first task for Social Efficiency educators, for as Tyler says,

> if an educational program is to be planned . . . it is very necessary to have some conception of the goals that are being aimed at. These educational objectives become the criteria by which materials are selected, content is outlined, instructional procedures are developed and tests and examinations are prepared. (1949, p. 3)

During the early stages of curriculum work, Social Efficiency educators devote "much time to the setting up and formulation of objectives, because they are the most critical criteria for guiding all the other activities of the curriculum-maker" (Tyler, 1949, p. 62).

Social Efficiency educators believe curriculum objectives must be stated in behavioral terms: as observable skills, as capabilities for action, as activities people can perform, as demonstrable things people can do. The need to state objectives this way provides several insights into the Social Efficiency ideology. First, the behavioral phrasing of objectives reflects the Social Efficiency conception of the nature of man: the essence of man is expressed in the specific behaviors he can perform. Important here are both the behavioral conception of man and the conception of man as a bundle of specific skills. As Bobbitt wrote, "human life, however varied, consists in the performance of specific activities." Second, the behavioral phrasing of objectives reflects the Social Efficiency conception of the nature of education. As Tyler wrote, "education is a process of changing the behavior of people. . . . [E]ducational objectives, then, represent the kinds of changes in behavior that an educational institution seeks to bring about in its students" (1949, pp. 5–6). The essence of education can be summed up by the phrase "changing behavior." Third, the behavioral phrasing of curriculum objectives allows them to be stated in a form that facilitates the efficient scientific development of curriculum: a form that "provides clear specifications to indicate just what the educational job is" (p. 62), a form that is "most helpful in selecting learning experiences and in guiding teaching" (p. 44), and a form that makes evaluation easy.

The second question Tyler asks educators creating curriculum or instructional programs is "What educational experiences can be provided that are likely to attain these purposes?" These "educational experiences" of Tyler's are the same as Bobbitt's learning "experiences which children . . . must have by way of attaining those objectives." The "experiences" from which the child learns comprise the substance of the curriculum and are the means of attaining the ends of the curriculum as defined in its "objectives." Learning experiences have this place in curriculum because it is believed that "for a given objective to be attained, a student must have [learning] experiences that give him an opportunity to practice the kind of behavior implied by the objective"

(Tyler, 1949, p. 65). Here, "the term 'learning experience' refers to the interaction between the learner and the external conditions in the environment to which he can react" (p. 63). Two aspects of this concept of learning experiences are crucial. First, "learning takes place through the active behavior of the student; it is what he does that he learns" (p. 63). Second, "learning takes place through the experiences which the learner has; that is, through the reactions he makes to the environment in which he is placed" (p. 63).

From this perspective, both the learner and the learning experiences are crucial. The learner is crucial to the learning process because he "himself must carry on the action which is basic to the experience" from which he learns, for "it is the reactions of the learner himself that determine what is learned" (Tyler, 1949, p. 64). Learning experiences are crucial because the actions and reactions of learners are controlled, molded, or shaped through their interactions with the environment in which they are placed. The significance of this for educators follows directly: They must control the learning experiences students have by "manipulation of the environment in such a way as to set up stimulating situations—situations that will evoke the kind of behavior desired" (p. 64). In particular, they must contrive an educational environment that contains the stimulus conditions that will elicit, stimulate, reinforce, and support the behavior (actions and reactions) desired of learners as specified by their curriculum's objectives.

Note that action that one performs is viewed as different from content stored in the mind. It is the former that is valued and not the latter. Social Efficiency curricula specify behavior that is learned, not content that is acquired.

The third question Tyler presents is "How can these educational experiences be effectively organized?" This is similar to Bobbitt's concern with creating an effective *series* of experiences that children encounter as they run the curriculum.

> In order for educational experiences to produce a cumulative effect, they must be so organized as to reinforce each other. Organization is . . . important . . . in curriculum development because it greatly influences the efficiency of instruction and the degree to which major educational changes are brought about in the learners. (Tyler, 1949, p. 83)

Important here is the word *efficiency*. Effective organization of learning experiences allows curriculum objectives to be *efficiently* accomplished by stimulating learning to take place in the most *efficient* manner possible—where efficiency is defined in terms of expenditure of time, money, and human resources.

The fourth question educators must answer is "How can we determine whether these purposes are being attained?" For the Social Efficiency ideology, "the process of evaluation begins with the objectives of the educational program" (Tyler, 1949, p. 110) and "is essentially the process of determining to what extent the educational objectives are actually being realized by the . . . curriculum" (pp. 105–106). Since "educational objectives are essentially changes in human beings," it follows that "evaluation is the process for determining the degree to which these changes in behavior are actually taking place" (p. 106). Important here is that the behavioral conceptions of man and education, which result in the stating of educational purposes as behavioral objectives, also result in a concept of evaluation limited to the overt behavior of the evaluee and the specific behaviors stated in the educational objectives. And since, as Bobbitt says, "the objectives of the curriculum . . . will be numerous, definite, and particularized," it follows that evaluation will be numerous, definite, and particularized.

In summary, the scientific technique of the Social Efficiency ideology consists of determining "educational purposes," "educational experiences . . . to attain these purposes," effective organization of these experiences, and evaluative measures to "determine whether these purposes are being attained" in accordance with a behavioral interpretation of the nature of man and education.

Programmed Curriculum and the Behavioral Engineer

The type of curriculum valued by Social Efficiency educators can be called programmed curriculum. Many types of programmed curricula exist, from individualized computer instruction to programmed courses taught to large groups of students; from mechanical teaching machines that offer students few learning choices to individually prescribed instruction where student interests, abilities, learning styles, and learning rates are accommodated; from environment simulators in which teachers are unnecessary to curriculum packages where the teacher is the center of attention; from programmed textbooks to multimedia courses. Description of one delivery system, the assumptions underlying it, and the procedures used in creating it will illustrate what is meant by programmed curriculum and the scientific technique.

Type to Learn is an individualized instruction curriculum designed to teach students to type using a computer (Sunburst Technology, 2001). The program begins with a movie that tells students about a time travel mission they are going on, introduces them to keyboarding ergonomics, and shows them the keyboard and how to place their hands on it. Students then begin the "mission," which includes 30 lessons, each including review of any previously learned keyboarding skills, demonstration of new keyboarding skills, practice using the new skills, assessments, and a reward in the form of a game when students pass the final assessment for the lesson. An early lesson teaches how to type using the f, j, and space bar keys. The lesson begins with the computer speaking to the student and demonstrating how to type f, j, and space using an animated image of a keyboard and three-dimensional hands. Immediately after the demonstration, students practice typing f, j, and space, with one keyboard stroke being introduced at a time. For example, students might have to type the following sequence of strokes: *fff jjj ffjj fjfj*. If a student makes a mistake, he or she is not allowed to continue until the mistake is corrected. If a mistake is made or the student does not respond in a certain amount of time, the computer first prompts the student with a visual and auditory cue; if this fails to stimulate the appropriate response, it demonstrates how to complete the task with an animated visual of the 3D hands typing the appropriate response. The computer constantly assesses students' accuracy and speed and presents this information to them as well as saves this information in a teacher management program. When students finish practicing typing the f, j, and space, they are given a test. If they pass the test—with sufficient typing accuracy and speed—they are given a reward in the form of a chance to play a game in which they practice the typing skills they have learned thus far. There are several types of games. Key Figures is a keyboarding speed– and accuracy–building exercise in which students meet 50 historical people. To play Dictation, students type exactly what they hear historical people say. Windshield Typers is designed to improve left- and right-hand coordination as students clear the sands of time from their windshield.

Type to Learn carefully sequences the skills students learn as they move from typing individual letters to typing pairs of letters, short words, longer words, sentences, and longer passages, including capital letters and punctuation marks. Students cannot progress to the next lesson until they have satisfactorily completed all previous lessons. As they work through the curriculum, their performance is saved in a teacher management program that records such things as typing accuracy, typing speed, and keys students have difficulty with. Teachers can thus review each student's records and individually adjust passing scores for tests, the amount of practice required, vocabulary levels, and so on.

Type to Learn was designed to provide students with the keyboarding skills they will need as adults to perform well in jobs that require the use of a computer—which are most jobs these days. A secondary benefit of the program is that it builds keyboarding skills that enable students to efficiently complete school and college assignments. The skills students acquire are carefully sequenced from less difficult to more difficult, until performance competency is achieved. The learning experiences students encounter directly simulate activities they will encounter as keyboarders—that is, they learn to type by typing on a computer keyboard. During the program, students are active learners who develop their skills by shaping their behavior in accordance with the requirements of Type to Learn. Students' progress is constantly assessed as they learn. During the program, the teacher is a manager of student progress who adjusts such things in the computer program as vocabulary levels.

Programmed Curriculum

Type to Learn is a programmed curriculum that consists of a carefully sequenced set of learning experiences, each representing a behavior to be learned. Each learning experience consists of one keystroke to be typed and the corresponding correct response. The learning experiences that make up the program are designed and sequenced in such a way as to gradually lead the learner from incompetence to competence.

The method of "behavioral engineering" used to design Type to Learn contains both a conceptual component that explains how programmed curriculum teaches and a methodological component that specifies how it should be created. Underlying both is the curriculum developer's conception of himself as a "behavioral engineer."

Understanding how programmed curriculum teaches requires an understanding of the Social Efficiency view of the nature of teaching and learning. The behavioral engineer views teaching as a process of shaping learners' behavior through the use of rewards or reinforcements. Learners' behavior is to be shaped in such a way that the occurrence of a specific stimulus automatically results in the emission of a desired response. The stimulus that Type to Learn produces for learners is the auditory and visual presentation of a letter, word, sentence, or (eventually) passage. The desired response is typing the corresponding keystroke or keystrokes to replicate the stimulus. Learners are provided several reinforcements and rewards for correct responses: presentation of the next stimulus, a window that constantly updates one's typing speed and accuracy, and, after each lesson's final test, a fun (skill-building) game. The behavior of learners is shaped both by arranging the rewards of learning in such a way that they reinforce the connection between the desired response and the specific stimulus upon which it is contingent, and by not letting a learner proceed to more advanced learning experiences until the desired response to a specific stimulus is automatically emitted.

Underlying this view of teaching and learning are several assumptions.

First, Social Efficiency educators assume that learning consists of a change in behavior, the new behavior being the emitting of a response to a stimulus that would not otherwise have taken place. Something is learned from Type to Learn when a learner responds to a stimulus—correctly typing the keystroke presented by the computer—in a way that he or she would not have prior to exposure to the curriculum.

Second, Social Efficiency educators assume that learning takes place only as a result of learners' practice of the behavior they are to learn, for it is what one does that one learns. The assumption is that people learn by constructing in their brains the connections that allow them to automatically respond appropriately to stimuli. In Type to Learn, learners practice the behavior they are to learn and in so doing learn, because they are required to respond to a stimulus by actually emitting the desired behavior so many times that the stimulus response connections they construct in their minds become automatic. Learning, in fact, takes place in three stages: a cognitive stage, an associative stage, and an automatic stage (Lauber, Robinson, Kim, & Davis, 2001). During the cognitive stage, Type to Learn presents a demonstration of the skill to be learned—an animated movie of hands typing the required keystrokes in response to a verbal and visual stimulus (the letters or other material to be typed) as well as a verbal description of how to type those keystrokes. During this stage, learners store in memory an image of the skill that is to be performed and try to execute the skill by talking or reasoning themselves through it. In the associative stage, learners gradually eliminate errors in performance. Here, connections between stimulus and response are strengthened by practice in such a way that reason can guide but does not need to be used in performance of a particular skill (in other words, understanding combined with the reason that leads to action is gradually transformed into procedural knowledge that leads to automatic performance of the required skill). During the automatic stage, skills learned in the associative stage become increasingly automatic as learners continue to practice typing keystrokes in response to the presentation of text in visual and verbal formats. At this stage, the need to use verbal knowledge, memory, and reason to perform a skill disappear as the connections between stimulus and response become automatic and occur with such ease that verbal mediation disappears. Learning results as learners construct the mental connections that allow them to automatically perform a keystroke in response to a verbal or visual stimulus.

Third, it is assumed that learning consists of acquiring specific responses to particular stimuli rather than general responses to vague stimuli. For example, in Type to Learn, it is assumed that one does not learn to type in general, but that one learns how to replicate specific letters seen or heard with specific corresponding keystrokes. Type to Learn presents one stimulus to learners at a time, to which there is only one specific and clearly defined response.

Fourth, it is assumed that learners acquire complex behaviors gradually by slowly building up ever more complex repertoires of behavior out of simpler ones. Programmed curricula move learners in finely graded steps through many unitary learning experiences, each of which develops a single behavior in such a way that successive, more complex behaviors build on the simpler behaviors preceding them. For example, Type to Learn first teaches individual keystrokes, then combinations of keystrokes, then words, and eventually teaches the learner to duplicate longer textual and verbalized passages. In addition, a programmed curriculum guarantees that learners will actually gradually build ever more complex repertoires of behavior, because it evaluates learners' responses to each learning experience and does not allow them to advance to subsequent levels of complexity until they have demonstrated that they have mastered the preceding material.

Fifth, it is assumed that all aspects of learning can be dealt with by using this view of teaching and learning. Complex behaviors, such as learning how to fly an airplane, simply require the development of complex teaching machines, such as the computerized flight simulators developed by the U.S. Air Force. Learning intellectual skills can also be taught. For instance, mathematical problem solving simply requires that learners be provided with (a) advanced organizers and problem solving demonstrations so that they can, with the aid of memory and reason, respond to stimuli and replicate the demonstrations when presented with new problems, and then (b) much practice internalizing the desired problem solving skills in such a way that they become automatic responses to certain types of mathematical problems.

Behavioral Engineering

Social Efficiency educators construct programmed curricula through the use of "behavioral engineering" (Holland, 1960, p. 275). Behavioral engineers engage in five basic tasks, which parallel Tyler's questions, while developing curriculum.

Their first task is to obtain educational purposes for their curricula. These are behaviorally phrased and specify the terminal performances learners are to acquire. Educational purposes are obtained from clients for whom programs are designed—behavioral engineers do not invent them themselves. Possible clients include society, scholarly organizations, parents, teachers, publishers, and businesses. Type to Learn was designed for an educational publisher who had determined that businesses, industry, and schools wanted workers and students to have keyboarding skills.

The second task behavioral engineers undertake is careful analysis of their program's educational purpose to find a sequence of specific behavioral objectives, each of which represents one stimulus-response contingency that a learner must acquire in order to gradually move from incompetence to competence. Different forms of this analysis are referred to as task analysis, activity analysis, and the construction of a learning hierarchy. Construction of a learning hierarchy

> requires that the behaviors that lead to terminal behaviors [be] carefully analyzed and sequenced in a hierarchical order such that each behavior builds on the objective immediately below it in the sequence and is prerequisite to those that follow it. (Holland, 1960, p. 275)

Robert Gagne describes the construction of a learning hierarchy this way:

> Analysis of a topic begins with the statement of the terminal objective—the performance or performances one expects the student to be able to exhibit after the learning of that topic has been completed. Once this objective has been satisfactorily defined, one can proceed to identify a subordinate set of subtopics, each an individual learning act, that must be considered prerequisites for the learning. Each of these subtopics in turn may be subjected to the same process of analysis, until one has arrived at performances that the students are known to possess, at which point the analysis stops. Each subordinate objective, then, is derived by systematically applying to the next higher objective the question, "What must the student already know how to do, in order to learn this performance?" The description of what the student must know—in other words, the prerequisite capabilities he must have—identifies the subordinate objectives. (1970, p. 329)*

This is not a simple endeavor, for creation of a program of any length requires defining and sequencing many specific behavioral objectives. Underlying each of the 30 units in Type to Learn are several subordinate objectives, such as "When presented with the letter *j* in written form, the learner will press the *j* key on a computer keyboard with the first finger of the right hand."

The third task behavioral engineers undertake is creation of the learning experiences that the learner will encounter while moving through the curriculum. Learning experiences consist of activities in which students engage that contain stimuli associated with the responses students are to learn. Each learning experience must be created to correspond to one of the clearly specified subordinate behavioral objectives previously defined as a result of task analysis. Larger learning experiences may consist of several smaller learning experiences. Each of the 30 units in Type to Learn presents students with several learning experiences, including demonstrations, practice of newly learned skills, practice of previously learned skills, and games.

The fourth task is to organize the learning experiences that the learner will encounter. This involves creating a linear sequence of experiences that parallels the sequence of specific subordinate behavior objectives derived as a result of task analysis. In Type to Learn, part of the sequence of each unit involves the repeated format of experiences that provide opportunities to review previously learned skills, demonstrate new skills to be learned, practice new skills, assess new skills, and practice new and old skills in the form of games. In the end,

> the actual instructional content of a program consists of a sequence of learning tasks or activities . . . through which a student can proceed with little outside help, and provides a series of small increments in learning that enables the student to proceed from a condition of lack of command of the terminal behavior to that of command of it. (Lindvall & Bolvin, 1967, p. 231)

The fifth task behavioral engineers undertake is designing evaluative measures to accompany each learning experience. Evaluative measures are developed to assess

---

*From *The Conditions of Learning* by Gagne, R. M., copyright © 1970. Reprinted with permission from Harriett T. Gagne.

whether or not learners acquire the desired behavior from each learning experience. They serve the following functions:

- They provide "rather immediate feedback to the student concerning the adequacy of his performance on each frame or element of the program" (Lindvall & Bolvin, 1967, p. 231) under the assumption that "learning is enhanced if students receive rather immediate feedback concerning the correctness of their efforts in attempting to approximate a desired behavior" (p. 249).
- They determine whether learners will be allowed to proceed to successive program experiences or whether they must do additional work before proceeding. They do so by assessing whether or not learners have acquired the desired behavior from each learning experience—that is, made the correct response to the program's stimulus.
- They provide a continual "monitoring function, both for the learner and the teacher" (Lindvall & Bolvin, 1967, p. 231) that can keep them both "rather continuously informed regarding [the learner's] goals and his performance" (p. 249).
- They provide the behavioral engineer with information about the effectiveness of a program in obtaining its educational purposes. Such information can be used as a basis for revising either the learning experiences or their sequence (formative evaluation) or for proving that the curriculum accomplishes its purposes (summative evaluation).

In summary, those who design programmed curriculum view themselves as behavioral engineers who use scientific techniques to design a series of experiences that shape the behaviors of learners to satisfy the needs of a client.

The Analogy

In an analogy comparing curriculum development to the industrial manufacture of steel rails, Franklin Bobbitt laid bare the essentials of the Social Efficiency ideology. The school is compared to a factory. The child is the raw material. The adult is the finished product. The teacher is an operative, or factory worker. The curriculum is whatever processing the raw material (the child) needs to change him into the finished product (the desired adult). The curriculum developer is a member of the research department who investigates what the consumer market (society) wants in terms of a finished product and finds the most efficient way of producing that finished product (Bobbitt, 1913).

Objectives and Standards

Curriculum workers, thus, have two tasks: they must determine what the consumer market wants in terms of a finished product, and they must determine the most efficient way of producing that product. Bobbitt describes these tasks in his first two principles of curriculum making:

Principle I. Definite qualitative and quantitative standards must be determined for the product [the desired adult].

Principle II. Where the material [man] that is acted upon by the labor processes [teacher] passes through a number of progressive stages on its way from the raw material [child] to the ultimate product [adult], definite qualitative and quantitative standards must be determined for the product at each of these stages. (1913, p. 11)

The first principle refers to the creation of a curriculum's terminal objectives, or what Tyler calls educational purposes. They designate the ends of the curriculum and the standards that indicate when the ends have been satisfactorily met. Social Efficiency educators between about 1910 and 1940—including Franklin Bobbitt—focused their efforts on fulfilling Principle I.

The second principle refers to the creation of progressive objectives, which consist of the series of specific behavioral objectives that collectively specify the step-by-step changes in learners that transform them from incompetence to competence and the standards that indicate when each progressive objective is accomplished. Social Efficiency educators between about 1950 and 1975 focused their efforts on Principle II. Robert Gagne is an example of such an educator.

Both of these principles refer to determining "definite qualitative and quantitative standards" that specify whether learners are meeting the requirements of objectives as they traverse the curriculum. From 1980 until now, some politicians and administrators promoting the Social Efficiency ideology have focused their efforts on establishing curriculum standards and performance-based accountability methods that hold learners, teachers, and schools accountable for meeting the requirements of such standards. The establishment of educational standards has been promoted by pressuring states to develop curriculum standards. Performance-based accountability methods have been promoted through political means and involve the use of management, accounting, and budgetary techniques to shape the behavior of educators. These are illustrated by the No Child Left Behind Act and the Teaching Commission report (2004).

Social Efficiency educators have emphasized the importance of terminal objectives, progressive objectives, educational standards, and accountability for almost a hundred years. However, differential emphasis has been placed on them at different times.

Social Orientation and Terminal Objectives

In Bobbitt's analogy, society is the source from which terminal objectives are determined. Since society does not realize the importance of specifically stating terminal objectives, it becomes educators' job to discover them. Educators, acting as agents of society, must determine the needs of society and the products that fulfill those needs. Just as a steel mill is no more than a contractor to do a job for railroads in making rails, so too are educators and schools no more than contractors to do a job for society in making suitable adults. Bobbitt puts it this way:

> It is well to note also, for our purposes, that the standard qualifications of the product are not determined by the steel plant itself. The qualitative and quantitative specifications are determined by those that order the product, in this case, the railroads. The steel mills are but agents of the railroad. . . . Now the relation of the school system to the various departments of the world's activity is exactly the same as the relation of the steel plant to the transportation industry. . . . It is the need of the world of affairs that determines the standard specification for the educational product. A school system can no more find standards of performance within itself than a steel plant can find the proper height or weight per yard for steel rails from the activities within the plant. . . . The standards must of necessity be determined . . . by those that use the product, not by those who produce it. . . . Standards are to be found in the world of affairs, not in the schools. (1913, pp. 12, 33–35)

Progressive Objectives

This is not the case for progressive objectives. Although society specifies the desired product of the schools, it is educators who determine the most efficient way of producing it:

> The progressive standards required by the second principle must be psychologically and experimentally determined by expert educational workers within the school system itself. This is a special professional problem requiring scientific investigation of a highly technical sort. It is a field of work in which the untrained layman can have no opinion and in which he has no right to interfere. Society is to say what shall be accomplished in the ultimate education of each class of individuals. Only the specialist can determine how it is to be done. (Bobbitt, 1913, p. 37)

Education

Within the Social Efficiency ideology, the production of an educated person through schooling is viewed in much the same way as the production of steel rails:

> Education is a shaping process as much as the manufacture of steel rails; the personality is to be shaped and fashioned into desirable forms. It is a shaping of more delicate matters, more immaterial things, certainly; yet a shaping process none the less. It is also an enormously more complex process because of the great multitude of aspects of the personality to be shaped if the whole as finished is to stand in full and right proportions. (Bobbitt, 1913, p. 12)

Scientific Instrumentalism

The central myth of the Social Efficiency ideology is "scientific instrumentalism" (Patty, 1938, pp. 6–7). This myth asserts that (a) curriculum should be developed in a "scientific" manner similar to the way industry produces its products and (b) curriculum development should be an "instrument" in fulfilling needs unassociated with its own vested interests in a manner similar to the way industry fulfills needs unassociated with its own interests.

The method is called "scientific" because educators attempt to use scientific procedures, placing their faith in what they conceive to be scientific method and technology. The method is called "instrumentalistic" because educators using it conceive of themselves as instruments and of their method as an instrument useful in fulfilling an end that is disjoint from themselves and their method.

Social Orientation

Society

The Social Efficiency ideology views education as a social process that perpetuates existing social functions. Bobbitt infers this when he writes,

> We are accustomed to say that education is a social process. It is the process of recivilizing, or civilizing anew, each new generation.

Each individual, we are told, is born on the cultural level of one hundred thousand years ago. He is but a bundle of potentialities. He brings with him no portion of our accumulated human culture. Literally, he is born a savage. Education is the process of so conditioning his activities and experiences that, as he grows up, he is shaped into the normally civilized man.

What is true of the individual is true of the whole new generation. . . . Society has the responsibility of so conditioning the growth of this new generation that it takes over and exhibits in its conduct the high and complex culture activities which man has been slowly inventing, accumulating, and habituating himself to during the long period of human history. Society's performance of this recivilizing function we call education. (1924a, p. 453)

Two Social Efficiency assumptions alluded to here are critical. First, society is viewed as consisting of a "system of activities" (Bobbitt, 1926, p. 1). Second, the essence of society is viewed as located in the activities its adult members engage in. Society is defined in terms of the "affairs of the mature world" and not in terms of the affairs of youth (Bobbitt, 1918, p. 207).

People in Society

People are first members of society and second individuals. As members of society, people have two characteristics.

First, people are conceived of as actors within society. Their essence is determined by the behaviors they can successfully perform. Bobbitt elaborates on this from the context of what Social Efficiency educators are reacting against:

A recently published book begins with the sentence "Education is the process of filling the mind with knowledge." In that single sentence we have the central conception of the old education. According to this conception, a human being, as he begins life, is mainly but an empty knowledge reservoir. The business of education is to fill this reservoir with the prepared facts of history, geography, grammar, science, and the rest. . . . Man is not a mere intellectual reservoir to be filled with knowledge. He is an infinitely complex creature of endlessly diversified *action*. His most salient characteristic is not his memory reservoir, whether filled or unfilled, but *action, conduct, behavior*. Action is the thing of which his life is made. In his activity he lives and realizes the ends of his existence[;] . . . his behavior is his life. Primarily, he is not a *knower*, but a *doer*. . . . Since he is primarily a doer, to educate him is to prepare him to perform those activities which make up his life. The method of the new education is not subject storage but *action*, activity, conduct, behavior. (1924c, pp. 45–47)

Second, people's essence is viewed as embodied in their mature adult behavior. As such, childhood is viewed as a stage of preparation for adulthood. Childhood is not important in and of itself. It is important because it provides a time to prepare for adulthood. Thus, education of the 6-year-old is to prepare for that of the 7-year-old, the education of the 7-year-old for that of the 8-year-old, and so on until maturity is reached. As Bobbitt says, "it is helpful to begin with the simple assumption, to be accepted literally, that education is to prepare men and women for the activities of every kind which make up, or which ought to make up, well-rounded adult life" (1924b, p. 7).

> Modern education . . . has discovered the child, but it does not see him merely as a child. . . . It sees the man within the child as clearly as it sees the child. It sees its task as one of bringing into full and complete being this man within the child. (Bobbitt, 1924c, p. 48)

The educator always keeps in mind "the man within the child," viewing the education of the child as preparation for his or her adulthood within society, for as Bobbitt insists, "education is primarily for adult life, not for child life. Its fundamental responsibility is to prepare for the fifty years of adulthood, not for the twenty years of childhood and youth" (1924b, p. 8).

Educating People to Live in Society

The aim of education is twofold: first, to perpetuate the functioning of society, and second, to prepare the individual to lead a meaningful adult life in society. An individual achieves an education by learning to perform the functions one must perform to be socially functional. In addition, the educated person is one who acts appropriately in society. Each of these statements needs clarification.

The necessity for perpetuating society is accepted unquestionably. The means of perpetuating society is preparation of the individuals who will constitute it to fulfill the social roles needed to sustain its functioning. This is the job of the school: "Society possesses the right to require that the school shall educate its offspring so that they will be prepared to carry on the work of society with efficiency" (Bobbitt, 1924b, p. 13).

Society is made up of people. And people take on their meaning, as well as their fulfillment and pleasure, by participating in society. The way to prepare individuals to lead meaningful adult lives in society is to provide them with the skills that will allow them to be constructive, active members of society. This is also the job of the school:

> It is this social organization that must transform the highly dependent young child into the adult who, in his own individual manner, lives a life that is satisfying to himself largely because it contributes to the goals of his society. (Gagne, 1965b, p. 237)

(Thus, children learn to type because keyboarding is a skill adults need to efficiently contribute to the goals of society and to their success as members of society.)

People are taught to perpetuate the functioning of society and to constructively function in society through "functional education," a term that applies both to teaching students to *function in the future activities* in which they will be engaged once they become mature members of society, and to teaching students to act in the desired way by having them *function in the desired way*. (Thus, children learn to type by typing with the correct fingering.) Functional education thus derives the means by which education is to take place directly from the ends of education: "One learns to act in desired ways by acting in those ways" (Bobbitt, 1924d, pp. 292–293). Bobbitt elaborates:

> One learns to act by acting. One learns to live by living. Behavior is not only the end of life but also the process of life and equally the end and process of education. . . . Education is preparation for life, and life is a series of activities. Education, therefore, is preparation for

the performance of those activities. Let us discover what the activities are which make up man's life and we have the objectives of education. . . . In discovering the objectives in terms of activities, however, one is also discovering the fundamental processes involved in achieving these same objectives, since, obviously, the way to learn to perform an activity is to perform it. (1924c, pp. 47, 49)

Finally, the educated person is one who functions appropriately and effectively in society. The ability to act correctly, rather than the knowledge of what the correct action should be, is what is important to learn. As Bobbitt puts it, "the business of education today is to teach to the growing individuals, so far as their original natures will permit, to perform efficiently those activities which constitute the latest and highest level of civilization" (1926, pp. 1–2). Education

has the function of training every citizen, man or woman, not for knowledge about citizenship, but for proficiency in citizenship. . . . We have been developing knowledge, not function; the power to reproduce facts, rather than the powers to think and feel and will and act in vital relation to the world's life. (Bobbitt, 1918, p. iv)

Education for a Future Better Society

Social Efficiency educators view themselves as instruments furthering the development of a future society superior to the existent one and not as proponents of the status quo. Although they see the school as the guardian of the system of values and institutions that the society has already evolved, their aims of education for both the child and the society are phrased in the future tense:

Education under the circumstances has, therefore, a double task to perform: (1) to act as a primary agency of social progress, lifting the world to a higher and more desirable level; (2) to do this by educating the rising generation so that they will perform their . . . functions in a manner greatly superior to that of their fathers. The task is to develop in the rising generation, not merely the degree of proficiency found in the world about them, but to carry them much beyond; to look, not merely to the actual practices, but rather to those that ought to be. It is so to train them that the . . . mistakes, weaknesses, imperfections, maladjustments, etc., that now appear so numerously in the . . . situations of their fathers shall be as fully as practicable eliminated in that more harmonious and more efficient . . . regime that they are to establish and maintain. (Bobbitt, 1918, p. 64)

The preparation of society for the future is based on precedents within current society. The strategy for change is not to look for new behaviors more appropriate than existing ones, but to reinforce strengths and desirable traits within current society while eliminating its weaknesses and deficiencies. The assumption is that cultural evolution takes place by training youth to do that which is done most efficiently and effectively in the culture and to avoid that which is done inefficiently and ineffectively. By this differential reinforcement-elimination it is believed that the betterment and evolution of society will be achieved.

Objectives

Several consequences of how Social Efficiency educators deal with terminal and progressive objectives require discussion. This requires that the form of objectives and the methods of deriving them be examined further.

Terminal objectives are the educational purposes of curriculum, the ends toward which educators directs their efforts in their attempts to perpetuate society by providing people with the skills needed to productively function within society. Their discovery and clear specification is the first task educators undertake.

Franklin Bobbitt defines progressive objectives when he states that "the material [man] that is acted upon by the labor processes [teacher] passes through a number of progressive stages on its way from the raw material [child] to the ultimate product [adult]." Progressive objectives are the specific behavioral objectives that designate the particular tasks ("progressive stages") the student must sequentially master ("pass through") in order to achieve competency in the activity inherent in the terminal objective (become "the ultimate product"). Deriving and sequencing progressive objectives is the second task of educators.

The Form of Objectives

The technology of scientific instrumentalism in combination with the behavioral conception of the nature of man requires that curriculum objectives be stated as behavioral objectives. There are several characteristics of behavioral objectives.

First, they must be stated in behavioral terms that specify observable behaviors, action capabilities, actions, skills, or cognitive processes. This excludes many things:

> To "know," to "understand," to "appreciate," to "gain insight into," and so on, are excellent words to convey general purposes, but they are not useful as descriptions of reliably observable behavior; nor are their intended meanings easily agreed upon by a number of individuals. (American Association for the Advancement of Science [AAAS], Commission on Science Education, 1968)

Second, to be useful, objectives must be self-contained, unitary in effect, "definite and particularized." Social Efficiency educators consider it impractical to attempt to accomplish vague and general objectives, such as teaching citizenship. As Bobbitt phrases it,

> education cannot take the first step in training for citizenship until it has particularized the characteristics of the good citizen. The training task is to develop those characteristics. It is not enough to aim at "good citizenship" in a vague general way. . . . The citizen has functions to perform. We are to develop ability to perform those functions. But first we must know with particularity what they are. (1918, p. 117)

Third, Social Efficiency educators endeavor to state objectives in a standardized form. From Gagne's perspective, an objective . . . is a verbal statement . . . having the following components: 1. A *verb* denoting observable action (draw, identify, recognize, compute, and many other words qualify; know, grasp, see, and others do not). 2. A description of the *class of stimuli* being responded to (for example, "Given the printed statement ab + ac = a(b + c)"). 3. A word or phrase denoting the *object used for action* by the performer, unless, this is implied by the verb (for example, if the verb is "draw," this phrase might be "with a ruling pen"; if it is "state," the word might simply be "orally"). 4. A description of the *class of correct responses* (for example, "a right triangle," or "the sum," or "the name of the rule"). (1970, pp. 326–327)

According to those who rewrote Bloom's *Taxonomy of Educational Objectives* in 2001, "educational objectives indicate that the student should be able to do something (verb) to or with something (noun)—a verb-noun relationship" (Anderson et al., 2001, p. 265). For the cognitive domain, this involves using one of the following verbs (or one of their many subtypes): *remember, understand, apply, analyze, evaluate, create.* Each specifies a "cognitive process," action, or behavior. Stating educational objectives this way also involves using one of the noun phrases of factual knowledge, conceptual knowledge, procedural knowledge, or metacognitive knowledge (or one of their subtypes) to specify a type of knowledge students are expected to acquire or construct.

Fourth, terminal and progressive objectives can take on meaning associated with many types of human activity, including cognitive, affective, and psychomotor activity. In addition, terminal and progressive objectives are discoverable or derivable. As Bobbitt says,

they can be discovered. This requires only that one go out into the world of affairs and discover the particulars of which these affairs consist. These will show the abilities, attitudes, habits, appreciations, and forms of knowledge that men need. They will be the objectives of the curriculum. They will be numerous, definite, and particularized. (1918, p. 42)

Social Efficiency curricula are, however, far more often designed to teach physical and cognitive skills than affective skills.

Fifth, the form of curriculum objectives is often of greater concern to Social Efficiency educators than their content. Educators view themselves as agents of clients, whose vested interests are in the content of the objectives. Social Efficiency educators' vested interests are in designing curricula that satisfy their clients. Educators focus their endeavors on clearly specifying the clients' desires, efficiently deriving objectives, and accurately assessing behavior. As Mager comments in *Preparing Instructional Objectives*, "this book is not concerned with which objectives are desirable or good. It concerns itself with the form of a usefully stated objective" (1962, p. 1).

Gathering Terminal Objectives

Essential to determination of terminal objectives is for educators to "go out into the field, actually study the men and women as individuals, and generalize on the basis of a numerical count of cases" (Peters, 1930b, p. 433). "Going out into the field" and "numerical count of cases" are critical because society has not delivered to schools a complete and definitive list of terminal objectives (except during the standards movement at the end of the 20th and beginning of the 21st centuries, when Social Efficiency adherents pressured states to adopt, adapt, or create content standards). As a result, educators must act as agents of society in discovering terminal objectives. Different approaches can be taken. Early in the 20th century, Bobbitt attempted to poll the whole of American society as a first step to discovering both what its needs were and how it felt such needs could be satisfied. During the middle of the 20th century, Gagne interviewed many scientists as he worked on *Science: A Process Approach* (AAAS, 1968). In so doing, he made heavy use of personal interviews as a means of collecting data. In both cases, it was necessary to "go out into the field . . . and generalize on the basis of a numerical count of cases."

In compiling terminal objectives, educators first determine "what are the major divisions or fields of human action?" and then "in each major field—whether six, ten, twenty, or fifty—what are the specific adult activities of the good type?" (Bobbitt, 1918, p. 5). This involves first specifying the major fields of human action and then partitioning each field into a set of specific behaviors, such that each specific behavior can be represented as a terminal objective to be aimed at. As Gagne says of terminal objectives, it is "necessary to *break them down into smaller units* representing fairly specific intellectual skills" (1970, p. 245). As Bobbitt states, these objectives will be "minute" and "numerous" (1924b, pp. 8–10). This has been the procedure used by many states and professional organizations in developing curriculum content standards since the end of the 20th century.

Acquiring Progressive Objectives

The process of formulating the "progressive stages" that the student must pass through in moving from incompetence ("raw material") to competence ("finished product") is called activity analysis. Activity analysis exists in a wide variety of forms. Two of them—Bobbitt's and Gagne's—will be briefly discussed.

Franklin Bobbitt's early form of activity analysis is based on an assembly line model of education. It includes three basic stages. First, the overall job to be completed—the performance necessary to achieve the terminal objective—is broken down into a finite set of tasks that need to be completed, the sum of which result in the completed job. Second, each task is analyzed to find the most efficient way of performing it. (Bobbitt used elapsed time as the criterion of efficiency.) Third, a flow chart is created that specifies the manner in which each task is to be performed, the time allowed to complete each task, the standards that each task must meet, and the sequence in which the tasks are to be completed.

Robert Gagne's form of activity analysis begins with the analysis of a terminal objective. Gagne begins by asking the question, "What must the learner already know how to do in order to achieve this performance, assuming that he is to be given only instructions?" (1963, p. 622). Let us say that the learner could not perform the task specified by the terminal objective unless he could first perform prerequisite tasks A and B. A pyramid begins, as illustrated in Figure 3.1.

❖ **Figure 3.1** Pyramid of prerequisite objectives.

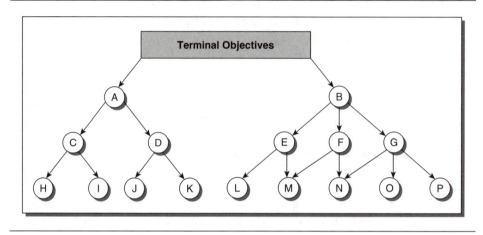

Tasks A and B are now the new objectives to be accomplished, which Gagne calls "prerequisite objectives." Gagne now asks his question again, this time regarding prerequisite objectives A and B: "What must the learner already know how to do in order to achieve this performance, assuming that he is to be given only instructions?" Let us say that the learner must be able to perform tasks C and D in order to perform task A, and that he or she must be able to perform tasks E, F, and G in order to perform task B. The learning pyramid grows, as illustrated in Figure 3.1. The process is then repeated with C, D, E, F, and G as the prerequisite objectives. The result of this next stage of analysis might produce the more complete learning pyramid illustrated in Figure 3.1.

In this manner, educators build a pyramid of prerequisites to the terminal objective. The process ends when the subordinate performances possessed by every learner for whom the learning program is intended are arrived at. This pyramid of prerequisite objectives capped by a terminal objective is called a learning hierarchy. Once the initial learning hierarchy is deductively derived, it is empirically tested to see if it is "psychologically" complete and accurately ordered. Then the two-dimensional hierarchy is broken down into a one-dimensional learning sequence that preserves the hierarchical prerequisite nature of the learning hierarchy. In running the curriculum, the student proceeds through this learning sequence to attain the performance abilities inherent in the terminal objective.

Atomism

To put objectives in a behavioral form that is self-contained, unitary in effect, and "definite and particularized," the aims of an educator's client must be broken down into unitary and self-contained entities. This breaking down of a general objective or partitioning of a complex behavior into its smallest unitary actions is called atomism. In creating terminal objectives, educators must atomize the field of action they are preparing individuals to function within. They must break up the field of action into sufficiently small units such that each is of the smallest convenient size. They must treat the behaviors they are formulating into terminal objectives as a set of independent actions, the sum of which make up the complete behavior. This means that one must conceive of human life and human activity as capable of being "broken up into a very large number of specialized activities, for the most part distinctly marked off from each other" (Peters, 1930b, p. 84).

Constructing progressive objectives through activity analysis also involves atomism. The process of transforming the raw material into the finished product involves breaking the desired activity up into a finite sequence of unitary subactivities, each of which is analyzed and treated as an individual atomistic process within the larger activity.

Underlying the Social Efficiency approach to curriculum is, thus, the belief that human life and human activity can be divided into a large number of self-contained, specialized activities, each distinct from the others. In addition, Social Efficiency educators treat the atomistic activities they construct as though they can be directly assembled into larger activities through a simple additive process. That is, the sum of the independent unitary subactions comprising progressive objectives is assumed to equal the complete terminal behavior.

Objective Reality

The necessity of collecting terminal objectives by "going out into the field, actually studying men and women as individuals, and generalizing on the basis of a numerical count of cases" raises questions about the types of reality Social Efficiency educators are concerned about. The distinction has long been made between the "subjective reality within man's mind" and the "objective reality in the world outside of man." Social Efficiency educators accept this dichotomy and concern themselves primarily with objective reality.

Terminal objectives refer to observable and measurable actions of people. They are to be found in objective reality and not subjective reality. When collecting terminal objectives, educators must "go out into the field" and actually study the actions performed by people, for terminal objectives are drawn from the actions people perform and the behavior repertoires mankind needs to successfully maintain the functioning of society. For these educators, the starting point is always the activities of mankind as manifested in objective behavior, rather than the needs of mankind as assumed to exist within the subjective mind.

The necessity of determining terminal objectives by "generalizing on the basis of a numerical count of cases" is also central to the Social Efficiency ideology. This is because the reality conceived to be of most worth is defined in a normative manner and not in an idiosyncratic manner. Social Efficiency educators' concern is what the majority of the members of society (or their client group) conceive to be "real" or "true" or "necessary." They care about social norms rather than individual uniqueness. Thus, there is an emphasis on statistical analysis during curriculum work. This results in an emphasis on concern for the individual with respect to achieving normative ends rather than on concern for the person with respect to achieving idiosyncratic ends. Social Efficiency educators focus on what the needs of the society *are* and not what men *think* they should be (Bobbitt, 1926, p. 20).

Progressive objectives are also determined by focusing on the observable and measurable actions in which a person engages rather than on the inherent nature of the person. Consequently, Social Efficiency educators (a) make a weighted distinction between the individual as a possessor of certain capabilities for action and the individual per se, (b) partition individuals' actions apart from the individuals themselves, and (c) deal with individuals' action capabilities as entities separate from the individuals themselves. As a result, only those aspects of people that can be atomistically observed and measured—the objective aspects—are considered; the subjective aspects of people, which are not readily observable, measurable, or atomistic, fade into the background.

Causality

Underlying the process of designing progressive objectives through the use of activity analysis are assumptions about causation, that is, how the raw material is transformed into the finished product. The basic assumption is derived from Newtonian mechanics; causation is conceived of within a context in which cause and effect, action and reaction, or stimulus and response are linked together in a deterministic pattern reducible by analysis to single and simple atomic transferences of energy. Three aspects of this assumption need elaboration.

First, planning for change in the human organism is thought of within a cause-effect, action-reaction, or stimulus-response context. This conception of human change requires that Social Efficiency educators use two types of planning while creating curricula: (1) they must predetermine the relationship between cause and effect, action and reaction, or stimulus and response, and (2) they must plan the causes, actions, or stimuli that in a direct and predictable manner will lead to the desirable effect, reaction, or response. As a result, the changes that are planned for during curriculum creation are only those that fit into a stimulus-response pattern and that can be observed to be directly behaviorally linked.

Second, this interpretation of causality is deterministic. Educators believe they can predetermine the changes that will take place in people's behavior as a result of their encounters with specified stimuli within the curriculum. That is, they assume that changed behavior resulting from exposure to the curriculum can be known in its entirety before the change takes place. Free will plays little part within this system— events are entirely determined by previous causes. Bobbitt expressed the spirit underlying the Social Efficiency posture toward determinism this way:

> In the world of economic production, a major secret of success is predetermination. The management predetermined with great exactness the nature of the products to be turned out. . . . They standardize and thus predetermine the processes to be employed, the quantity and quality of raw material to be used for each type and unit of product, the character and amount of labor to be employed, and the character of the conditions under which the work should be done. . . . The business world is institutionalizing foresight. . . . There is a growing realization within the educational profession that we . . . too, must institutionalize foresight, and, so far as conditions of our work will permit, develop a technique of predetermination of the particularized results to be obtained. (1920, p. 738)

Third, change in human behavior is conceived of as a shaping process. It is "a shaping process as much as the manufacture of steel rails" (Bobbitt, 1913, p. 12). The behavioral engineer aspires to manipulate the human shaping process with the same degree of control the industrial engineer exercises as he molds steel rails into the form he desires them to be. Within this context, the human beings who will undergo the shaping process are treated as though they have about as much to say about what is happening to them during the shaping as the steel has to say about what is happening to it during its shaping. Free will and self-determination do not have a prominent place in the Social Efficiency ideology.

Ends, Means, and Instrumental Values

One of the distinctive aspects of curriculum creation within the Social Efficiency ideology is the clear dichotomy that exists between terminal objectives and progressive objectives, between the social orientation and the methodological orientation, between the ends of the curriculum and the means of creating the curriculum. Terminal objectives are associated with the ends of the curriculum: they are discoverable in society. Progressive objectives are associated with the means of creating curriculum: they are derived using the methodology of "scientific instrumentalism." Ends must be clearly specified, and their value lies in their ability to reflect the needs of society. Means must also be clearly specified, and their value lies in their ability to achieve the ends efficiently.

In both cases, the criterion of value is independent of the curriculum. Ends are judged in terms of their ability to reflect the needs of society and not in terms of anything inherent within themselves. Means are judged in terms of their efficiency in meeting the ends and not in terms of anything inherent within either themselves or the ends.

Thus, in both cases, educators ask that the value of their work be defined in terms of a criterion independent of the work itself, and that criterion is essentially one of efficiency. In the case of ends, efficiency is measured in terms of optimal reflection of social needs in the terminal objectives. In the case of means, efficiency is measured in terms of optimal cost (time, money, natural resources, etc.) in achieving the ends. Ends and means are both to be judged as instruments that contribute to the attainment of goals external from themselves, and instrumental values based on the ethically neutral concept of efficiency are to be used as the criteria for judging them. As a result, there is no criterion of value for judging "good" or "bad," "just" or "unjust," or "sane" or "insane" ends for the curriculum. Neither is there a criterion of value for judging "kind" or "unkind," "moral" or "immoral," or "responsible" or "irresponsible" means of creating the curriculum. Bobbitt points out the pervasiveness of this system of instrumental values when he writes that "any instrument or experience which is effective . . . is the right instrument and right experience; and . . . anything that is not effective is wrong" (1918, p. 283).

Historical Context

The Social Efficiency ideology has its origins in four movements: social reform, utilitarian education, behavioral psychology, and scientific methodology (Callahan, 1962). These movements are still active in promoting the Social Efficiency ideology today.

Social Reform

Muckraking journalism during the first two decades of the 20th century developed a reform-conscious population that put social needs above all else. Bobbitt expressed the spirit of the times when he exclaimed,

> The ideal of social service is rapidly becoming the corner-stone of faith in every department of human affairs—in none certainly more than in the field of education. In this service, "social efficiency" is becoming the chief watchword and the chief aim. (1913, p. 50)

Muckraking journalism and the accompanying social reform movement influenced the Social Efficiency ideology by inspiring it to make the needs of society its highest priority and to conceive of society as the sanctioning body in which individuals take meaning.

As we enter the 21st century, the successors of earlier muckraking journalists continue to stir public discontent with education (Bracey, 2003). Currently, "there is a distinct rhetoric of blame, shame, and punishment throughout the conversation about quality [education], with the frontline classroom teacher and his or her students bearing much of the day-to-day brunt of this tactic" (St. Pierre, 2006, p. 241). In 2004, the Teaching Commission asserted that it wanted to "bring a national sense of urgency" (p. 5) to "the sorry state of American Schools" (p. 12). It attempted to do so by pointing out that "academic achievement" in the U.S. is inadequate, as measured both by the National Assessment of Educational Progress and international comparisons ("which show that American teens continue to lag behind high-school students in many other industrialized nations," p. 13). The following statement sums up the tenor of the national discussion on education: "The capacity of America's educational system to create a 21st-century workforce second to none in the world is a national security issue of the first order. As things stand, this country is forfeiting that capacity" (p. 20).

Utilitarian Education

The movement for utilitarian education during the last quarter of the 19th century and the first quarter of the 20th century emphasized the importance of making schools useful and relevant to the life of individuals and the nation. Utilitarian education was an outgrowth of the agricultural education, manual training, industrial education, trade school, and vocational education movements and the increasingly popular business ideology (Kliebard, 2004, chaps. 4–5). This was Bobbitt's "functional education," which trained "man for the performance of the functions or activities which constitute his life" (Bobbitt, 1924c, p. 45). It involved providing students with job training skills that would allow them, as adults, to function constructively in an industrial society (as was the intent of Booker T. Washington's Tuskegee Normal Institute, which focused on the manual training of African Americans). The utilitarian education movement also embodied a reaction to academic education in schools, which consisted of generally useless textbook memorizing that prepared people only for life in the university.

The movement for utilitarian education during the beginning of the 21st century is considered by Social Efficiency advocates to be related to the economic health of society—in particular the economic health of business and the U.S. economy: "A quality educational system is an absolute essential to the economic, political, and social welfare of the United States. . . . There is a consensus that students need employable skills for the new economy" (Lessinger & Salowe, 2001, pp. 11–12). Education must do its job in training highly productive workers for business, whose continued health will support a strong U.S. economy. According to the Teaching Commission (2004), the goal, as before, is to help children learn "to become successful, contributing citizens," because "around the world . . . the most vibrant and stable economies draw their strength from a well-educated, highly skilled citizenry"; "in a competitive global economy, all citizens must continually race to obtain new, higher skills" for a "highly skilled citizenry"; and "student achievement . . . is directly related to . . . national economic growth" (pp. 12–14).

Even so, Schultz, in an article in the journal of the Association for Career and Technical Education regarding the reform movement that took place between 1985 and 2005, asks "was it good for you?" (2006). His answer, from the perspective of utilitarian education, is that "one would suspect not" (p. 44). During this period, the percentage of students enrolled in utilitarian courses decreased greatly as students in academic courses increased.

Behavioral Psychology

During the first two thirds of the 20th century, behavioral psychology provided the Social Efficiency ideology with a psychological context in which to frame its endeavors. The deemphasis on the subjective behavior of people, the interpretation of mind as the total behavioral response of people, the emphasis on the effect that controllable conditions of learning have in molding behavior, and the concern with accurate statistical evaluation provided Social Efficiency educators with an ideal tool. Behavioral psychology, as first interpreted by John B. Watson (1878–1958) and Edward L. Thorndike (1874–1949) and later reinterpreted by B. F. Skinner (1904–1990), was rapidly accepted as the psychological base of the Social Efficiency ideology.

By the late 1960s, cognitive psychology began to replace behavioral psychology. However, most of the assumptions underlying the behavioral psychology that mid-20th-century Social Efficiency educators used continue to be relevant to Social Efficiency endeavors in the 21st century. Social Efficiency cognitive psychologists working on curriculum design emphasize that "the modern information-processing approach in cognitive psychology would recommend careful analysis of the goals of instruction" and "decomposing knowledge into its elements for purposes of study and decontextualizing these elements for purposes of instruction" (Anderson, Reder, & Simon, 1996, p. 1); that "learning requires a change in the learner, which can only be brought about by what the learner does" (p. 13); that "learning is strongly influenced by the sequence of stimuli and the feedback that tells the system when responses are correct, and when they are wrong" (p. 12); and "that real competence only comes with extensive practice" (p. 12).

Scientific Methodology

"Scientific methodology" became popular in education at the beginning of the 20th century. It referred to the methodology of technology and connoted a collection of techniques such as statistics, accurate measurement, task analysis, efficiency engineering, and industrial management (Parker, 1912; Taylor, 1911). Social Efficiency educators adopted scientific methodology both as a reaction against the existing inefficiency of education and in alliance with the successful use of "scientific techniques" in the business and industrial worlds. At the beginning of the 20th century, Bobbitt modeled his "scientific methodology" after "scientific management" in the world of material production. In the middle of the 20th century, Gagne derived his approach to "scientific methodology" from his training in task analysis as a behaviorist psychologist. And in the 1970s, Lessinger modeled his approach to "educational engineering" after successful scientific and technological endeavors of the aerospace industry (St. Pierre, 2006, p. 240).

As we enter the 21st century, "science" continues to be a magic word for Social Efficiency educators: "The fundamental idea is that better science will make better schools—that 'quality' science will enable us to finally reengineer schools so they work" (St. Pierre, 2006, p. 240). Heavy use of statistics, technology, and measurement, along with faith in man's ability to comprehend the complexities of what goes on in schools through objective assessment, underlies both the accountability and standards movements and many of the ways in which these two movements interact. For example, the use of statistical analysis of standardized tests scores to pressure educators to improve student, teacher, school, and state educational performance (in ways that are aligned with state content standards) is derived both from beliefs in scientific methodology and scientific approaches to organizational management. For example, the No Child Left Behind Act has "111 references to 'scientifically-based research'" (Feuer, Towne, & Shavelson, 2002, p. 4). Social Efficiency educators also continue to be attracted to the scientific procedures of cognitive psychology. They continue to assume that prestige and usefulness are automatically accorded their work if they use "scientific" techniques.

A Century of Forgetting

Social Efficiency educators at the beginning of the 20th century believed that the client for whom they worked was society. Their focus was on the preparation of the individual for a balanced and constructive life in society. Part of the initial impulse underlying the development of the Social Efficiency ideology was a reaction against education's servitude to special-interest groups—particularly "the dictation of the special predilections of selfish academic interests" (Bobbitt, 1924c, p. 49). Education was to serve society as a whole.

Things changed as time passed and Social Efficiency educators discovered the difficulty of drawing comprehensive objectives from society. By the middle of the 20th century, the clients for whom Social Efficiency educators worked became any group desiring their services. For example, Gagne, a strong Social Efficiency advocate, worked for the American Association for the Advancement of Science to develop the curriculum *Science: A Process Approach.*

By the beginning of the 21st century, with the rise of the standards and accountability movements, there was a further shift of emphasis from fulfilling social needs to what Bobbitt called raising the "qualitative and quantitative standards" that determined the products of schools. The shift involved taking as a given the academic programs condoned by state departments of education and emphasizing that high standards be used to assure that the academic goals of state curricula are met, that academic achievement is promoted, and that "no child is left behind" (The Teaching Commission, 2004). As a result, the raising of student academic performance became the terminal objective of Social Efficiency educators.

In only a century the Social Efficiency ideology forgot its anger over academia's domination of the school curriculum and came to embrace the academic interests that controlled the school curriculum. In the transition, this original socially oriented curriculum development system became an academically oriented curriculum development system and its major client became the academic disciplines.

Accountability Movement: From Educational to Administrative and Political Initiatives

The 21st century accountability movement—as illustrated by the No Child Left Behind Act—provides an example of how an educational ideology concerned with issues of curriculum and instruction can be transformed into a political movement based in administrative (rather than educational) agendas, for the current "accountability [movement] is not primarily a pedagogical movement. It is an administrative system, and as such it is impervious to . . . educational concerns" (Martin, Overholt, & Urban, 1976, p. 32).

Precursors of today's accountability movement exist. The English "payment by results" method of administering education (1862–c. 1892) rewarded educators whose students performed well on standardized tests (Coltham, 1972). The efficiency movement within educational administration early in the 20th century was the first American attempt at imposing "scientific" industrial accountability methods on schools (Callahan, 1962). It elevated "budgetary values over education concerns" (Martin et al., 1976, p. 38).

The current accountability movement "seems so reasonable and simple. You specify the changes in learners that should result from schooling. You evaluate the extent to which the changes have taken place. You use the results of the evaluation to improve the schooling process" (Anderson, 2005, p. 103). This viewpoint follows the Social Efficiency ideology with only a few changes in emphasis.

First, there is increased emphasis on accountability to taxpayers who pay for education: "Schools, like other sectors of our society, are accountable to the public for what they do—or fail to do" and "taxpayer[s] . . . have a right to know what educational results are produced by a given expenditure" (Lessinger, 1970, pp. 3–4). In other words, the public deserves information related to student performance, teacher effectiveness, school efficiency, the school district's annual progress in meeting goals, and the state's progress in providing "guaranteed acquisition of basic skills by all of our children" (p. 12). To demonstrate accountability, educators should provide taxpayers with an annual report card on school effectiveness that describes changes in student achievement on standardized tests that reflect national, state, or local curriculum standards and that "relate learning to its cost" (p. 9) in terms of "measurable relationships between dollars spent and results obtained" (Lessinger, 1971, p. 8). "Independent auditors" should create the tests using scientific procedures to accurately reflect changes in student performance, and they should be designed and administered in a way that eliminates "bias resulting from race, ethnicity, sex, or income" (Fenstermacher, 2001, p. 333). Teachers (and school officials) should be held accountable for their students' performance on the tests.

Here, it is assumed that (a) curriculum standards reflect the educational aspirations of the taxpayers to whom educators are accountable, (b) curriculum standards include everything children need to learn in school, (c) school curricula reflect "curriculum standards . . . [that] are simply mandated objectives . . . that teachers are expected to teach regardless of how important the teachers themselves believe them to be" (Anderson, 2005, p. 104), (d) standardized test questions reflect the content of curriculum standards, and (e) learning consists of a change of learner behavior that can be easily assessed by standardized tests.

Second, the accountability movement emphasizes that the educational effectiveness of teachers, schools, school districts, and states rests solely on measurable gains in student test scores resulting from teachers' instructional endeavors. It is assumed that teachers are the only ones responsible for and contributing to the education of children and that children's education is entirely under the control of teachers. This deterministic view of direct causes and effects excludes the effects social and economic factors outside the classroom have on children's education.

Third, it is emphasized that "data-based decisions" based on the annual report card of student, teacher, school, school district, and state curriculum effectiveness should "drive" (Hanson, Durton, & Guam, 2006, p. 18) a process of "educational engineering" (Lessinger, 1970, p. 12) that uses "modern management and budget techniques" (Fenstermacher, 2001, p. 333) "currently employed by business and industry" (Lessinger, 1971, p. 7) to shape the behavior of all involved in children's education in our public schools by the distribution of "penalties and incentives" (Lessinger, 1970, p. 35), both in the form of tax dollars and public recognition of achievement or failure.

Fourth, it is emphasized that "full disclosure of information to all parties regarding school effectiveness" (Fenstermacher, 2001, p. 333) based on aggregated student test scores will pressure states, school districts, schools, teachers, and students to focus intently on preparing students to perform well on standardized tests that assess their achievements. Here is where political pressure (in terms of competition among schools, school districts, and states and in terms of parental and community pressure to provide children with an adequate education) and economic pressure (in terms of competitive seeking of monetary rewards for student achievement) come into play. Here the political and economic agendas of the accountability movement tie all of public education to the rights of taxpayers both to know the results of their tax expenditures and to determine how their tax dollars are spent.

Fifth, it is emphasized that society can be maintained and improved through this administrative approach to education. This is because children who succeed in this system will be prepared to function as adults in the jobs that provide our nation's economic foundation, since curriculum standards reflect the skills needed for full adult participation in jobs at varying levels of employment.

Discussion of the Social Efficiency ideology will now shift from examining the context in which educators' work to examining the concepts that mold their view of curriculum.

Aims

Social Efficiency educators consider their aim to be the efficient carrying out of a task for a client. In fulfilling this aim, they see themselves as educational engineers who design and implement educational programs that shape the behavior of people in much the same way as industrial engineers design and manufacture railroad rails from steel. This analogy involves the assumptions that the educational engineer and the industrial engineer both obtain their tasks from a client; both are evaluated by the ability of their product to fulfill the needs of a client (both are accountable to a client in the final analysis); both use a precise, particularized, and atomistic approach to accomplishing their purposes; both plan with a high degree of care and explicitness; both pay rigorous attention to empirical events and standards; both value sophisticated use of scientific techniques; and both take a programmatic approach to transforming their raw material into a finished product.

Whether the task Social Efficiency educators engage in is the discovery of terminal objectives, the design of a sequence of progressive objectives, the creation of learning experiences, or the construction of standards for assessing performance, their aims are not directly associated with the content of the curriculum per se, but rather with the efficient and effective design and implementation of the curriculum and the resulting student achievement. Their vested interests are not as much in what is achieved as in *how well* it is achieved, and they are more concerned about the means of accomplishing the ends than they are about the ends themselves. The criterion used to assess their endeavors is efficiency, whether they are designing curriculum ("Activity analysis seeks to discover the quite specific types of human activity which men should perform efficiently" [Bobbitt, 1924c, p. 45]), determining how to best perform an activity ("The business of education today is to teach growing individuals . . . to perform efficiently those activities which constitute the latest and highest level of civilization" [Bobbitt, 1926, p. 1]), or facilitating learning ("Such a procedure should, if systematically followed, bring about the required learning in the most efficient possible manner" [Bobbitt, 1926, p. 1]).

Knowledge

The knowledge most valued by Social Efficiency educators has two characteristics. First, it is by nature a capability for action that can be taught to learners. Second, its identification and its worth demand the acceptance of the duality of subjective and objective reality.

The Nature of Knowledge

Knowledge is a capability for action identifiable as the "successful performance of a class of tasks" (Gagne, 1962, p. 355). It is a skill. It is something that a person can learn to do.

Knowledge is defined in behavioral terms. Social Efficiency educators equate such things as "knowledge," "wisdom," "insight," and "understanding" with behavior. This is partially because the only tangible evidence we have of knowledge, wisdom, insight, and understanding is behavioral evidence, and partially because the only way to determine whether or not people "know" or "don't know" something is to see how they behave in certain situations.

The emphasis on the behavioral interpretation of the nature of knowledge results in a corresponding deemphasis on the informational interpretation. The possession of the correct *behavior* is emphasized over the possession of the correct *information*. There is certainly a relationship between having the necessary information to act and being able to act, between "knowing that" and "knowing how." However, for Social Efficiency educators, the ability to act is more important than the ability to be informed. For example, in the debate over whether it is more important "to understand" or "to do" mathematics, Social Efficiency educators, while not denying that both are important, will always behave as though acquiring mathematical "skills" is more important than acquiring an "understanding" of mathematics. Bobbitt speaks of this in comparing the "old education" with the "new functional education." He writes that, according to the old education, "the well educated man is to be defined as a walking body of knowledge. The more swollen the bulk of information that he carries about with him, the better educated he is" (1924c, p. 45), whereas within the new functional education, "man is not a mere intellectual reservoir to be filled with knowledge. He is a creature of . . . *action*. His most salient characteristic is not his memory reservoir, whether filled or unfilled, but *action, conduct, behavior*" (p. 46). Gagne supports this behavioral versus informational interpretation when he writes, "The most striking characteristic of these materials is that they are intended to teach children the *processes* of science rather than what may be called science content" (1966, p. 49) and

> that an emphasis on process implies a corresponding de-emphasis on specific science "content." . . . [C]hildren . . . are not asked to learn and remember particular facts or principles. . . . Rather, they are expected to learn such things as how to observe . . . and how to perform experiments. (AAAS, Commission on Science Education, 1967b, p. 3)

Some confusion exists regarding the behavioral interpretation of the nature of knowledge. For example, are the facts of Newtonian mechanics knowledge? For Social Efficiency educators, information alone is not knowledge. By itself, the possession of information by an individual does not mean that the individual possesses knowledge. However, the ability to state a fact when appropriately stimulated does fall within the behavioral context. The ability to act in accordance with the ability to state a fact falls even more within the behavioral context. The relevant criterion is whether the possessor of information is capable of acting on the knowledge represented by the information.

Let us take, for example, the case of knowledge about "honesty." It is one thing to have memorized what society considers honest behavior. It is another thing to be able to state what society considers honest behavior. But it is another thing yet to be able to act in an honest manner. It is the ability to act in the appropriate manner which Social Efficiency educators call knowledge, rather than the ability "to know," "to understand," or "to appreciate" what the appropriate behavior should be. What is in peoples' heads is not as important in the Social Efficiency ideology as the ability to translate what is in peoples' heads into behavior in which they engage.

Social Efficiency educators also believe that knowledge can be atomized, or broken up into specific unitary behaviors: that "large tasks decompose into nearly independent subtasks" (Anderson, Reder, & Simon, 1996, p. 3). Activity analysis is the method of decomposing knowledge into specific atomistic elements and is one of the major components of the Social Efficiency approach to curriculum design. A consequence of atomism can be seen in the debate over using a "phonics" versus "whole language" approach to reading instruction. While not having to deny that both approaches are of value, Social Efficiency educators emphasize the phonics approach, in which words are decomposed into groups of letters, which in turn are decomposed into individual letters (each of which is an atomistic unit with a sound associated with it). This approach may be compared to the whole language approach, in which comprehensive meaning is emphasized.

One consequence of Social Efficiency educators' conception of themselves as instruments in achieving the ends of a client needs mention. The educator is concerned about the means of achieving the ends more than about the ends themselves, about the means of achieving knowledge more than about knowledge itself, and about learning more than about knowledge. As a result, Social Efficiency educators pay more attention to learning than to knowledge. In many ways they view knowledge from the perspective of learning. Thus, they are more likely to write about *The Conditions of Learning* (Gagne, 1965b) than they are about the conditions of knowing and are more likely to speak about the nature of learning than they are about the nature of knowledge.

Knowledge and Objective Reality

Social Efficiency educators accept the duality of subjective and objective reality, and they believe that objective reality is the more significant of the two. Accordingly, they deal with their world as an empirical entity. Behavior that cannot be observed or measured is treated as though it does not exist—more to be ignored than denied. Attention is directed toward those aspects of reality that can be observed. That which cannot be observed, such as some of the "spiritual" dimensions of people's being, is simply not dealt with.

Curriculum knowledge has its origin in the objective reality of a client population—in the normative aspects of a particular social group—and is discoverable by taking a numerical count of the needs of the majority of the members of that group.

Knowledge derives its value from its ability to fulfill needs in the objective world of mankind. Its worth is determined by the consequences that can result from its possession. As such, curriculum knowledge is identified by evaluating the potential consequences of its possession on those who possess it and the society in which they function. The important criteria for identifying worthwhile knowledge are not the insights into themselves that the possessors derive from its possession or the sources from which the knowledge is derived, but rather the power such knowledge gives curriculum clients to fulfill their needs and the power it gives those who possess it to fulfill their own needs by fulfilling the needs of the curriculum client. If something furthers the client's aims, it is worthy of inclusion in the client's curriculum.

This view of knowledge is represented in Figure 3.2. Knowledge has its source in the normative objective reality of members of a curriculum developer's client population (ΣO where Σ represents the normative aspect of objective reality, O). Knowledge's worth for inclusion in curriculum is tested by determining the consequences that result from its possession by the client population. Once curriculum knowledge is determined, learners (S) can acquire it.

❖ **Figure 3.2**   The Social Efficiency process of obtaining curriculum knowledge.

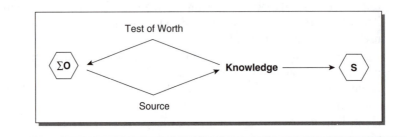

Learning

Learning is a central concept in the Social Efficiency ideology and is synonymous with change in behavior.

> Learning exhibits itself as a change in behavior[;] . . . the inference of learning is made by comparing what behavior was possible before the individual was placed in a "learning situation" and what behavior can be exhibited after such treatment. (Gagne, 1970, p. 3)

In other words,

> a learning event . . . takes place when the *stimulus situation* affects the learner in such a way that his *performance* changes from a time *before* being in that situation to a time *after* being in it. The *change in performance* is what leads to the conclusion that learning has occurred (Gagne, 1970, p. 5).

Learning is not viewed in terms of the natural growth or development of children, societal acculturation or socialization of children, or filling the minds of children with information. It is viewed in terms of changes in the observable behavior of learners, of training learners to perform specific activities.

A Behavioral Viewpoint

The learning theory used by Social Efficiency educators is essentially that of behavioral psychology. This may seem strange, for by the late 1960s cognitive psychology began to replace behavioral psychology in the field of psychology. However, the changes were evolutionary and, from the point of view of Social Efficiency educators, enriched the previously accepted tenets of behavioral psychology rather than refuted them (Anderson et al., 1988, p. 227).

For the Social Efficiency ideology, the development from behaviorism to information processing and cognitive psychology "was an awakening to the complexity of human cognition" (Anderson et al., 1996, p. 10) accompanied by postulation of the existence of "mental structures and processes" (Anderson et al., 1988, p. 228). Now, rather than having to consider the mind a black box about which nothing could be assumed, educators could posit the existence of mental structures and processes of thought (such as long-term memory, working memory, and schemas). Now they could offer explanations for how children learn and what happens between the time children are exposed to stimuli and the time they respond. However, the explanations of what happens in children's brains did not significantly affect the way Social Efficiency educators treated learning while they developed and used curriculum. They have continued to treat learning in essentially the same way as they did while using behaviorism, for changes in psychological *theory* have not yet significantly impacted curriculum *practice*.

The emphasis in the learning theory utilized by Social Efficiency educators is not on the learner, but on the stimuli that cause the learner to change (S), the responses that indicate that the learner has changed (R), and the relationships between the stimuli and responses that account for the transformation that takes place within the learner (→). The stimulus situation (S) is of primary importance, because it can be controlled and deliberately manipulated by educators to produce the desired learning in the student; it is "*outside the learner* and can be identified and described in the terms of physical science" (Gagne, 1970, p. 6). Therefore, it is the focus of educators' attention while they are developing curriculum. The behavioral responses (R) are the specific acts that can be identified as occurring as the result of learners' exposure to the stimulus situation (S). They are what indicate to educators whether or not the student is learning and whether learning experiences (S) are producing the desired results. They can be observed in a learner's behavior. The relationship between the stimulus and the response (→) represents the transformation that takes place within the learner. It tells educators how to get the results they desire. "The learning change is from stimulus → (nothing) to stimulus → response" (p. 6). The Type to Learn program discussed earlier provides an example of these elements. The presentation to the learner of a letter in either visual textual or verbal auditory form is a stimulus (S). The typing of the letter by the learner is the response (R). The relationship between the stimulus and the response may be postulated to be the activity within working memory of the dual linguistic and graphic subprocessors (Baddeley, 1986), which allow the learner to associate sight of the letter (by the graphic subprocessor) or the sound of the letter (by the linguistic subprocessor) with the action of typing the letter. It may be postulated that when a learner is just beginning to learn, it takes working memory considerable effort to produce the connections between S and R that produce the desired response. Once learning has been automated and schemas have been formed in long-term memory, the connection between stimulus and response (→) is automatic and the desired typing skill has been learned (Chandler, Cooper, Pollock, & Tindall-Ford, 1998).

Note in this example that, under the behavioral psychology of the 1960s, nothing would have been said about the nature of the connection between S and R, because they would not have been able to be directly observed. Note also that, for all practical purposes, the nature of the connections currently postulated are irrelevant to most of the instructional designs of Social Efficiency educators. During curriculum and instructional design, educators focus on analysis of the skill to be learned, division of the skill into its component tasks, design and sequencing of learning experiences (S) that result in the desired response (R), and assessment of whether or not learning has taken place (R). During Social Efficiency educators' administrative and political (accountability) endeavors, they focus on making sure curriculum standards have been satisfactorily met by publicly reporting student achievement test scores (S) in order to shape teacher behavior (R) so that teachers more directly teach to the standards.

Assumptions About Learning

Several assumptions about the Social Efficiency view of learning need elaboration.

First, learning is an active process and "only the active learner is a successful learner" (Anderson et al., 1996, p. 18). That is, "learning requires a change in the learner, which can only be brought about by what the learner does" (p. 13). Learners must make the responses they are to learn. They learn what they do. This refers to Bobbitt's "functional education," in which learners must practice the behaviors they are to acquire or make the responses they are to learn—that is, learn to function by functioning in the desired manner. (For example, students learn to type by actually typing.) Skilled performance develops only as a result of "learning-by-doing," during which "cognitive structure accommodates to experience" (p. 13). It is learners who shape their behavior (and schema) in accordance with the requirement of the curriculum (its stimulus, reinforcement, and response conditions), not the curriculum that shapes the learner.

Second, learning skills requires practice: "Real competence only comes with extensive practice" (Anderson et al., 1996, p. 12). The stimulus → response connection is strengthened with practice. (For example, in running the Type to Learn curriculum, students engage in many activities that allow them to practice typing.) One must be careful with the types and amount of practice required of learners: "The instructional task is not to 'kill' motivation by demanding drill, but to find tasks that provide practice while at the same time sustaining interest" (p. 13).

Third, "learning is strongly influenced by the . . . feedback that tells the system when responses are correct, and when they are wrong" (Anderson et al., 1996, p. 12), and learning progresses as correct responses to specific stimuli are reinforced. This assumption refers to Thorndike's law of effects (or Skinner's contingency of reinforcement theory) and pertains to the belief that the way to get learners to acquire a behavior is to arrange the conditions in which they learn so that they are immediately rewarded or given reinforcement when they emit the desired behavior. There are three component assumptions making up this belief: (1) correct responses are strengthened by being followed by immediate reinforcement, (2) incorrect responses are weakened by not being followed by a reward, and (3) complex behaviors are built up gradually through the reinforcement of prerequisite behaviors that gradually approximate the desired terminal behavior. (All three assumptions are embedded in Type to Learn.)

Fourth, acquiring skilled performance requires that responses to stimulus conditions be put under the control of particular stimuli in such a way that these stimuli automatically generate the responses. This refers to the Social Efficiency belief that, to be "efficient," a learned behavior must become so ingrained that the learner responds automatically and in a predetermined manner to the presence of specific stimuli—without the contemplation or internal thought processing in working memory that typically occurs when a behavior is just being learned (as in Type to Learn).

Fifth, Social Efficiency educators assume learning is atomistic. This shows up in their concern with devising specific stimulus conditions that will condition the learner to emit specific behavioral responses (as in Type to Learn). Associated with this is the assumption that the total learning of a child with respect to a complex task is a summative accumulation of specific learnings associated with that task. Activity analysis, during which knowledge is decomposed, uses this assumption.

Sixth, there is the assumption that not all learning is of the same level of complexity: "Most complex skills are hierarchical in structure, with component skills within component skills, and so on" (Anderson et al., 1996, p. 18). Curriculum developers both derive unitary actions to be learned and define the hierarchical relationships among those actions during activity analysis.

Readiness

Social Efficiency developers are primarily interested in learning versus growth. As Gagne says, "learning is a change in human . . . capability which . . . is not simply ascribable to the process of growth. . . . [I]t must be distinguishable from the kind of change that is attributable to growth" (1970, p. 160).

As a result, these educators reject readiness arguments based on developmental perspectives. "Readiness" to undertake learning is viewed as a function of the presence or absence of the necessary prerequisite learnings. Gagne phrases it this way:

> The acquisition of knowledge is a process in which every new capability builds on a foundation established by previously learned capabilities. The convenient escape mechanism that the student is not "mature" enough to learn any particular content needs to be studiously avoided, since it is valid for only the very earliest years of life. A student is ready to learn something when he has mastered the prerequisites. (1970, pp. 26–27)

Thus, "at any given age, a child may be unable to perform a particular intellectual task because he has not acquired the specifically relevant intellectual skills as prerequisites to that task" (p. 290). However, "such learning may be readily accomplished if the learner has acquired, or will undertake to acquire, the intellectual skills prerequisite to the task" (p. 290). In particular, it is assumed that "children can learn any intellectual thing we want them to learn, provided they have learned the prerequisites" (p. 300). In terms of Figure 3.1, for example, when learners are competent in tasks C and D, they are ready to learn task A. Until they are competent in tasks C and D, they are not ready to learn task A.

Partitioning learning apart from growth and conceiving of learning as atomistic in nature raises the question of what the relationship between the learning required by a curriculum and the self-evolving nature of the child's life is. That is, how is the organic life series within the child united or meshed with the atomistic learning series of the curriculum? The concepts of transfer, curriculum integration, and curriculum continuity are used to account for the relationships between the parts of the atomistic curriculum and the organic life of the child. Transfer refers to generalizing specific learnings so that they will be useful to the learner in contexts other than the specific situations in which they are acquired. Lateral transfer "refers to a kind of generalizing that spreads over a broad set of situations of roughly the same level of complexity" (Gagne, 1970, p. 335). It involves the integration of (a) learnings that take place within a curriculum and activities that take place in the learner's everyday life and (b) learnings within separate curricula that the learner is simultaneously experiencing. Vertical transfer "refers to the effects that learned capabilities at one level have on the learning of additional ones at higher levels" (p. 335). It promotes continuity by providing for (a) the natural flow of learning from activity n to activity $n + 1$ and (b) the revisitation of related learnings at several different levels of complexity.

The Child

Lack of Concern

Social Efficiency educators show little concern for the child per se while developing and using curricula. When they do show concern for the child, it is not concern for the person but for the potential adult who possesses behavioral capabilities and can provide an energy input into the educational endeavor (Gagne, 1966, p. 51).

Children are not viewed as entities who of themselves have meaning. Instead, they have meaning because they can develop into adults and can serve their society. They are first members of society capable of fulfilling social needs and only secondarily individuals with needs. They are first potential adult members of society—"the man within the child"—and only secondarily children. They are first bundles of action capabilities and only secondarily persons possessing the ability to act.

If a distinction is made between the *acts* of a person and a *person* acting, it is the former, not the latter, with which Social Efficiency educators are primarily concerned. They are interested in the *activity* people engage in rather than *the person* engaged in activity. People and their attributes are dichotomized in a manner similar to the way objective and subjective reality are dichotomized, with emphasis being placed on the attributes of people in contrast to people themselves.

Educators conceive of their endeavors as contributing to the next stage of development of the child. They are constantly working on activity n so that activity $n + 1$ can be accomplished and constantly thinking of children learning capability n so that they will be able to learn capability $n + 1$ in the future (where n is a positive integer). Educators' concern is always the future learning of the child rather than the present growing of the child.

The Child as a Worker

Within the Social Efficiency ideology, children are viewed as workers capable of providing energy inputs into the educational endeavor:

> Looking at a school system as a large organization of individuals for the purpose of turning out certain necessary human products, the pupils are in fact the ultimate workers. They are the

rank and file over whom the teachers stand in supervisory capacity. The work is a development of the potential abilities which the pupils carry around within themselves into actual abilities of a given degree. These actual abilities are the educational products. It is the work of the student, not the work of the teacher, that produces these products. (Bobbitt, 1913, p. 32)

From this perspective, children are the ones who do the work in school. They provide the energy inputs that work to transform them into suitable educational products. They know what work to perform on themselves and the standards they must reach because of the supervision given by teachers and curricula.

Individualized Programmed Instruction

The stance of Social Efficiency educators toward individualized programmed instruction highlights both of these points. First, individualized programmed instruction is designed to help children achieve a set of standard capabilities, to teach *tasks* rather than *students*. It deals with a very limited part of children's total functioning; it is not intended to give students a complete, well-rounded education but to provide them with a set of specialized skills. Second, instructional materials sit idle until they are activated by students. Children provide the primary energy input that takes them through the materials, which educate them at a rate proportional to the amount of energy they expend on learning.

Teaching

Role of the Teacher

The teacher's job is to make sure that learners appropriately work through curricula and acquire their terminal performances. "The teacher is the *manager of the conditions of learning*" (Gagne, 1970, p. 324) who both prepares the learning environment for learners and supervises their work in that environment.

Part of the teacher's job is to prepare the environment in which students learn (do their work on themselves). This consists of doing whatever is necessary to prepare the curriculum for use by students. Once students engage the learning environment, the teacher's job is to supervise student work, much as the manager of an assembly line supervises the workers on the assembly line. As Bobbitt phrases it,

the teacher is supervisor, director, guide, stimulator, of the rank and file of the workers [students] in order to bring about on the part of the latter the development of these various abilities. The teaching problem is in fact a supervisory problem at the first level. (1913, p. 32)

In a school system . . . the pupils are the ultimate workers . . . [and] teachers rank as foremen. It is their business not to do the work that educates, but to get it done by the pupils. In doing this, they must know the pupils: know their varying mental capabilities, their interests, their aptitudes and abilities, their states of health, and their social milieu. They must know how to arouse interest; how to motivate them from within; how to adjust the conditions of the work to child-nature; how to keep up an abundant physical vitality in the children; and how to employ community influences for vital stimulation of the pupils. (1918, pp. 84–85)

Managing, directing, and supervising student work involves guiding them, motivating them, and assessing them. Guiding students (as workers) involves indicating to them what they are to learn (the work they are to do). In guiding students, the teacher must be knowledgeable of the students and the curriculum so that appropriate help can be given to students as needed.

Motivating students (as workers) involves knowing them and appropriately interacting with them in such a way that they become persuaded to work through the curriculum and acquire its competencies.

Assessing students involves monitoring students' work as they progress through the curriculum and maintaining quality control so that they acquire all of its prerequisite and terminal competencies.

The job of teaching is to fit the student to the curriculum and fit the curriculum to the student. It involves stimulating students to run the curriculum and adjusting the curriculum to the capabilities of students. This entails knowing students and taking into account their idiosyncratic natures. The curriculum developer designs curriculum for a standard student; the teacher makes adjustments for particular students.

Consequences

There are three important consequences of this view of teaching.

First, the teacher's role as manager, similar to that of a foreman managing an assembly line, removes the teacher from having any input in determining the ends toward which the student's work is being directed or the learning activities in which students engage. Teachers are not to question the ends or means of the curriculum or implement their own ends or the ends of children in their care. Thus, although teachers' functions are different from those of curriculum developers, teachers are considered instruments of ends other than their own in the same way curriculum developers are. That is, teachers are instruments who implement curriculum created by developers, developers are instruments who create curricula to fulfill client needs, and, thus, teachers are instruments who fulfill client needs.

Second, excluding teachers from designing curricula to meet the idiosyncratic needs of their students has the effect of guaranteeing that "a 'quality control' of the choice of instructional conditions is insured and maintained" (Gagne, 1970, p. 325). That is, allowing only curriculum developers to design curricula guarantees to the greatest degree possible that the "ultimate product" resulting from the educational process will measure up to the "definite qualitative and quantitative standards" required to fulfill the needs of the curriculum client by making sure that "quality does not suffer from variations in teachers' skills" (p. 332). But this also produces a standardization of educational processes and products and an inhibition of classroom flexibility, responsiveness, and innovation.

Third, "the objective of this management [teaching] is to insure that learning will be efficient, that is, that the greatest change in the student's behavior will occur in the shortest period of time" (Gagne, 1970, p. 325). Teaching is evaluated in terms of both student achievement and the efficiency with which the teacher produces student achievement rather than in terms of how humane, creative, enlightening, or insightful it is. When this is taken in combination with the emphasis on providing students feedback during learning, it should be no surprise that one of the recommendations of the current accountability movement is that teachers should "be measured and compensated [as part of their salaries] based on their classroom performance, including the academic gains [amount of learning produced over a specified period of time] made by their students" (The Teaching Commission, 2004, pp. 10–11). This includes using a "value added" (The Teaching Commission, 2004, p. 27) method to assess "the rate of improvement in student performance each year, as measured by state tests" and basing "a significant percentage of teachers' total compensation on improvements in student performance" (p. 26). This is consistent with the Social Efficiency view of learning, for

> our failure to link pay to performance [stimulus to response] . . . removes the possibility of reward for success and accountability for failure [reinforcement through reward or punishment]. Until teachers are rewarded and given responsibility for what really matters—their impact on student achievement—we cannot expect to see a marked change for the better in student performance [learning]. (The Teaching Commission, 2004, p. 23)

Evaluation

Reasons for Evaluation

Within the Social Efficiency ideology, it is essential to assess curricula, learners, and teachers. Key concepts during evaluation are accountability and standards. There are five primary reasons why evaluation is important in the Social Efficiency ideology.

First, educators conceive of themselves as instruments who fulfill the needs of a client. They hold themselves accountable to their clients, and they demonstrate their accountability by evaluating the efforts of curriculum developers and teachers to produce evidence that the needs of the curriculum client have been fulfilled. To assess their efforts, developers evaluate their curricula to demonstrate that terminal objectives have been achieved. To assess the endeavors of teachers, individual schools, school systems, and states, aggregated student achievement—as determined by standardized tests—is used to provide evidence of success, failure, or annual yearly progress toward meeting curriculum standards.

Second, Social Efficiency educators see their endeavors within the mainstream of science. One aspect of the scientific endeavor is conceived to be the demand for reproducibility, validity, reliability, and proof. As such, educators believe they must use evaluation in order to demonstrate that their endeavors possess these qualities and are therefore scientific. Mathematical and statistical procedures are viewed as powerful scientific tools, and they are used on individual or aggregated standardized test scores to "scientifically" determine educational success or failure of students, teachers, individual schools, school districts, states, and the nation as a whole.

A third reason why evaluation is important in the Social Efficiency ideology is related to the nature of sequenced progressive objectives, which represent the sequence of unitary learnings children must acquire one by one to move from incompetence to competence. Learners' mastery of each progressive objective in its turn guarantees that they will reach competence. Their performance must be continually monitored and evaluated to ensure that they do not proceed to successive objectives before mastering previous ones. A

> primary reason for direct measurement of the outcomes of a learning exercise session is to insure that instructional objectives have been met. If a student fails to exhibit the performance required on such a test, he needs to undertake additional learning covering the same ground. It is inefficient, even useless, for him to try to proceed to the learning of advanced topics, in view of the hierarchical nature of knowledge. . . . [T]he defined objective must somehow be achieved if subsequent learning is to be even minimally efficient for this student. (Gagne, 1970, pp. 342–343)

A fourth reason why evaluation is important has to do with the effect that feedback has on children's endeavors to learn. It is believed that the results of evaluation constitute an important source of feedback to learners that helps them appropriately shape their behavior, whether the feedback (and the accompanying rewards or reinforcement) is positive or negative. The same holds true for teachers, individual schools, school districts, states, and the nation as a whole.

The fifth reason why evaluation is important is related to the role of standards in assessing students, teachers, and school systems. Teacher tests certify that teachers meet certain standards and are qualified to enter the classroom. In many states, student achievement tests certify that students are qualified to graduate from high school because they meet certain standards. Under the No Child Left Behind Act, the results of aggregated student testing viewed in the light of specific standards determine whether or not schools should be certified as achieving or underachieving.

The Nature of Evaluation

Social Efficiency evaluation involves comparing a curriculum, student, or teacher to a predetermined standard through the use of criterion-referenced tests. Such comparisons are made with respect to criteria decided on before evaluation takes place. Evaluation does not involve comparisons that depend on population norms discovered during or after testing. As Gagne says, evaluation's "purpose is to compare each student's performance with an external standard representing the defined objective" (1970, p. 342).

The data obtained from evaluation come in a "pass or fail" form, not a ranking form. The important thing for evaluation of students and teachers is whether they pass or fail their tests and thus whether they meet certain standards, not that they are seventh or eighth from the top. The important thing for summative curriculum evaluation is whether the curriculum achieves the standards set for it, not how well it achieves them. The important thing for formative curriculum evaluation is decisions such as "the curriculum is acceptable" or "more refinement is needed."

Objectivity and Atomization

Two characteristics of evaluation need mention.

First, evaluation involves objective, unbiased measurement of objective reality. Two different perspectives on this are (1) that "accurate . . . assessment . . . requires . . . that the competence being tested for . . . be specified precisely without undue reliance on subjective judgment" (Anderson et al., 1996, p. 17) and (2) that "the outcomes of learning, the achievements of the learner, need to be assessed by an agent 'external' to the student, in order to ensure that they are objective and unbiased" (Gagne, 1970, pp. 27–28). Statistical assessment is the preferred type of evaluation.

Second, evaluation takes place within the context of atomization. The total learning or achievement to be evaluated is partitioned into specific atomistic events, each of which is evaluated separately. When each of the partitioned events is evaluated, it is examined in terms of characteristics inherent in the partitioned element. The question asked is whether or not the partitioned characteristics are present in the curriculum, child, or teacher, and whether they meet their respective standards.

Appropriateness of Evaluation

Three characteristics of the Social Efficiency ideology facilitate evaluation.

First, curriculum aims are stated as behavioral objectives that specify human performances. Behaviors are observable and thus easily measured.

Second, learning is conceived within the context of an identifiable change in behavior resulting from an identifiable stimulus condition. It is a change from the absence of a behavior to the presence of a behavior. Conceptualizing learning this way facilitates evaluation.

Third, the Social Efficiency conception of causation as deterministic facilitates evaluation. One must simply show absence of behavior, display a stimulus-response linkage, show the stimulus, and show the response to demonstrate that learning took place as the result of a specific intervention. If causation were not so direct and easily analyzable, evaluation would be more difficult.

Concluding Perspective

The Social Efficiency ideology has done much to make American education practical over the last century. Its insistence that education operate efficiently and accountably, prepare people for many years of productive adult life within society, and prepare them to perform useful skills rather than simply fill their minds with information, has done much to make American education relevant and useful. Its views that the most useful knowledge is the ability to perform skills, the teacher is a manager of classroom activity, the child is a doer, and educational objectives must be specified in terms of student performances, along with its broadening of our view of evaluation to include criterion-referenced testing, have done much to make schools more efficient, accountable, and relevant to the future lives of students. This is the ideology that has brought us behavioral objectives, behavioral management techniques, and objective quantitative research methods.

The Social Efficiency ideology first gained influence on American education during the last quarter of the 19th century and the first quarter of the 20th century with the rise of concern about utilitarian education (including agricultural education, manual training, industrial education, and vocational education). It became increasingly prominent during the second decade of the 20th century as a result of its influence on the field of school administration through the efforts of men like Franklin Bobbitt. It continued to gradually gain influence as it adopted the "scientific" statistical techniques of educational assessment and research. Ralph Tyler (with his systematic approach to curriculum and instruction) and behavioral psychologists (with the learning theory that was adopted by the ideology) did much to promote the Social Efficiency agenda in the middle of the 20th century. Between 1940 and 1980, Social Efficiency advocates became the major group of faculty teaching within schools of education and greatly influenced generations of teachers. With the rise of other ideologies in the last third of the 20th century, the replacement of behavioral psychology by cognitive psychology, and the replacement of Social Efficiency faculty in schools of education by those holding other ideologies, the Social Efficiency ideology declined in influence. At the end of the 20th century, as American society began to fear that the economic prominence of the U.S. might be eclipsed and the inefficiency and ineffectiveness of American education was made the scapegoat, the ideology again began to reassert its influence on education with its views on accountability, efficiency, and the federal No Child Left Behind mandates. Figure 3.3 provides a rough estimate of those times when advocates of this ideology have been most active, with respect to their own norms, in attempting to influence American education.

❖ **Figure 3.3** Times of relative high and low activity of the Social Efficiency ideology.

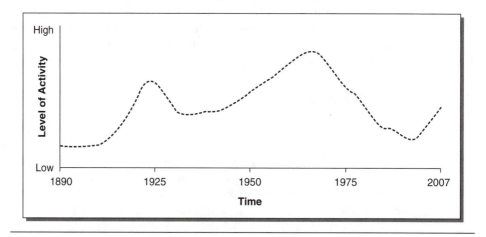

Activities designed to extend what is written here and provide additional insight into the ideology are located on the Sage Web site at www.sagepub.com/schiroextensionactivities.

Learner Centered Ideology

The Ideal School

Underlying the thoughts and endeavors of Learner Centered educators is an image or vision of an ideal school: a "school of tomorrow," as John Dewey wrote in 1915 (Dewey & Dewey, 1915). To the uninitiated visitor, the ideal Learner Centered school would look nothing like a traditional school. This is the way Rugg and Shumaker described it in 1928:

> Is this a schoolhouse . . . ? These cheerful rooms—walls colorful with children's paintings, floors spotted with bright rugs, light, movable tables and comfortable chairs. . . .
>
> Here is a group of six and seven year olds. They dance; they sing; they play house and build villages; they keep store and take care of pets; they model in clay and sand; they draw and paint, read and write, make up stories and dramatize them; they work in the garden; they churn, and weave, and cook.
>
> A group is inventing dances, which, we are told, are for a pageant. In a darkened room films are being shown. A high school class is teaching the seventh grade how to use the library. . . . A primary class is getting ready for an excursion . . . to a bakery. . . . At the end of the hall is a toy shop where industrious members . . . ply lathe and saw, pattern and paint, in fashioning marvelous trucks and horses. . . . Here is a nature-study laboratory with green things growing. A breathless group is stocking a new aquarium to be sent to the third grade; while over in the corner white rabbits, mice, and guinea pigs—even a turtle—loll in well-attended ease.
>
> . . . [W]e come across a shop where. . . . [o]ver all the walls are blueprints, maps, and posters and models of things made and in the making—ships, steam engines, cars, airplanes, submarines, sets for scenes, and even the swords and bucklers of medieval armor. (pp. 2–4)*

What a contrast this picture of the ideal school presents when compared to the Learner Centered view of the traditional school:

> In that pattern children are pigeonholed in long rows of desks, filed in stereotyped class-rooms. . . . Children must sit quietly, study their lessons silently, obey the teachers promptly and unquestioningly. . . . The listening school is a place where the chief weapons of education are chalk-talk on a dismal blackboard, a few intensely dull required texts, and a teacher's tired voice. . . .
>   Think of children sitting with arms folded, eyes front, putting up a hand for a begrudged permission to move, chanting lessons in unison. . . . There *memorize, recite, pay attention* are the keynotes. Not "What do you think?" but "What does the book say?" directs the educative process. (Rugg & Shumaker, 1928, pp. 2–4)

Although this particular contrast between the ideal school and the traditional school may sound oversimplified, making such a clear distinction is central to the Learner Centered ideology. An important dimension of Learner Centered educators' vision of their ideal school is that they perceive it to be dramatically different from the traditional school. It is "different in atmosphere, housing, furniture; different in its basic philosophy and psychology; different in the role that it assigns to pupil and teacher initiative" (Rugg & Shumaker, 1928, p. 2).

Ideal Schools for All Learners

The ideal schools envisioned by Learner Centered educators have existed in the past and exist today. They exist at all levels of education. Montessori and Reggio Emilia schools are currently popular at the preschool level. Learner Centered schools have been popular at the elementary through secondary school levels for more than a hundred years. Francis Parker promoted them at all educational levels in the 1890s in the Quincy, Massachusetts, public schools. Marietta Johnson promoted her organic school, which educated elementary through secondary school students, during the first several decades of the 20th century (and it is still in operation today). "Progressive education" had become popular by the 1920s and was widely practiced in public and private elementary and secondary schools. In 1942 the results of the Eight-Year Study, which examined the effects of Learner Centered secondary schools on college performance during the 1930s, were published. During the 1960s and 1970s, the open education movement promoted Learner Centered education in Grades K through 12. The Sudbury Valley School currently promotes Learner Centered education from elementary through secondary school. Learner Centered education is also practiced in higher education; the free university movement of the 1970s and 1980s provides one example, and Bennington College provides another. In addition, many adult education centers align themselves with this approach.

Thus, Learner Centered schools have been a reality for a few individuals, but Learner Centered educators believe they should become the schools of tomorrow for all people.

Most of the educators quoted herein speak of "children" as young people in school from preschool through college. In this chapter, I also speak of "learners," "people," "students," and "individuals"—not all of them children—to remind the reader of the broad applicability of this approach.

The ideal school envisioned by Learner Centered educators is different from the traditional school because it is a learner-centered school, an activity (or experience) school, an organic (or developmental) school, and an integrated school. Each of these dimensions of the ideal school will now be discussed.

The Learner-Centered School

The learner-centered ideal school is different from the traditional school because it is based on "nothing less than the reorientation of the entire school around the child" (Rugg & Shumaker, 1928, p. 56). In the learner-centered school, the needs and interests of learners, rather than those of teachers, principals, school subjects, parents, or politicians, determine the school program.

First, learner-centered schools are "child-centered institutions in contrast to the teacher-centered and principal-centered schools of the conventional order" (Rugg & Shumaker, 1928, p. 56). The interests, needs, and desires of learners dictate the nature of the school program, the content of the curriculum, and (to as large a degree as possible) the governance of the classroom. "These schools believe that boys and girls should share in their own government, in the planning of the program, in the administering of the curriculum, in conducting the life of the school" (p. 57). In the learner-centered school, "the routine needs of the school, as well as the lesson assignments, the planning of excursions and exhibits, and the criticism of reports are taken over by the pupils" (p. 57). This is very different from the traditional school, where teachers and principals dictate all aspects of student education and students must obey their every wish promptly and unquestioningly.

Second, learner-centered schools are organized around the needs and interests of individuals rather than the demands of the school subjects:

> In the formal schools . . . the program of the child's education is organized about school subjects. Not so in the new schools. . . . There is a . . . new article of faith—child interest as the orienting center of the school program. . . . The new school is setting up a program of work which has a personal connection with the immediate life of the child. It starts from his needs and interests. The units of the new program approximate as nearly as possible what to children are real-life situations. Hence the new school organizes its program around the centers of interest rather than around academic subjects. (Rugg & Shumaker, 1928, pp. 60–61)

In the learner-centered school, centers of interest such as clay boats, worms, care of a flock of chickens, musical instruments, and building and using a radio dominate the school curriculum. In contrast, academic subjects such as mathematics, English, science, and history dominate the school program in the traditional school. In learner-centered schools, "the having of wonderful ideas" (Duckworth, 1987) is important, while in traditional schools the acquisition of information and skills is valued.

Third, learner-centered schools orient themselves around the needs and interests of children rather than around parental expectations for their children. Here a distinction is made between the "self expressed needs of the child" and the "needs of the child as inferred by adults" (that is, what adults think the needs of children are; Noddings, 2005a, pp. 147–148). This is difficult for many parents to accept, as Marietta Johnson wrote 70 years ago of some parents of children in her School of Organic Education:

> He is afraid that the desired amount of "subject matter" will not be acquired. To think of growth in other terms than reading, writing, arithmetic, science, history, and geography is impossible for him. . . . The idea that education is a preparation for something in the future has such a strong hold upon the imagination that few parents can believe that if the need of the present is met fully, the future is assured. (1974, pp. 17, 25–26)

The learner-centered school concentrates on meeting the needs, interests, and desires of children and insists that "children should not be conscious of [or subjected to] adult expectancy. This is a source of self-consciousness and waste in childhood" (p. 25).

The Activity School

The ideal school is a school full of activity, a school where experience is the medium through which individuals grow and learn, a school where, indeed, "experience [is] the keynote of . . . education!" (Rugg & Shumaker, 1928, p. 5). Here it is believed "that knowledge comes . . . through the interaction of an individual with the surrounding world, both inanimate and social" (Hein, 1975, p. 2) and that "children naturally *think* through experience—through activity" (Johnson, 1974, p. 10). Here it is proclaimed, "I would have a child say not, 'I know,' but 'I have experienced'" (Rugg & Shumaker, 1928, p. 60). "I know" is taken to be the slogan of the traditional school, whose program is based on reading and silence, on sitting and reciting, on listening and acquisition of facts. In contrast, "I have experienced" is the slogan of the activity school.

The activity school program is based on four practices: direct firsthand experience with reality, experience with physical materials and people, experience involving physical activity, and experience both inside and outside the classroom. Each practice needs elaboration.

Firsthand Experience With Reality

The activity school provides learners firsthand experiences with reality and avoids the traditional school's practice of providing only secondhand experiences through reading, writing, listening, and viewing. Those who maintain activity schools "feel it is necessary for the student to confront the real world and its physical materials directly, rather than through intermediaries such as textbooks" (Education Development Center, 1966, p. 3):

> One mandate is imperative for our style of work: there must be personal involvement. The child must work with his own hands, mind, and heart. It is not enough for him to watch the teacher demonstrate or stand in line to take a hurried glimpse of the reflection of his own eyelashes in the microscope eyepiece. It is not enough for him to watch the skillful classmate at work, not enough to follow the TV screen. He needs his own apparatus, simple, workable. (Morrison, 1964/1970, p. 111)

Activity school educators emphasize direct, firsthand experiences with reality because they believe that growth, learning, and knowledge come through individuals' personal interactions with their world.

Experience With Physical Materials and People

Since learners must personally experience reality in order to grow, learn, and construct meaning, it becomes necessary for the activity school to provide them with the "reality" they need to experience. It does this by furnishing them with a multitude of activities involving physical materials and social encounters. Physical materials of both animate and inanimate form are prominent in the activity school. Children experience the growing of plants firsthand in the activity school instead of reading about them as they would in the traditional school. They care for and personally handle animals in the activity school instead of looking at pictures of them as they would in the traditional school. Adolescents personally make things such as tables, model airplanes, radios, dresses, cakes, and sets for plays instead of listening to lectures about how to make such things as they would in the traditional school. Adults paint, dance, work on political campaigns, write and discuss poetry, and work in archaeological digs instead of listening to lectures or reading books on such as they would in the traditional school. The belief is that

> the child must discover the fact for himself. . . . He will do this if the relevant material is available to him in sufficient quantity and variety, if he is given many opportunities of handling it and trying it out. (Blackie, 1971, p. 87)

This is in contrast to beliefs operating in the traditional school, where students are expected to learn facts that others have discovered by reading books and listening to teachers.

In the activity school, "manipulative materials are supplied in great diversity and range with little replication" (Walberg & Thomas, 1971, p. 90). For example, one might find a tape recorder to tell stories into, a stove for cooking, a computer on which to access the Internet or run a simulation, a camera for taking pictures of interesting occurrences or projects just finished, a play store from which things can be bought and sold, old clothes in which one can dress up and make believe, a multitude of books, bottle caps, spools, seashells, peas, buttons, string, wire, rope, ribbon, rulers, scales and balances with which to weigh and measure, and magic markers, crayons, and paints with which to create pictures. As a result, the traditional school, with its desks, its chairs, and its standardized books neatly arranged, is very different in appearance from the activity school.

In the activity school, encounters with peers and adults are also in abundance. These are real social encounters where people work together, explore together, exchange ideas with each other, play together, dispute ideas with each other, construct meanings about their physical and cultural world together, and construct social and individual meanings together. Sudbury Valley School emphasizes this social orientation on its Web site:

> The school teems with activity. Adults and students of all ages mix freely. People can be found everywhere talking, reading and playing. Some may be in the photolab developing

or printing pictures. Some may be in a dance class or building a bookshelf in the wood-shop. There are almost always people making music of one kind or another, usually in several places. . . . People may be at computers, doing administrative work in the office, playing chess, rehearsing a show, or participating in role-playing games. People will be trading stickers and trading lunches. A group may be selling pizza that they made to raise money for new equipment. . . . Always there are people playing happily and busily, indoors and outdoors, in all seasons and all weather. Always there are groups talking, and always there are individuals quietly reading here and there. (n.d.-c, ¶ 2–3)

This social activity does not take place by accident:

> In preparing the space [in which children learn], teachers offer the possibility for children to be with the teachers and many of the other children, or with just a few of them, or even alone when they need a little niche to stay in by themselves.
>
> Teachers are always aware . . . that children learn a great deal in exchanges with their peers, especially when they can interact in small groups. Such small groups of two, three, four, or five children provide possibilities for paying attention, for hearing and listening to each other, for developing curiosity and interest, for asking questions and for responding to them. It provides opportunities for negotiation and dynamic communication . . . [and for] planning and decision making. This type of small group also favors the emergence of cognitive conflicts; such conflicts can initiate a process in which, while children find a res-olution, they construct together new learning and new skills. (Gandini, 2004, pp. 17–18)

Social, as well as individual, construction of knowledge is encouraged in the activ-ity school. This is in contrast to what is encouraged in the traditional school, where students are expected to "do their own work" and where sharing ideas, answers to ques-tions, and solutions to problems is often considered cheating.

Experience Involving Physical Activity

The ideal school is full of activity: physical, verbal, social, and emotional. It radiates the belief that healthy intellectual, social, and emotional growth must be accompanied by physical and verbal activity. It is a school where "children move freely about the room without asking permission," where "talking among children is encouraged," and where "many different activities go on simultaneously" (Walberg & Thomas, 1971, p. 90). It is a school where one finds "a large amount of actual physical exertion, of overt bodily movement, of a wide variety of sensory contracts, of the type of energy-release which is ordinarily designated as play" (Rugg & Shumaker, 1928, p. 58). In the activity school it is believed that one must "free the legs, the arms, the larynx of a child" in order to "take the first step towards freeing his mind and spirit" to grow and learn (Rugg & Shumaker, p. 55). This is because adherents of the Learner Centered ideology believe that perhaps the "most deep-seated tendency in human life is movement, impulse, activity . . . that the basis of all learning is . . . action" (Rugg & Shumaker, p. 59). As a result, the activity school is very different from the traditional school, which encourages stillness and quiet. "Where the [traditional] school maintained . . . silence as the ideal classroom atmosphere, the new [activity school] removes the ban from speech, [and] encourages communication as a vehicle for social understanding and personal develop-ment" (Rugg & Shumaker, p. 66).

In the activity school, for example, one might find adolescents acting out Greek and Roman myths through improvisational drama rather than just studying classics from a textbook; children telling each other stories rather than just writing language arts essays; adults dancing old English folk dances and singing old English ballads rather than just reading English literature; adolescents building a model railroad rather than filling in a worksheet on the history of railroads; adolescents exploring and mapping gullies, streams, and bays near the school rather than just listening to a lecture about physical geography; children measuring the height of their school rather than just writing in an arithmetic workbook; and adolescents discussing surface tension as they play with water rather than just watching the teacher perform a physics demonstration. In the activity school, all of these activities might occur simultaneously, in contrast to the traditional school, where one thing happens at a time.

Experience Inside and Outside the Classroom

The activity school is designed to provide learners with experiences that occur both inside and outside the classroom. Teachers within the activity school frequently take children outside the classroom and the school to explore phenomena within their everyday natural and man-made world (Fayerweather Street School, n.d.). By doing so, they make available many rich and stimulating learning experiences from which children can learn. Nature study offers experiences with animals, plants, geological formations, pond water, and observations of the moon. The man-made world offers the ability to explore different types of transportation, buildings, and the local community. When children are taken outside the classroom to learn, a whole world of rich learning experiences opens up as part of the instructional environment.

Because the activity school provides learners with educational experiences outside the classroom—in the halls of the school, in the schoolyard, and in the school neighborhood—it is strikingly different from the traditional school. In the traditional school, students are viewed as learning only in their classroom at their desks, while in the activity school people are encouraged to learn wherever interesting occurrences present themselves.

The Organic School

The Learner Centered ideal school is an organic, or developmental, school: a school designed to further the natural growth of the developing human organism (hence the term *organic*). It is founded on the belief that "life—growth—education—are synonymous" (Johnson, 1974, p. 18) and with the "idea that education is growth and that the school program must minister to growth" (p. 37), and it is organized to "respect the inner movement of growth" (p. 22) of learners as they self-actualize themselves and to provide them with educational experiences compatible with their stage of social, emotional, and intellectual development. The organic school is different from the traditional school in three ways.

First, the organic school is different because its curriculum is based on the natural developmental growth of people, rather than on demands external to them. Marietta Johnson says of her School of Organic Education, "Our school has always been an effort to work with children from the point of view of meeting their needs rather than getting them to meet the demands of any system" (1974, p. 15). The organic school does not pressure people to acquire academic skills and knowledge before they are developmentally ready to do so. The differing approaches taken to reading and writing instruction in organic and traditional schools provides an example. Organic school educators do not force children to learn to read or write before their bodies and minds are ready to voluntarily do so—and a whole language approach to literacy is taken. In traditional schools, children are encouraged, or required, to read and write as soon as they can—and a phonics approach to reading is taken. The issue here is the difference between training and growing:

> "Training" and "growing" are quite different. In training, we often dominate or force in order to accomplish certain definite external results. In growing, we provide the right conditions and the end is human and immediate—included in the process—and the moving power is within . . . the child. (Johnson, 1974, pp. 8–9)

It is the task of the organic school to provide the medium for growth—an intellectually rich, physically interesting, socially humane, emotionally joyous, and aesthetically pleasing instructional environment for individuals to experience, and teachers who facilitate those individuals' interactions with that environment—and it is the task of those individuals to grow in their own natural self-actualizing ways. In contrast, the traditional school fills children's minds and trains them by imposing knowledge and skills upon them.

Second, the organic school is different from the traditional school because it believes people evolve through a series of qualitatively different growth stages as they develop from infancy to adulthood. Hence, the organic school views children as different from adults, treats them differently, and bases its curriculum on the nature of children as children rather than as potential adults.

The organic school endeavors to educate people in the manner most appropriate to their stage of development. This involves ministering directly to people as they experience their nature at a particular stage of growth. By doing this, the organic school cherishes childhood and "stresses the present, not the future; living, not preparing for life; learning now, not anticipating the future" (Barth, 1972, p. 97) under the belief that to live life fully "as a child is the best preparation for adulthood" (Walberg & Thomas, 1971, p. 85).

The issues here are how people are treated and the activities in which they are encouraged to engage. The organic school treats children as children and provides them with "childlike" activities designed to be congruent with, to nurture, and to elaborate on their stage of development. In contrast, the traditional school treats children as potential adults and provides them with "adultlike" activities designed to prepare them for and speed them on their way toward adulthood. For example, the organic school provides the child with activities that might be classified as having the essence of "play" under the belief that

> if the need of the present is met fully, the future is assured. Growth has no external end. The end and the process are one. If the child is happily engaged in wholesome activity, he is growing, he is being educated. (Johnson, 1974, pp. 25–26)

In contrast, the traditional school is perceived to provide children with activities that might be classified as having the essence of "work" under the assumption that "school-work" is the work of children, and that as work it is often unpleasant and difficult and often requires both strenuous intellectual exertion and the painful activity of sitting still.

In the organic school, "play is not distinguished from work as the predominant mode of learning" (Barth, 1972, p. 24). In fact, the distinction between work and play is considered inappropriate. It is more appropriate to distinguish between involvement and lack of involvement in an activity, since it is believed that if people are actively engaged in an activity, they are constructing meaning, learning, and growing—which is viewed as both play and work. As a result, the atmosphere of the organic school fosters voluntary, happy, and active involvement in experiences. In contrast, the atmosphere of the traditional school is viewed as one that forces students to partake in tedious work.

Third, the organic school is different from the traditional school because it believes individuals grow and learn intellectually, socially, emotionally, and physically in their own unique and idiosyncratic ways and at their own individual rates rather than in a uniform manner. The school is organized and conducted in a way that supports differences among individuals in all their qualitative richness. Three practices follow:

1. Individualized instruction in organic and traditional schools is different. In organic schools, many different activities take place simultaneously and learners choose among them based on their personal needs, interests, and learning styles. In traditional schools, only one activity usually takes place at any one time and all students must participate in that activity regardless of their personal needs and interests. In the organic school, "activities do not arise from predetermined curricula," for "the teacher plans instruction individually and pragmatically, based upon reflective evaluation of each child's particular needs and interests" (Walberg & Thomas, 1971, p. 91). In the traditional school, a predetermined curriculum determines what will occur in the classroom independent of students' needs, interests, abilities, and learning styles.

2. In organic schools, "children have the right to direct their own learning, to make important decisions regarding their own educational experience" based on their own felt needs, interests, abilities, and learning styles (Walberg & Thomas, 1971, p. 93). Learners exercise this right by deciding which activities they will become involved in, how long they will spend on an activity, whether they will work alone or in a group, and, if they work in a group, who will be the members of the group. The organic school "is a place where people decide for themselves how to spend their days. Here, students of all ages determine what they will do, as well as when, how, and where they will do it" (Sudbury Valley School, n.d.-b, ¶ 1). In contrast, the traditional school is a place where the teacher decides all of these things.

3. Organic schools are conducted with the dual belief that "there is no set body of knowledge which must be transmitted to all" learners (Walberg & Thomas, 1971, p. 93) and that the knowledge individuals construct as a result of their unique, personal, and idiosyncratic interactions with their world is a function of their developmental stages, learning styles, and thinking styles. As a result, organic school teachers believe that what individuals learn in their school is a function of their own unique organic nature at their particular stage of development. In contrast, traditional school educators predetermine the knowledge students will learn without taking into account the students' individual organic natures.

In essence, the organic school is organized and conducted in such a way as to support the multitude of differences that naturally exist among individuals—differences in interest, learning style, rate of learning, and the specific meaning each has acquired from previous experiences. In contrast, the traditional school is perceived to suppress individual differences and attempt to establish uniformity in learning among students.

The Integrated School

The ideal school is an integrated school. It takes a unified rather than an atomistic approach to people's education. It is integrated in many ways.

First, it is integrated because it treats people as integrated organisms. People are dealt with as inseparable conglomerates of intellectual, social, emotional, and physical components rather than as creatures whose attributes can be partitioned and dealt with separately (Noddings, 2005b, p. 12). The integrated school takes "a holistic view of personality" that requires one to "look at the whole child" and deal with all of their attributes simultaneously (Hein, 1975, p. 2). Unlike the traditional school, the integrated school

> does not see "skill development" [or concept development] as a separate activity which can be isolated, studied, and improved independent of the rest of the child. . . . [I]ntellectual growth cannot take place without growth and development of the whole personality of the child. (Hein, 1975, p. 2)

Rugg and Shumaker phrase it this way while pointing out how the diversity of materials in the activity school support its integrated approach, that is, the education of all aspects of the child simultaneously:

> The whole child is to be educated. Hence the materials of education are as broad and interrelated as life itself. For experience is not only an intellectual matter, it is physical, rhythmic, emotional. Thus the vocabulary of the new school has coursing through it a unitary, integrating theme. (1928, p. 5)

Second, the ideal school is integrated because it integrates knowledge of the school disciplines. It does this by taking an interdisciplinary approach to knowledge in which the separate "school subjects are rejected in favor of broader and more integrated centers of work" (Rugg & Shumaker, 1928, p. 61). Integrated schools do not view knowledge as broken up into separate disciplines. For example, if children are exploring what can be found in pond water, they are not asked to categorize what is being learned as technology, science, mathematics, art, reading, and writing when they collect pond water from a nearby pond, build microscopes to observe small living "creatures" in the collected pond water, measure and paint what they observe, locate the creatures they have observed in books and read about them, and then write about their observations and discoveries. Further, it is assumed that children will integrate their understanding of the meanings they create in their own unique ways, and that the ways they interrelate the meanings they construct will not necessarily correspond with the ways universities have partitioned knowledge into the separate academic disciplines. Here it is assumed that it is the learner's job to integrate knowledge, and that configuring what goes on inside learners' minds is not the job of the teacher or the curriculum. The job of the teacher and the curriculum is to create engaging learning experiences that naturally integrate the content of the different academic disciplines in holistic ways that do not atomize and partition knowledge.

Third, the ideal school is integrated because it has few fixed periods during the day when particular events occur. There is a fluidity of time in the integrated school; learners begin activities, end their involvement in activities, and move on to new activities when it feels proper and natural to them. In contrast, in the traditional school time is broken up into segments for specific purposes under the belief that students' interests and intellectual development can fit into neatly arranged time periods.

Fourth, the ideal school is integrated because many different activities take place simultaneously. This is in sharp contrast to the traditional school's practice of partitioning the day in such a way that only one activity takes place at a time. Activities naturally become integrated into each other in the following two ways: (1) activities that simultaneously take place in different parts of the room merge together, as when, for example, several children's involvement with mice merges with other children's involvement with building blocks, resulting in mice running through block structures and thus a study of animal behavior in mazes; and (2) activities that take place at one point of time naturally flow into later activities, as when, for example, work with plants leads to a search for information in the classroom library, which leads to reading.

Fifth, the ideal school is integrated because it attempts to integrate people's home and school lives. In the integrated school,

> the boundaries most American children carefully draw between "school" and "home" are blurred. Children, like teachers, take things and ideas of interest home to ponder, just as they bring things and ideas of interest from home to school. The result is a more fully "integrated day." (Barth, 1972, p. 75)

The integrated school, unlike the traditional school, fosters in learners a sense that the world is not fragmented into the isolated places of "home" and "school."

These five aspects of integration are not viewed in isolation from each other. The simultaneity of activities in an undifferentiated classroom time schedule, a simultaneity that supports the continuity between home and school life while cutting across subject areas, is directed toward fostering to the fullest extent possible all aspects of people's growth.

Learners

The Learner as Central Focus

Learner Centered educators see the world through the eyes of learners, who are their central concern. In 1894, Francis Parker affirmed, "The centre of all movement in education is the child" (1894/1964, p. 383). In 1967, the opening sentences of the Plowden Report declared,

> At the heart of the educational process lies the child. No advances in policy, no acquisitions of new equipment have their desired effect unless they are in harmony with the nature of the child, unless they are fundamentally acceptable to him. (Plowden, 1967, p. 9)

An assumption of the Learner Centered "approach is that children constitute the basic resources of the educational process. In contrast to those educational theories which 'assume' the presence of a child during instruction," the Learner Centered "approach 'requires' the presence of a child to define instruction" (Bussis & Cluttenden, 1970, pp. 14–15).

The Learner Centered approach to curriculum involves an effort to create and use curriculum in such a way that the child's organic nature, "the child's own needs," and "his immediate interests . . . furnish the starting point of education" (Rugg & Shumaker, 1928, p. 58). Learner Centered educators are concerned about people rather than theories regarding people, about sensitivity and responsiveness to people rather than scholarly rigor in the study of people, and about helping people learn the things of greatest concern to them rather than teaching people what they "need" to know. This involves an effort, in creating and using curricula, to "apply to the education of children the lessons learned from the study of children themselves" (Jersild, 1946, p. 1).

The first consideration of Learner Centered educators in creating and using curricula is learners' needs, interests, and concerns as learners themselves feel them. Lillian Weber describes the centrality of learners to educators' endeavors this way:

> Central to the conversations [of Learner Centered advocates] was always a child: What does he need? What is he interested in? What is he ready for? What are his purposes? How does he follow them? What are his questions? What is he playing? These questions about children seemed to be uppermost in developing plans for the classroom, for plans were made not from the vantage point of a syllabus of demand which a child had to meet, but with relevance to children in the most immediate way. A plan fitted itself to a child. It was developed in response to the pace and internal pattern of his own growth and in support of his own purposes. It was developed through watching a child, studying him at his moments of deepest involvement in play. (1971, pp. 169–170)

This means that whatever knowledge educators possess about people is to be used to help these people further their own ends. Knowledge of people is not to be used to manipulate them to learn content not inherently deriving from their nature, to maneuver them to endure styles of learning not natural to them, or to further ends other than their own. The curriculum is to organize itself around individuals' intentions to learn rather than educators' intentions to teach them; around what individuals want to learn rather than around what educators want them to learn; and around individuals' learning styles rather than around teachers' preferred teaching styles. Marietta Johnson aptly states, "Our constant thought is not what do children learn or do, but what are the 'learning' and the 'doing' doing to them" (1926, p. 350).

The Nature of the Learner

The Learner Centered ideology sees people as naturally good. It also sees the stages of life known as childhood, adolescence, and adulthood as naturally and inherently good. It believes that people's natural modes of growth and impulses for action will be good and constructive if they are not inhibited or distorted, and that children will naturally grow into happy, constructive, well-functioning adults if they are allowed to do so. In addition, Learner Centered educators believe that people's "capacity for self-fulfillment is good, that the ability of humans to command their own educational destinies is good, that a child's search toward fuller understanding is normal, natural, and good" (Rathbone, 1971, p. 113).

People are also conceptualized as self-activated makers of meaning, as actively self-propelled agents of their own growth and not as passive organisms to be filled or molded by agents outside themselves. A person is viewed as "an active agent in his own learning process. He is not one to whom things merely happen: he is one who by his own volition causes things to happen . . . [through] his own self-initiated interaction with the world" (Rathbone, 1971, p. 100). People's inherent capabilities for growth are activated by their own endeavors.

As a result, education is seen as an enterprise involving the drawing out of the inherent capabilities of people. It is a facilitator of people's natural growth in that it allows learners to, as Rogers and Maslow would say, "self-actualize" themselves. It will result in healthy, virtuous, and beneficial learning if what is drawn out is allowed to come out naturally.

The Growing Individual

Growth

Because Learner Centered educators believe people contain their own capabilities for growth, are the agents who must actualize their own capabilities, and are basically good in nature, a central theme of their endeavors is the concept of "growth." They proclaim, "Not 'what do they know' but 'how do they grow' is our slogan" (Johnson, 1974, p. 15). These educators' devotion to growth leads them to believe that "ministering to growth, meeting the needs of the organism, is the sole function of the educational process"(p. 18). Growth of the learner in terms of his (or her) unfolding in "conformity to the law of his being" (Parker, 1894/1964, p. 383) through self-actualization becomes the objective of the Learner Centered approach. This doctrine of growth demands that education of each individual be in harmonious resonance with the inner "being" of that individual: that "education . . . respect the inner movement of growth" of the individual (Johnson, 1974, p. 23), that education be "organic education," that learning be in vibration with the "rhythms of life," and that growth occur through creative self-expression. This perspective emphasizes the development of individuals and their individuality, for it is assumed that each individual has a unique being and must grow in accordance with that unique being.

Freedom and Individualism

Learner Centered educators insist on individuals' "freedom to develop naturally, to be spontaneous, unaffected, and unselfconscious" (Rugg & Shumaker, 1928, p. 56). In the freedom-versus-control debate, Learner Centered educators insist on freedom: freedom of individuals to determine the nature of their education, and, as a result, freedom of individuals to develop into the unique people that correspond to their inner being.

The crux of the issue surrounding the freedom-versus-control debate concerns which agent will decide the nature of an individual's education: the individual, society, academic subjects, teachers, parents, politicians—in other words, the individual or someone else. Learner Centered educators declare that each individual learner must be the agent of his or her own learning, growth, education, and life (Sudbury Valley School, n.d.-a).

Learner Centered educators believe individuals should determine the directions their education will take by responding to their own innate natures, felt needs, and organic impulses. The desire of these educators is to let individuals grow naturally into the people they will become. This requires that society, parents, school subjects, teachers, and politicians not attempt to control individuals' growth or to mold individuals to conform to their expectations. Rather, they must allow individuals the freedom to determine their own directions for growth, their own education, and their own lives: "It is the creative spirit from within [individual learners] that is encouraged, rather than conformity to a pattern imposed from without" that involves "social adjustment, adaptation to the existing order . . . [or] compliance with social demands" (Rugg & Shumaker, 1928, pp. 62–63).

Insisting that individuals be the prime agents of their own education—independent, self-reliant, self-actualizing learners who are capable, on their own, of directing their own growth—leads Learner Centered educators to a belief in individualism. This belief asserts that learners are different from one another, that their own unique inner impulses motivate them to grow in different manners, and that, as a result, education must be individualized. Seeing individuals as the prime agents of their own education also leads Learner Centered advocates to a position where they "not only acknowledge but deliberately attempt to foster individual differences among children" (Barth, 1972, p. 72). This individualistic view extends far beyond simple conceptions of individualization based on learning style, thinking style, or rate of conceptualization, for it sees all learners as fundamentally unique and independently self-directed in ways that make them somewhat autonomous from all teachers and codified information.

Autonomy

Inherent in Learner Centered educators' belief in freedom and individualism is a belief in the autonomy that must be accorded to people, who have the right to determine what they will learn and the competence to direct their own learning. Thus, the Learner Centered "school provides a setting in which students are independent, are trusted, and are treated as responsible people" (Sudbury Valley School, n.d.-b, ¶ 4). Conceptualizing people as autonomous learners means that it is up to them to determine what they will learn, how they will grow, and how they will self-actualize their potential. It means that when a "child firmly decides against doing what the teacher thinks is best, the teacher often will make the decision to honor the child's position and give up, for the time being, this particular opportunity to extend his understanding" (Rathbone, 1971, p. 112). This is because an important aspect of Learner Centered educators' view of autonomy is the belief that it is often "more important for a child to have the experience of receiving someone else's *respect* for him and for his wishes than to have the experience of *submitting* to someone else's notion of 'what's good for him'" (Rathbone, 1971, p. 112). The need for individuals to actually *recognize* and *feel* that they are in charge of their own lives and learning, and to be respected as human beings in doing so, is essential to the way Learner Centered educators construct the instructional environment in which individuals grow and learn.

This view of learners' autonomy is a delicate one to handle, for on one hand it is believed that learners' needs and desires as they express them should guide curriculum creation, while on the other hand Learner Centered educators have goals in mind for the learner—such as competence in reading, writing, and arithmetic. The problem is really one of priorities. Educators must have objectives, but they must embed them in their curricula in such a way that learners' needs and desires always take priority over the teacher's objectives when the two come into conflict. In addition, educators must embed their objectives in their curricula in such a way that learners are given real choices as they encounter the curricula—choices involving which direction to proceed, choices regarding the type of knowledge to construct, and choices from a rich array of learning styles and rates of proceeding.

Learner Centered educators handle the issue of individuals' autonomy in such a way that their objectives can be implemented when they correspond with the needs and desires of the individual. Educators' objectives are implemented more frequently than might be expected, for educators proceed under the assumption that what teachers make available to learners has a powerful effect on their interests, what they become involved in, and thus what they learn and how they grow. For example, by bringing into a classroom a boa constrictor and books on snakes, a teacher can make it more likely that children will become interested in snakes, read about snakes, learn about snakes, and thereby improve their reading skills. If no snake were available, children might not become interested in them. If no books about snakes were available, children might not explore what scientists have learned about snakes and learn that science. If no books were available on a subject about which children were interested, children might not want to learn to read or improve their reading comprehension.

In general, individuals' autonomy is nourished within the Learner Centered ideology through the creation of learning environments in which educators' control of the learning environment and learners' autonomy within the learning environment are both respected. The success of Learner Centered classrooms thus depends

> not on adults giving up of control to children but on a deliberate and conscious sharing of responsibility for learning on the part of both child and teacher. The adult, to a large extent, determines the nature of the school environment; the child decides with which . . . materials he will work, to which problems he will address himself, for how long, and with whom. (Barth, 1972, pp. 27–28)

As a result, curriculum developers create curricula and teachers instruct students in such a way that students' autonomy is preserved and direction for students' growth and learning is provided.

The Learner in the Present Tense

Learner Centered educators dedicate themselves to the growth of people in the present moment, to children as children rather than to children as potential adults, and they refuse to sacrifice the here and now of childhood to the requirements of the future. Educators view children as qualitatively different from adults and focus their endeavors on enhancing the lives of children as children, undergoing growth as children, in the moment during which they are undergoing the growth. Their assumption is that "each day's activity is important and enough in itself" (Johnson, 1974, p. 26) and that "if the child is wholesomely, happily, intelligently employed, he is being educated!" (p. 9). While creating curricula, Learner Centered curriculum developers design materials and activities that stress the present in people's lives and not the future, living life and not preparing for life, growing now and not worrying about how to reach some predetermined future goal.

Developmental Viewpoint

Two major assumptions underlying the work of Learner Centered educators are that people grow through distinctly different developmental stages and that people's thoughts are different at different developmental stages. Whether the stages are psychological, social, cognitive, or moral in nature, people are believed to evolve through a sequence of qualitatively different development stages from infancy to old age. People at different stages of growth are thought to perceive, understand, think about, and interact with their world in different ways. For example, 8-year-olds in Piaget's "concrete operational" stage of cognitive development are viewed and treated differently from 14-year-olds in Piaget's "formal operational" stage. It is important to curriculum developers and teachers to design and use curricula so that they "respect the inner movement of growth" of people and complement their developmental stages (Johnson, 1974, p. 23). Since people are basically different at different stages of growth, the curricula designed for and used with people at different stages of growth will also be different.

To ascertain the nature of people's stages of growth, Learner Centered educators look to developmental learning theories. Marietta Johnson explains:

> The main work of the child is to grow. To be able to recognize the signs of growth in children at any age is a great art! One must study the results of the experts—must respect the findings of authorities—and then one must study at first hand the reaction of children. (1974, p. 10)

Important here is that, after studying "the results of the experts," "one must study at first hand the reaction of children." A critical component of Learner Centered educators' endeavors is their firsthand observations of people.

Viewing people's growth developmentally goes beyond just making sure that the instructional activities match people's intellectual, social, and psychological attributes. The developmental viewpoint also assumes that people's evolution from infancy to old age takes time. Learner Centered educators interpret this to mean that people are not to be hurried from stage to stage, but that they are to be allowed to evolve at their own rate from one stage to the next. Curricula are created and taught so as to allow people to evolve naturally, each according to his or her own personal developmental timetable and rate of learning. Curricula are not designed or taught to efficiently accelerate people's progress through stages of growth. From the Learner Centered perspective, the purpose of curricula is to enrich people's growth within a developmental stage.

In addition, the developmental viewpoint includes the belief that people's thoughts and thinking processes evolve from concrete to abstract. As a result, Learner Centered educators assume that real, concrete, personal experiences in one's environment form the roots out of which thoughts and thinking processes grow. This means that within Learner Centered curricula, "verbal abstractions should follow direct experience with objects and ideas, not precede them or substitute for them" (Barth, 1972, p. 33).

> Thus there is a stress on experience, materials, "stuff" of the world, as well as concern that people have time and opportunity to assimilate these experiences, to "work" on them internally so that they increase their capacity to learn, to reason, to think. (Hein, 1975, p. 1)

The Learning Person

Learning: The Person in an Environment

The potential for growth lies within people. However, people grow, their thoughts develop, and their thinking processes evolve as a result of stimulation that comes from their interaction with their environment. Learner Centered educators believe both the weaker assumption that people's learning is facilitated by active interaction with an environment rich in physical, social, and intellectual stimuli and the stronger assumption that "learning depends upon direct interaction with materials and one's social and physical environment" (Weber, 1971, p. 93). The underlying belief is that "all children naturally *think* through experience" (Johnson, 1974, p. 10), and, as a result, "learning is seen as a consequence of the interaction between the child and the real world—be it an idea, a person, a gerbil, a book, or a can of paint and a brush" (Barth, 1972, p. 63).

Learning is a function of the interaction between people and their environment: it takes place when inquiring learners engage a stimulating environment. People are not passive agents during this interaction; they are active agents of their own learning. Learning is not something transferred from the environment *to* people but something created *by* people in response to their environmental interactions. Learning is people's "creative self-expression" that results from their active exploration of and response to their environment.

Learning Theory

The learning theory underlying the Learner Centered ideology is a form of constructivism.

Learning takes place when people interact with learning environments. People engage their environments with already existing cognitive structures. Their cognitive structures consist of previously acquired meanings and an organizational structure that relates the meanings. Learning takes place when people interact with their environment and perceive sensory information as a result of the interaction. This sensory information might come from social, physical, emotional, or intellectual experiences.

Incorporating new perceptions into an already existing cognitive structure involves the twin processes of accommodation and assimilation. On one hand, new perceptions are altered so that they are consistent with the individual's existing meanings and can fit into the individual's organization of existing meanings. This involves constructing new meanings by transforming perceptions. On the other hand, people's preexisting cognitive structures are changed when new perceptions are incorporated into them in order to eliminate any inconsistencies and discontinuities that might exist with previously created meanings and in order to adjust the organization of previously created meanings to give the new knowledge a place in the organization. This means that people reconstruct their existing cognitive structures by transforming themselves. That is, in learning, people construct and reconstruct meaning by transforming both the new meanings they are acquiring and their preexisting cognitive structures—by transforming both their new understanding of their world and themselves.

Learning Leads to Knowledge

Learner Centered educators are much less interested in knowledge than they are in growth and learning. This is because their concern is, first, facilitating the growth of individuals, and second, providing them with learning experiences through which they can make meaning. Knowledge enters the scene because it is an inevitable by-product of learning, and thus of growth. It results from individuals making meaning out of their experiences.

From the Learner Centered perspective, the process by which an individual learns—learning—yields the product of learning—knowledge. As such, "knowledge is seen as an integral part of learning rather than a separate entity" (Barth, 1972, p. 47), which individuals must go out of their way to acquire. Put another way, learning naturally leads to the construction of knowledge, and individuals do not need to do anything other than learn to construct knowledge. It is not that knowledge is of no importance to Learner Centered educators, but rather that it is considerably less important than growth or learning. It is not seen as an end of education—as is growth—but rather as a by-product of growth. Knowledge is viewed as the secondary consequence of growth, and it derives from learning, which is viewed as the primary consequence of growth. How children learn is thus linked to what children learn, the knowledge children construct, and meanings that children comprehend. The Learner Centered

> model advanced for explaining the *process* of a child's learning clearly implies that the product of his learning results from the particular interactions he and he alone has experienced. This further implies that what a child learns is not only his *but may well be his alone*, even though it closely resembles the learning of someone else. (Rathbone, 1971, p. 101)

Two important assumptions flow from these beliefs. First, knowledge is a personal creation of individuals who engage in learning by interacting with their environment. Second, the knowledge the "child learns is not only his but may well be his alone." This is because knowledge, which is the result of learning, is something personal that "results from" an individual's "particular interactions" with his environment that "he and he alone has experienced." The results of these assumptions are the twin beliefs that "forming a conception of the way things are is an individual act based on experiences that can never be identical to anyone else's" and that "one must admit not only the possibility but the inevitability of individual differences of conceptualization" (Rathbone, 1971, p. 102). In other words, the knowledge individuals possess is a personal creation unique to each of them.

As a consequence of holding these beliefs, Learner Centered educators do not express the objectives of education in terms of knowledge—since knowledge is unique to the individuals who create it—but in terms of the experiences they desire learners to have. One cannot give knowledge to other people in nice, neat packages, but one can provide other people with experiences out of which they can construct knowledge. Learner Centered educators are not givers of knowledge, but rather givers of experiences out of which people will—with some degree of unpredictability—create knowledge for themselves. Knowledge is thus rarely spoken of in terms of "to know" but often in terms of "to experience."

In addition, since "knowledge is a function of one's personal integration of experience," knowledge "does not fall neatly into separate categories or 'disciplines'" (Barth, 1972, p. 45). Although it may be useful to Learner Centered educators to think of certain materials or experiences as associated with specific disciplines, such thinking is not used for the purpose of influencing people's categorization of experience and knowledge into traditional disciplines but rather for the purpose of (a) enabling curriculum developers to organize materials and experiences into curriculum and (b) helping teachers to organize their classrooms so that they and their students will know where to locate materials. Learner Centered educators believe that knowledge does not have to be partitioned into academic disciplines and organized in the ways currently conceptualized by scholars.

Teaching

Within this context, teaching has three basic functions. First, teaching involves careful observation of students and diagnosis of their individual needs and interests. The next two functions of teaching result from these observations of students and are designed to stimulate their growth based on their needs and interests. Second, teaching involves setting up the physical, social, emotional, and intellectual environment in which people learn. It is students' interactions in that environment that stimulate them to grow, learn, and make sense of their world. Third, teaching involves facilitating students' growth by intervening between them and their environment to assist them as they learn:

> Teachers also act as recorders (documenters) for the children, helping them trace and revisit their words and actions and thereby making the learning visible. . . . They provide instruction in tool and material use as needed, help find materials and resources, and scaffold children's learning. (Edwards, 2002, p. 9)

What this means in terms of classroom performance is that the Learner Centered ideology deemphasizes the role of the teacher as a deliverer of knowledge, possessor of information, transmitter of answers, mediator between curriculum and learner, conductor of children's activity, and evaluator. Instead, it emphasizes the

> teacher as trained observer, diagnostician of individual needs, presenter of environments, consultant, collaborator, flexible resource, psychological supporter, general facilitator of the learning requirements of an independent agent. This means that . . . the teacher is mainly *assistant to* not *director of* the child's activity. (Rathbone, 1971, pp. 106–107)

The Curriculum: Unit of Work Versus School Subject

Central to Learner Centered educators' views about curriculum are issues of how to organize instructional materials and activities to maximize the growth of children, adolescents, and adults. Curriculum is not thought of as subject-matter-set-out-to-be-learned but rather as environments or units in which people can make meaning. Curricula are often associated with Kilpatrick's *The Project Method* (1918), physical materials, or learning centers. Learner Centered educators often contrast their type of curricula—here called units of work—with traditional curricula—here called school subjects.

Scope

The first difference between a school subject and a unit of work is one of scope. The school subject is thought of as a relatively narrow and logically arranged body of predetermined knowledge associated with established conventions (be they academic, social, or otherwise). The unit of work is thought of in much broader terms, assembling for study material often found in several subjects. Compare, for instance, the names given the two types of curricula. Units of work display titles such as "Peas and Particles," "Boats," "Batteries and Bulbs," and "Water." School subjects have names such as arithmetic, history, geography, and science.

The school subject is thought of as one-dimensional subject-matter-set-out-to-be-learned, whereas the unit of work is thought of as a multidimensional area of investigation in which children can explore different directions and make choices among the things they will learn. Either type of curriculum could be developed by a mathematician hoping that the child would learn, for example, graphing. In creating a school subject, curriculum developers first (a) delineate all the things the student *must* know and then (b) lay them out to be learned. Here (a) and (b) are sequential. Developers create a unit of work by (a) delineating all the things that *might* be learned about graphing and (b) creating activities from which students *might* learn them. Here (a) and (b) need not be sequential. As a result, a curriculum as designed by Learner Centered developers and the same curriculum as experienced by students are different: for students, the curriculum is the sum of the particular growth experiences they encounter, whereas for the developer it is the range of activities that might bring about students' growth.

Sequence

A second difference between a school subject and a unit of work is one of internal organization: sequence, integration, and continuity. Educators organize school subjects within their minds with the assumption that their own organization of knowledge will be preserved in students' minds. Educators organize units of work for presentation to students, but the organization of knowledge is the students' job. Learner Centered educators believe students integrate into their conceptual structures in unique ways the knowledge they construct as a result of engaging in a unit of work. There is no one correct means of organization, and it is the job of students—not educators—to meaningfully organize that which is learned.

Flexibility

A third difference between a school subject and a unit of work is what might be called flexibility. School subjects are thought of as content rigidly laid out in scope and organization, ready to be learned by students. Units of work are designed for spontaneous activity and maximum flexibility based on the interests and needs of learners; they are intended to operate through learner-initiated direction in a teacher-prepared environment. School subjects do not allow room for learners to make meaningful choices. Units of work present learners with opportunities for decision making based on their needs and interests.

Concern for the Whole Person

A fourth difference between a school subject and a unit of work is the range of learner capacities affected by the curriculum. School subjects are designed to affect only a narrow range of students' capabilities, usually only the cognitive (and generally intradisciplinary), although the purely physical is dealt with in physical education. Units of work show concern for the whole person and are designed to affect cognitive, affective, and psychomotor aspects of growth—to help people grow socially, emotionally, physically, and intellectually so that they develop "a fine body, an intelligent mind, and a sweet spirit" (Johnson, 1974, p. 30). Units of work are designed to avoid isolating people's intellects from the rest of their being.

Movement From the Concrete to the Abstract

A fifth difference between a school subject and a unit of work is the range of learning experiences students are exposed to. School subjects present students with abstractions of experience and emphasize the learning of symbolic concepts. Units of work emphasize the necessity of moving from personal, concrete, and physical learning experiences to abstract, verbal, intellectual conceptualization. They often incorporate physical experiences designed to actively involve the learner. Units of work are thus associated with respect for physical activity and materials and with the belief that symbolic abstractions should grow out of direct experience with objects, people, and ideas. However, Learner Centered curricula, particularly those designed for adolescents and adults, need not necessarily make use of physical materials.

Responsibility

A final and crucial difference between a school subject and a unit of work involves the question, who is responsible for what is learned in the curriculum? In school subjects, educators make all the decisions related to curriculum content and bear full responsibility for what students do or do not learn. In units of work, responsibility for what is learned is borne jointly among curriculum developers, teachers, and students. Curriculum developers are responsible for designing activities from which students learn. Teachers are responsible for intervening between activities and students to facilitate growth and learning. Students are responsible for providing the initiative, decision making, and capabilities that shape the substance and content of the curriculum. Thus, both educators and students are responsible for the student's education: educators through the presentation of activities and facilitation of growth and students through their responses to same. Curriculum thus has "the quality both of adult initiation and uniformity and of student initiation and diversity" (Barth, 1972, p. 50).

Historical Context

Four early Europeans who contributed to the Learner Centered ideology deserve mention.

John Amos Comenius (1592–1670) emphasized that learning is developmental and that it progresses from concrete experience to abstract thought. He wrote that people learn by doing: "Artisans learn to forge by forging, to carve by carving, to paint by painting, . . . let children learn to write by writing, to sing by singing, and to reason by reasoning" (Comenius, 1657/1896, pp. 100, 152).

Jean-Jacques Rousseau (1712–1778) wrote *Emile* in 1762 (Rousseau, 1762/1979), which is frequently credited with being the source of Learner Centered ideas. Rousseau viewed children as naturally good and society as corrupt. He believed that education's purpose is to nurture children's natural goodness and powers of constructive development in such a way as to keep them free from corruption by society's evil ways until they are adults and can withstand society's corrupting influences. Since children are naturally curious and good, intrinsic motivation in a world full of rich experiences is what is needed to facilitate their growth. Rousseau insisted that children are not miniature adults; that childhood is a unique and valuable stage of life and should be nurtured, enjoyed, and not hurried through; that learning should proceed developmentally from direct experiences with nature to sensory experiences with concrete objects to abstract ideas; and that children's natural growth should be the focus of education.

Johann Heinrich Pestalozzi (1746–1827) transformed Rousseau's theory into practice. He popularized his ideas in *How Gertrude Teaches Her Children* (1801/1898). He emphasized that children should be free to explore their own interests, draw their own conclusions, and have a role in directing their own education. He promoted spontaneity and play during learning, sought to educate the whole child, and advocated a balanced education that equalizes concern for head, hands, and heart. He was troubled by the tyranny of abstract language in children's education and emphasized the importance of experience and observation as sources of understanding. He emphasized children's inner goodness and dignity and maintained that we should educate children in an atmosphere of love and kindness.

Friedrich Froebel (1782–1852), a student of Pestalozzi, invented kindergarten. He emphasized the education of children's senses and perceptions in ways that are playful, enjoyable, and spontaneous. In doing so, he invented "gifts" and "occupations" that allow children to perceive the order and beauty of nature as a result of interacting with it and acting on it. Gifts are structured physical manipulatives that children can play with and personally interact with and include such things as building blocks and parquetry tiles. Occupations are creative materials that children can shape and manipulate as they desire and include such things as clay, sand, and paints. Froebel also emphasized the use of games, songs, stories, and crafts.

Many educators contributed to the evolution of the Learner Centered ideology in the U.S.

G. Stanley Hall (1844–1924), the president of Clark University, founded the child study movement in the 1880s. This movement encouraged educators to study children as they actually were—to watch them carefully, to listen to them intently, and to collect data about them so that instruction could be designed based on observations of children's nature, needs, and interests.

Colonel Francis W. Parker (1837–1902), a Civil War hero, is known for his work as public school superintendent in Quincy, Massachusetts, and (beginning in 1875) his work at the Cook County Illinois Normal School (which John Dewey's children attended). Dewey called him the "father of progressive education" (*Who Is Francis W. Parker?* n.d.). Parker is best known for his desire to move children to the center of education; his urging of educators to base curriculum on intense study of children; his developmental view of children; his eagerness to nurture children's growth, to make schools enjoyable places, to emphasize the value of understanding, and to integrate school subjects; his view that teacher-prepared learning environments that allow children to explore nature and their world through self-activity are central to instruction; his emphasis on intrinsic motivation and the shunning of grades as punishment or rewards for learning; his promotion of "freedom" as a goal of education; and his belief that a social function of education that "stands higher than subjects of learning" is to erase prejudice and "make the public school a tremendous force for the upbuilding of democracy" (Parker, 1894/1964, p. 420).

John Dewey (1859–1952), the great American education philosopher, inspired many teachers with his work at the Laboratory School of the University of Chicago between 1896 and 1904 (Mayhew & Edwards, 1966) and with his book *Schools of Tomorrow* (Dewey & Dewey, 1915). Learner Centered educators believe his work supports many of their beliefs:

- Children and not content should be the focus of teaching.
- Children learn by doing (Dewey, 1938/1963).
- Children make meaning and construct knowledge through the continuous reconstruction of their existing meanings as a result of new experiences they encounter (Dewey, 1948).
- Learning best takes place when children actively initiate and explore problems arising in their world and solve them themselves because of their own interest and motivation.
- "The child's own instincts and powers furnish the material and give the starting point for all education" (Dewey, 1897, p. 77).
- The teacher's job is to prepare experiential environments that engage children and challenge them to learn and make personal meanings.
- School subjects should be integrated through project learning.

- Education should be concerned with children's total (intellectual, social, emotional, physical, and spiritual) growth.
- Social interaction and learning are central to the educational endeavor.

The Progressive Education Association was founded in 1919 as an umbrella organization for the many Learner Centered educators working in private Country Day Schools (such as Marietta Johnson's School of Organic Education in Fairhope, Alabama) and public schools (such as those in Winnetka, Illinois, which implemented the Dalton Plan). One of its important contributions was the Eight-Year Study, which compared the effectiveness of Learner Centered and traditional schools. It found that students from Learner Centered high schools performed better in college than students from traditional high schools and that students who attended high schools that integrated content from different disciplines did better in college than students who attended high schools that kept the content of different disciplines separate (Aiken, 1942).

The Great Depression, World War II, and McCarthy-era politics largely halted development of the Learner Centered ideology. The ideology was reinvigorated in about 1965 in response to the resurgence of the Scholar Academic ideology and generous funding of curriculum projects by the National Science Foundation (NSF).

During the 1960s, the Elementary Science Study, funded by NSF, provided energy for resurgence of the Learner Centered ideology. It discovered and widely publicized British Infant Schools, which had continued to develop in the Learner Centered tradition over the previous 25 years while the ideology stalled in the U.S. It developed many physical manipulatives (such as pattern blocks) and instructional units (such as "Batteries and Bulbs") consistent with the project method (promoted by Kilpatrick in the 1920s). And it promoted open education.

Open education flourished between about 1965 and 1980. It promoted many of the same educational practices as Parker and Dewey. In the late 1970s, *New York Times* editor Fred Hichinger began an extended attack on open education, claiming that it was a failed experiment (Ellis, 2004, p. 44). Open education gradually atrophied. It was not until 1984 that Walberg's research concluded that the academic progress of students in open education schools was equal to or better than that of students in traditional schools.

During the 1960s, the psychological (and epistemological) work of Jean Piaget was "rediscovered." Between 1960 and 1990, his views on the developmental stages through which people develop an understanding of their world, genetic epistemology describing how children's understanding is different from that of adults, and constructivist theories concerning how people construct knowledge through the processes of assimilation and accommodation provided major contributions to Learner Centered educational theory.

During the 1960s and 1970s, the counseling theories of Carl Rogers and Abraham Maslow were also discovered by Learner Centered advocates and later elaborated by educators such as Nel Noddings. Their emphasis on client-centered therapy was transformed into an educational theory of learner-centered instruction, and their emphases on the following ideas provided major support for the Learner Centered approach to education: self-actualization; self-directed learning; lifelong learning; the prizing and valuing of the learner's opinions, feelings, and person; concern for the whole person; empathy for the learner; importance of the learner's subjective understanding; and the role of the educator as a facilitator of growth who is genuine or real in his or her relationship with the learner.

During the 1970s, 1980s, and 1990s, the whole language movement provided stimulus to the Learner Centered ideology with its emphasis on constructivism, student interpretation of text, learning in a social context, student meaning making, and curriculum integration. Educators such as Ken and Yetta Goodman, Brian Cambourne, and Donald Graves extended the earlier work of Louise Rosenblatt on how learners make meaning by transforming the objective written word into idiosyncratic, personal, subjective meaning.

During the 1980s and 1990s, Howard Gardner's theories on multiple intelligences stimulated Learner Centered educators to extend his ideas into ways to differentiate instructions by accounting for different types of learning and thinking styles.

During the last decades of the 20th century, the Learner Centered ideology continued to be nurtured and promoted by educators (such as Eleanor Duckworth), schools (such as the Sudbury Valley and Fayerweather Street Schools), and organizations (such as Patricia Carini's Prospect Center in Vermont and the North Dakota Study Group). In addition, over the last 40 years, several versions of the Learner Centered approach that were developed in Europe have been transformed to suit American needs. Among these are the increasingly popular American Montessori schools and the Reggio Emilia approach, which have been described this way:

> They are built on coherent visions of how to improve human society by helping children realize their full potential as intelligent, creative, whole persons. In each approach, children are viewed as active authors of their own development, strongly influenced by natural, dynamic, self-righting forces within themselves, opening the way toward growth and learning. Teachers depend for their work with children on carefully prepared, aesthetically pleasing environments that serve as a pedagogical tool and provide strong messages about . . . respect for children. (Edwards, 2002)

During the 1980s and 1990s, other educational movements arose that continued the Learner Centered ideology by promoting such things as developmentally appropriate practice. The following list of a few of the basic principles and practices of developmentally appropriate practice illustrates its continuity with Learner Centered ideas.

- Curriculum facilitates the growth of the whole child (the predictable sequences in physical, emotional, cognitive, and social development) as well as the self-actualization of individuals' unique potentialities (of personality, learning style, interests, disposition, cultural orientation, etc.) in ways that encourage self-directed, lifelong learning.
- "Curriculum planning is based on teachers' observations and recordings of each child's special interests and developmental progress" (a) so teachers can prepare rich instructional environments in which children can construct meaning through self-initiated, self-directed, playful, "active exploration and interaction with adults, other children, . . . materials," and experiences located both inside and outside of school, and

(b) so teachers can determine how to best interact with individuals and groups to provide "support, focused attention, physical proximity, and verbal encouragement" to facilitate their growth (Bredekamp, 1987).

- Teachers "respond quickly and directly to children's needs, desires, and messages and adapt their responses to children's differing styles and abilities" in such a way as to "facilitate the development of self esteem by respecting, accepting, and comforting children" in a loving and caring environment (Bredekamp, 1987).

Several developmentally appropriate practices include hands-on learning; the use of concrete manipulatives and learning and activity centers; thematic unit study; the use of integrated curriculum; cooperative learning; mixed-age grouping; family, school, and community partnerships; authentic assessment; portfolio assessment; celebration of multiple intelligences; and culturally responsive teaching (Novick, 1996).

During the last years of the 20th century and first years of the 21st century, the standards movement and the mandates of the federally supported and politically fashionable No Child Left Behind law (which were "deeply incongruent with . . . child-centered . . . education"; Davson-Galle, 1998, p. 303) resulted in great animosity toward advocates of child-centered education and thus a decline of emphasis on Learner Centered initiatives in public schools. However, Learner Centered education continues to flourish in private schools and its initiatives continue to be promoted by organizations such as the Association for Supervision and Curriculum Development (whose September 2005 issue of *Educational Leadership* was on "the whole child").

Aims

The aim of Learner Centered educators is to stimulate and nurture growth in students, teachers, and others involved in education—to help all engaged in helping students grow create meaning for themselves. One creates meaning by engaging in stimulating experiences. Growth in students, teachers, and other educators is brought about by preparing stimulating curricula and instruction for students and teachers to engage in and by having others (for example, parents, school administrators, and curriculum developers) interact with and grow along with students and teachers. The doctrine of growth provides both the ends and means for Learner Centered workers.

The design of the educational environments in which students and teachers grow is the responsibility of the curriculum developer. Students and teachers also have responsibilities. They must engage the educational environments designed by curriculum developers, initiate the directions of their growth, and make meaning for themselves by understanding their personal involvement in the educational environment. This does not mean that developers present students and teachers with opportunities for experience without expectations. They create curricula based on careful study of students and teachers with certain growth goals in mind, and in so doing develop clear expectations for what might or might not occur when students and teachers engage their curricula. These expectations are furthered by the careful inclusion and omission of curriculum activities, structuring of the curriculum, and suggestions of possible directions for growth within the curriculum.

The Child

The Child as an Integrated Person

Learner Centered educators view children (and learners of any age) as integrated organisms possessing an integrity as complete people. They view the child as a "whole child," as an inseparable conglomerate of intellectual, social, psychological, and physical dimensions.

The Learner Centered ideology values children because they are unique individuals. Educators are concerned about each child's uniqueness rather than his or her ability to conform to standardized norms. They believe that a child's innate nature is one of goodness and that children's natural impulses for growth and capabilities for growth will mature constructively if they are not hampered or distorted by "corrupting outside forces." Educators value children because of who they are in the here and now, not because of the behaviors or attributes they possess or because of what they might become at some future time.

The Child as a Meaning-Making Organism

Learner Centered educators view children as meaning-making organisms. That is, they see children as organisms who naturally create meaning—and thus knowledge—for themselves as a result of interacting with their environment. They assume that children contain within themselves their own capabilities for growth and that they are the ones who activate those capabilities through their own efforts: "The assumption [is] that children are innately curious and predisposed toward exploration and are not dependent upon adults, for either the initiation or perpetuation of learning" (Barth, 1972, p. 20). Children are not considered empty organisms to which things happen; they are vibrant organisms who by their own activity cause meaningful things to happen to themselves. As Rugg and Shumaker say, "personality evolves from within. It cannot be imposed from without. Individuality develops only through growth in the power of self-propulsion" (1928, p. 5).

Children's capacity to grow, their motivation to learn, and their ability to make meaning occur because of their innate capabilities and exploratory inclinations and impulses. From the Learner Centered viewpoint, it is crucial that the adult "trust in the innate abilities of children, in their capacity to energize and direct their own exploration, and in their wanting to explore and learn," for it is believed that children "will display natural exploratory behavior if" they are "not threatened" by adults and that they will learn and grow in ways that are best for them if they are not pressured to learn by adults (Barth, 1972, pp. 20–21).

The Child's Subjective Being

Learner Centered educators speak about processes and states of being that are internal to children (and learners of any age). These internal processes and states form the child's subjective reality. They make up what educators consider to be the most significant aspects of the child's being.

Using conceptualizations such as those of Piaget, the Learner Centered educator speaks of children as if one could look within them to see the inner workings of their minds. It is not children's behavior resulting from stimuli that is of interest to these educators, but rather what goes on between the stimulation and the response, what is "happening 'within' the individual" (Carini, 2005, p. 3). It is not "what the child knows" or "what the child can do" that is important to these educators, but what is behind the knowing and doing, or what structures internal to children support that knowing and doing.

As a result, these educators are interested in parameters such as the state of children's cognitive structures, their meaning-making abilities, their self-esteem, their self-concept, their self-confidence, their creative spirit, and their dignity, rather than in specific knowledge and skills children might possess (Carini, 2001, p. 100). As Rugg and Shumaker say, "witness the little girl of five . . . who said of her painting, 'It looks *the way* you feel inside.' It's the feel inside [that] . . . the new education seeks to evoke and to build upon" (1928, p. 6). How children feel about themselves, their ability to construct personal meanings, their ability to actualize themselves, and their disposition to be lifelong learners are considered crucial. Critical here is the child's self-concept, for it is believed that children will initiate and take responsibility for their own learning, growth, education, and lives only if they have robust self-concepts, healthy respect for themselves, and strong confidence in their abilities.

Learning

Learning as Natural

Learner Centered educators consider learning to be what happens to people while they make meaning out of their interactions with their social and physical world—the "undergoing" phase of learners' growth. It is natural to people: both the impulse to learn and the ability to learn are innate characteristics of the human species. People are naturally self-activated constructors of meaning. Learning needs no justification. It should be enjoyed in and of itself.

Natural learning takes place spontaneously and is congruent with people's inner nature. It occurs as a natural response to people's interaction with their environment and is in rhythm with their organic personalities. Learning is not an artificial construction of an agent other than the learner; rather, it is a natural function of living that happens in the present tense and not the future tense, an innate response to experience that does not have to be artificially forced on people.

The Mechanics of Learning

Learner Centered educators view learning from a constructivist perspective.

Learning takes place when people interact with the world around them and make meaning for themselves out of those interactions. It takes place when a receptive, inquiring learner engages a stimulating environment. Three things are required for learning to occur: a learner, an environment, and the learner's act of involvement with that environment through direct experience. The learning results from the process of making meaning for oneself out of one's experiences with one's environment. It is the "making meaning" process that is important here, for learning is not viewed as a process of discovering, memorizing, or in any way absorbing information that already exists outside of and independent of the learner. Figure 4.1 portrays the nature of learning. Stimuli from an environment (the dotted straight arrows) impinge on the learner, some of which are perceived by the learner. Many things can be located in the learning environment that can stimulate learning, including other learners, teachers, books, learning materials, and natural occurrences and phenomena (such as animals). In response to the stimulation, the learner actively engages the stimuli (the solid curved arrow) and makes meaning out of the interaction based on his or her own personality, stage of development, learning style, and cognitive structure (which consists of prior meanings learned, the relationships among them, and the ways they are organized). In learning, learners construct meaning by transforming what is perceived so that it can be assimilated into their cognitive structure, and reconstruct their previously existing cognitive structure so that it can accommodate the newly created meaning. This construction and reconstruction process is unique to each individual's existing cognitive structure and particular experiences with his or her learning environment. The learning arrow also represents a process that is unique to the learner because it originates within the learner, engages the environment that stimulates that learner, and returns to the learner. It is unique because each individual is unique, because each individual has unique learning capacities, because learning results from an individual's active engagement in his or her environment under unique circumstances of time and place, and because what individuals learn is the result of their own creative self-expression to themselves of their experiences.

❖ **Figure 4.1** The mechanics of learning in the Learner Centered ideology.

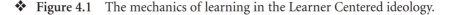

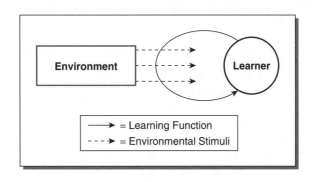

Learning is a function of the unique interaction of an individual with his or her environment. The more active and personally engaging the individual's exploration and the richer the environment in which the exploration takes place, the greater the potential for learning. Although both the learner and the environment are important during learning, each has a different significance.

People learn when they experience the involvement and engrossment connected with wholehearted play. Learning does not result from passivity. It results from people's absorbed involvement with their environment that comes from their innate impulse to understand and to make sense out of interactions with their world. Learners' active and personal engagement in making meaning out of their experiences for themselves is the crucial variable during learning.

For curriculum developers and teachers, however, it is the environment in which individuals make their meaning that is of crucial importance, for it is the environment that they can control. The developer and the teacher help people learn by arranging the learning environment in such a way as to stimulate the desired learning. The developer and teacher must stimulate people to learn in this way because it is not viewed as appropriate to predictably manipulate the inner nature of people, indoctrinate people, or inject information into their minds.

Stages of Learning

As previously mentioned, while growing, people develop through a sequence of learning stages. The meanings people construct from that which is learned are different at each stage of growth. Further, educators emphasize enriching the learning within a growth stage rather than stimulating people to move to more advanced growth stages.

In addition, a distinction is made between concrete and abstract learning. Educators assume the following:

- People's learning should proceed from concrete to abstract.
- "Premature conceptualization based upon inadequate direct experience" is unhealthy (Walberg & Thomas, 1971, p. 94).
- Concept formation progresses from concrete to abstract slowly (Featherstone, 1968).
- "All of us must cross the line between ignorance and insight many times before we truly understand. Little facts, 'discoveries' without the growth of insights are *not* what we should seek to harvest" (Hawkins, 1965/1970).

Learner Centered educators also make several other assumptions:

- People have different learning styles (that instruction should accommodate).
- "Children's innate curiosity and self-perpetuating exploratory behavior should form the basis of their learning in school" ("they should have the opportunity to pursue interests as deeply and as long as they find the pursuit satisfying"; Walberg & Thomas, 1971, p. 94).
- "Individual children often learn in unpredictable ways" (and instruction should accommodate such; Walberg & Thomas, 1971, p. 94).
- "Children are capable of making intelligent decisions in significant areas of their own learning" (and should be able to do so; Walberg & Thomas, 1971, p. 94).
- "The function of school is to help children learn to learn" (Walberg & Thomas, 1971, p. 94) and to become lifelong learners.
- "Learning is facilitated by relationships of openness, trust, and mutual respect" (and schools should provide "an accepting and warm emotional climate"; Walberg & Thomas, 1971, p. 94).

Teaching

Learner Centered educators view teaching primarily as nurturing the growth of individuals. Within the overarching role of nurturer, teachers have three critical roles: observer and diagnostician of learners, provider of the environment for learning, and facilitator of learning.

The Teacher as Diagnostician

To plan the environment in which a person will learn and to determine how to interact with that person in the learning environment, teachers must first understand such things as the person's interests, concerns, needs, fantasies, thought processes, learning and thinking styles, intellectual development, social inclinations, emotional profile, and physical abilities. As such, one of the first, and continuing, tasks of teachers is to carefully observe and chronicle the nature of the students in their care. Data about students are collected by watching what they do and say during instruction and at play, gathering together the artifacts and productions they create, and consulting with parents and other adults who care for them. Data are recorded in teacher diaries, student portfolios, and individual learner histories. Based on analysis of the data collected, teachers make decisions about the education of students. Studying and analyzing the behavior of the students in one's care is a critical component of what teachers do on a daily and continuing basis. Based on their ongoing reflective evaluation and analytical assessment of each student, teachers modify the content, arrangement, and structure of the classroom; group students for instruction; gather the class for activities such as storytelling and discussion; suggest, change, extend, or redirect student activity; and interact with students to support their learning, growth, and development.

The Teacher as Provider of the Environment for Learning

One of the functions of the teacher is to provide the instructional environment in which learning takes place. The environment is to be designed with personal, social, material, psychological, and intellectual considerations in mind in order to provide students with the experiences that will stimulate their intellectual, social, emotional, and physical growth.

In designing the instructional environment, the teacher must do such things as select curricula; choose and position instructional materials in the classroom in such physical, emotional, and temporal contexts that they become maximally available to student engagement; group students for learning activities; direct the flow of instructional activity over the course of the day; and structure and maintain classroom rules that promote an atmosphere of warmth, openness, and respect for one another and a sense of community and cooperation. Based on diagnosis of their students' needs and characteristics, teachers also set up interdisciplinary learning centers; place a diverse assortment of physical manipulatives, books, and common environment materials (plant life, rocks, animals, etc.) in activity centers; plan and supervise field trips; arrange classroom furniture into spatial configurations with different learning atmospheres (quiet reading centers, noisy construction centers, etc.); and create activities for individuals and small groups to work on. In doing so, teachers attempt to

> organize environments rich in possibilities and provocations that invite the children to undertake extended exploration and problem solving, often in small groups, where cooperation and disputation mingle pleasurably. . . . [and where a] classroom atmosphere of playfulness and joy pervades. (Edwards, 2002, p. 9)

The planning, construction, and maintenance of instructional environments in which people learn and the tailoring of those environments to each student's unique nature, based on each student's interests and needs and the teacher's desires for each student's development, is a crucial role of Learner Centered educators. It is crucial because providing the instructional environment that stimulates students to interact with their world and to construct and reconstruct meaning is one of the major ways in which teachers influence students' growth and learning.

While providing environments in which people learn, teachers must design those environments in such a way that they encourage people to feel that they are making the important decisions about what they learn, are engaged in explorations of their own choosing, and are pursuing those explorations in accordance with their own inner direction and felt needs—even though they know that the teacher has structured the learning environment and is supplying the learning alternatives they can pursue.

The Teacher as Facilitator of Learning

The teacher also functions as a facilitator, assistant, aid, advisor, and consultant to people during their learning. As an assistant to students during learning, the teacher intervenes between students and the environment (or ideas) they are exploring to facilitate their growth and learning. The interventions are based on diagnosis of the needs, interests, and natures of the students and on diagnosis of the nature and potential of the work in which they are engaged.

Teachers also act as resources or consultants to students during their learning. In this role, teachers are consulted by students on how to learn something, complete an activity, answer a question, or reach a goal. Acting in this capacity, the teacher "is, in a sense, a *travel agent*. He helps the child go where the child wants to go. He counsels on the best way of getting there" (Leitman, 1968).

Four examples illustrate the range of ways in which teachers can act as facilitators of learning:

- Teachers can intervene when students are learning by helping them verbalize to themselves the meaning of their experiences. By doing so, teachers can help students make sense out of their experiences by helping them find language to reflect on those experiences, acting as evaluators who reflect back to students their thoughts, or prodding students to move from more concrete toward more abstract meaning making.
- As a result of observing the interests, questions, and concerns students raise as they engage in an activity, teachers can place carefully chosen books, manipulatives, environmental materials, or other students in their presence to enrich, amplify, extend, or redirect their growth and learning. Teachers can also facilitate students' growth by

asking questions, making suggestions, adding their ideas to the conversation, or increasing "the difficulty, complexity, and challenge of an activity as children are involved with it" (Bredekamp, 1987, pp. 7–8).

- As a result of observing students with common interests, teachers can ask students to work together, ask them to teach each other or learn for each other, put them in small groups to discuss their interests together, provide special activities for them, have discussions with them, or provide them with demonstrations or direct instruction.

- Teachers can "facilitate a child's successful completion of tasks by providing support, focused attention, physical proximity, and verbal encouragement" as a result of simply being present, attentive, and engaged while the child is learning (Bredekamp, 1987, p. 16).

While acting as facilitators of learning, teachers frequently "give individual children small concentrated amounts of [their] time [through individualized conversation and attention] rather than giving [their] *general* attention to the children as a class all day" (Walberg & Thomas, 1971, p. 90).

And teacher behavior is always to be based on careful observation of the nature of the learners and diagnosis of their needs and interests: "Interactions are based on adults' knowledge and expectations of age-appropriate behavior in children balanced by adults' awareness of individual differences among children" (Bredekamp, 1987, p. 13).

Characteristics of the Teacher

Learner Centered educators view the teacher's main roles to be diagnostician, provider of an instructional environment, and facilitator of growth. Several characteristics aid teachers in carrying out these roles.

Teachers must be able to spontaneously respond to children. They must be available, accessible, and capable of responding quickly and appropriately to children at all times as they constantly scan "the horizon of children's interactions, with materials and with one another, for situations when a response, an appropriate intervention, will contribute to a child's learning" and growth (Barth, 1972, p. 107). Teachers directly respond "to children's needs, desires, and messages and adapt their responses to children's differing styles and abilities" (Bredekamp, 1987).

Teachers must be generalists, rather than specialists, with respect to knowledge. They need to be knowledgeable about all of the school subjects, have one or two subjects in which they have "special interest, experience, and competence," and be "capable of growing in *any* area as the need and interest of the children dictate" (Barth, 1972, p. 68).

The teacher must be a *person* within the classroom rather than a paragon, exemplar, or ideal representing inhuman virtues. Teachers are

encouraged to be themselves: to be honest, angry, loving, upset, tired, happy—to be real. . . . [F]rom the teacher's honest expression of feeling, children learn to respect, expect, and handle the wide range of behavior which they find in others, and to acknowledge and accept it in themselves. (Barth, 1972, p. 65)

Teachers must take "an involved interest in what the child is doing" and must become "actively involved in the work of each child . . . as one who seeks to help him realize his goals and potential" (Walberg & Thomas, 1971, p. 91). This means that teachers must be capable of becoming involved in children's learning, interested in what they are learning, and excited about what they are learning—and able to share their involvement, interest, and excitement with children as they learn.

Knowledge

Personal Meaning and Knowledge Construction

Within the Learner Centered ideology, worthwhile knowledge takes the form of personal meanings. These personal meanings are idiosyncratic to each individual who possesses them, because knowledge has personal significance to its creator within the meaningful context of previously acquired knowledge, because the unique environmental context in which it is acquired is the result of a learner's experience in a particular learning environment at a particular time, because it is not an internalized representation of the real world that everyone views in the same way but a personal construction of a meaning maker, and because it is basically subjective rather than objective in nature.

Personal meanings are created when sensory information is perceived by a learner and incorporated by the learner into his or her existing cognitive structure through the twin processes of accommodation and assimilation. Meaning making—or knowledge construction—enables learners to understand and adapt to their world. New knowledge constructed by learners, which produces new cognitive structures that learners reconstruct out of their existing cognitive structures, is unique to each learner, because the new knowledge and cognitive structures are based on a learner's uniquely constructed existing cognitive structure and because they carry contextual connections to the specific environments in which they are learned. That is, Learner Centered educators assume that new knowledge acquired by learners does not float free from the environment in which it was learned, but rather that it carries with it many connections to that environment. For example, a child who first sees a doe in a black-and-white drawing in a book has a very different experience from that of a child who first sees a doe in a field next to his grandparents' house early on a cool morning while holding a cup of hot chocolate and sitting on his grandmother's warm lap. Knowledge carries with it all sorts of emotional, social, and other contextual meanings associated with where, when, and how it is learned.

Four things are important here.

1. Knowledge is *constructed* by learners because of the way in which newly perceived information is transformed through the processes of assimilation and accommodation so that it can fit into the learners' existing cognitive structures.

2. Knowledge is repeatedly *reconstructed* by learners, because their previously existing cognitive structures are constantly altered and updated as new knowledge is constructed through the twin forces of assimilation and accommodation.

3. Knowledge takes the form of personal *meaning* because of its personal significance to its creator (and possessor) within the meaningful context of previously acquired knowledge.

4. Knowledge takes the form of *idiosyncratic personal* meanings because of how it is related to a learner's uniquely organized set of previously acquired meanings and because of the unique context in which it is acquired.

Knowledge is not an internalized representation of the real world that everyone views in the same way. It is "a function of a synthesis of each individual's experience with the world" (Barth, 1972, p. 45). It is the result of an individual's personal creative self-expression and based in conceptual structures comprehensible only within the context of the meaning maker's experiences. It is idiosyncratic to the individual who creates it. Theoretically, no two individual's knowledge can be identical. This means that what individuals learn is not only their own personal possession, but that it may well be theirs alone, even though it closely resembles the learning of other individuals. That is, people's conceptions of "house" or "justice" or "red" will not be so different as to exclude communication, but there will be inevitable differences in conceptualization.

The following assumptions are also important to note:

- Knowledge cannot be separated from the process of meaning making—or knowing. Nor can it be isolated from the experience of the person who constructs it, for it is based in its creator's conceptual structures and prior experience.
- Knowledge is actively constructed, invented, created, or discovered by learners. It is not passively received by them and stored in their minds as photographic images of objective reality—it does not magically appear in their mind in a form identical to what a teacher, book, or real life experience might have transmitted to them.
- Learners are constantly constructing and reconstructing their cognitive structures, both as a result of newly acquired knowledge and as a result of their reflection on previously acquired knowledge. Reflection on previously acquired meanings is an important way of constructing knowledge.
- Social interaction with peers and adults in a cultural context is extremely important in individuals' construction of knowledge. In most situations, the individual construction of knowledge cannot be isolated from social and cultural influences. For example, when peers (or teachers) challenge an individual's previously accepted meanings and explain their reasons for the challenge, the verbal exchanges are a type of experience that can stimulate the individual to reconstruct those meanings. As Vygotsky (1979) has suggested, when an individual constructs knowledge in the presence of others, those others enrich the individual's learning environment through their use of language, their concepts, and the learning and thinking styles they use to create and judge the worthiness of their knowledge.
- Children go through the process of rediscovering meanings and reconstructing their conceptual structures continuously over an extended period of time as they learn about their world and themselves and reconcile new information with past meanings. Understanding is built up only gradually as children go through different developmental stages, each of which influences their conceptual structures and how they make meaning. Meanings that make sense at one developmental stage frequently become misconceptions at later developmental stages, because children's evolving development influences what and how they understand their world. For example, simple ideas of number are reinterpreted numerous times by children as they move through the Piagetian preoperational, concrete operational, and formal operational stages of development. As a result, the knowledge children possess

changes over time. Both the nature of children's "knowledge" and their "way of knowing" are assumed to evolve as the child grows through different developmental stages.

These views put the Learner Centered ideology within the epistemological context of the constructivist movement, which became popular among American educators in the 1980s.

Knowledge as a Derivative Concept

Learner Centered educators are concerned less with knowledge than with learning and growth. They assume that knowledge is an integral part of learning rather than a separate entity to be learned: that the process by which a person learns—learning—implies the nature of the product of learning—knowledge. Knowledge is the creative response of unique individuals to their personal interactions with their environments, a derivative of individuals' learning and growth. Consequences of these assumptions have already been discussed:

- Knowledge is not seen as a universal, abstract, impersonal quantity but as unique to the individual knower.
- The goals of education are not expressed in terms of knowledge, since one has little control over the idiosyncratic meaning individuals generate when they encounter an experience.
- Because the child is viewed in the context of growth, it is assumed that the nature of both the child's knowledge and the child's "ways of knowing" evolve as the child grows.
- It is believed that there is no one way of organizing or categorizing knowledge for learning (such as into academic disciplines), because it is learners who must organize meaning in correspondence with their unique conceptual structures.

Knowledge and Reality

Learner Centered educators make a distinction between subjective and objective reality. Worthwhile knowledge is considered to be person centered and not object centered—to be within the province of the individual's subjective reality and not within the province of objective reality. Knowledge exists only within the individual knower—it is not a thing apart from the individual knower. It is personal and not objective. Even though the creation of knowledge depends on individuals interacting with their objective environment, knowledge itself is subjective and idiosyncratic to the individuals who create it. This belief does not deny the existence of the external world of objective reality; what it denies is that the meanings created by individuals can accurately mirror objective reality.

Knowledge is not viewed as a universal, abstract, impersonal quantity. It is unique to the individuals who create it for themselves and does not exist outside of individual knowers. The information found in books, in libraries, and on the Internet is not viewed as the same as the meanings that people construct—as the personal knowledge that people create for themselves. Although individuals can memorize and repeat the information found in books, in libraries, and on the Internet, abstract and impersonal knowledge requires a more personal connection to the lives of individuals before it can become "real" to knowers. This does not mean that people cannot create situations that allow them to somewhat imprecisely share their knowledge with others through such media as language, books, and film. But Learner Centered educators do not confuse an individual's construction of a medium or environment that facilitates the creation of knowledge by another individual with the direct transmission of knowledge itself.

The Learner Centered assumptions about knowledge's subjectivity and derivativeness are reinforced by the belief that "the quality of being is more important than the quality of knowing; knowledge is a means of education, not its end. The final test of an education is what a man is, not what he *knows*" (Barth, 1972, pp. 44–45). The Learner Centered educator emphasizes the learning person rather than knowledge, the quality of people's conceptual structures and meaning making abilities rather than the knowledge of objective reality that they possess.

Evaluation

Assessment for Growth

Assessment is critical within the Learner Centered ideology. Teachers need to constantly assess learners' growth and interests by "observing, recording, and documenting the learner's progress" (Cruz-Acosta, 2006, p. 1) so that they can plan the instructional environment in which students will learn and plan the ways in which they will facilitate students' growth by interacting with them. Students need to constantly assess their interactions with their world so that they can assimilate and accommodate new experiences to previously developed cognitive structures as they make personal meaning and construct knowledge. Curriculum developers need to constantly assess their curricula so that they can be revised to meet students' developmental needs, individual learning characteristics, and interests. In all cases, assessment is primarily for the benefit of students and for the purpose of facilitating their growth, development, and learning. Evaluation is not looked on favorably when it is used to inform someone other than students (such as school administrators or politicians) about students or their growth. Specifically, evaluation is not to be used for the purpose of comparing students to externally prescribed curriculum standards, except when mandated by state or federal legislation or college entrance examinations—and even then it is viewed unfavorably. Also, since valid assessment instruments are difficult to find, most assessment relies heavily on portfolio assessment and direct observation of students:

> Assessment of individual children's development and learning is essential for planning and implementing developmentally appropriate programs, but should be used with caution. . . . Accurate testing can only be achieved with reliable, valid instruments and such instruments . . . are extremely rare. In the absence of valid instruments, testing is not valuable. Therefore, assessment of young children should rely heavily on the results of observations of their development and descriptive data. (Bredekamp, 1987, p. 22)

Standardized Objective Testing

Learner Centered advocates are opposed to the "psychometric philosophy of education, which posits that the learner possesses measurable abilities," that "individual differences in performance are regarded as reflecting differences in amount of ability," that "education is seen as imparting quantifiable knowledge and skills which can be measured objectively on standardized tests," and that "answers are either right or wrong" (Novick, 1996, pp. 34–35). As a result, Learner Centered educators are opposed to standardized objective achievement testing. They believe such tests

> fail to describe children's growth, development, and progress; measure a restricted view of intelligence; are unrelated to classroom activities; provide no information to individualize and improve instruction; limit the breadth and depth of content coverage; create stress for children; label and stigmatize some children; are culturally biased; . . . emphasize lower order thinking[;] . . . [pressure] teachers [to] teach to the test[;] . . . [dumb] down instruction[;] . . . [and place] emphasis on drill and practice of decontextualized skills. (Novick, 1996, p. 35)

Learner Centered advocates also give other reasons for viewing standardized achievement tests unfavorably. One reason is that students frequently understand things that they cannot verbalize as abstract symbolic expressions publicly displayable in a form that can be objectively assessed on standardized achievement tests. Another reason is that the dimensions of student learning that can be accurately measured are usually not the most important ones. The important things, such as a student's self-concept, curiosity, and initiative, are difficult to measure and are seldom measured in most schools, while trivial things such as students' ability to recall when Columbus discovered America tend to be repeatedly measured because they are easy to assess. A third reason is that taking and confronting the results of standardized achievement tests can have a negative effect on students' learning. At the high school level, this is seen in the rise in student dropout rates in states that require students to pass a standardized achievement test to graduate.

Grading

Giving letter or numerical grades to children is avoided. Lengthy written reports describing children's development, learning, and activity is the preferred mode of providing parents and school records with a description of children's growth (Edwards, 2002). Letter and numerical grades are avoided because it is believed that learning should have intrinsic value and that the intrinsic value of learning is diminished when it is extrinsically rewarded, because the reward does not come from the completion of the task but from pleasing the teacher. What is valued is the possibility of present learning empowering the children to engage in a lifelong love of learning rather than simply pleasing a teacher (Hein, 2005). As Dewey and Dewey wrote,

> rewards and high marks are at best artificial aims to strive for; they accustom children to expect to get something besides the value of the product for work they do. The extent to which schools are compelled to rely upon these motives shows how dependent they are upon motives that are foreign to truly moral activity. (1915, p. 297)

One of the central issues emphasized within the Learner Centered ideology is the necessity for children to learn how to evaluate their own learning as well as to learn when it is or is not possible for them to do so. It is assumed that whenever possible, children's work is best assessed by children themselves through their direct interactions with materials, other students, and adults from and with whom they are learning, rather than from authorities who are spatially and temporally removed from the children's learning interactions.

Student Evaluation

Since the 1880s, when G. Stanley Hall started the child study movement, the preferred Learner Centered method of assessment has been through teacher observation of students during instruction and collection of artifacts created by students. In current day language, authentic assessment that describes students' performance during typical instructional activities is the preferred form of student evaluation. Authentic assessments include, for each student, portfolio assessment, teacher notes, teacher diaries, developmental checklists, learning logs and journals, student self-assessments, student peer assessments, and informal anecdotal narratives.

Portfolio assessment is one form of authentic assessment:

> Portfolios are an organized collection of children's work that provide a continuous record of a child's progress over time. . . . One of the strengths of portfolios is that they reflect multiple voices and perspectives: that of children, parents, and teachers. They [can] include writing samples, art work, self portraits, stories, audio tapes of children's oral reading and speaking, photographs, self-portraits, math papers, teacher and parent reflections, summaries of progress, and children's self-reflective comments about their work. Based on the assumption that children should be active *participants* in their own assessment . . . , children are encouraged to make judgments about their own work and reflect on their progress during frequent individual and group conferences. . . Teachers and parents can focus on what children can do, rather than what they can not and children are able to see themselves as successful learners. . . . [P]arents are able to compare their children's work at different times and understand that their children are learning. . . . Unlike many traditional assessments, that are external to or even in conflict with instruction, portfolios may become an integral part of the learning process. (Novick, 1996, p. 37)

Learning logs and journals are often kept on each student over an extended period of time. These anecdotal records chronicle students' activities and growth over time and also contain comments and observations about such things as students' relationships with peers, learning styles, thinking styles, interests, physical demeanors, self-concept, and social, emotional, physical, and cognitive growth. These logs and journals are used to apprise children, parents, and teachers of individuals' progress in school.

Learner Centered educators believe that

> authentic assessments provide a more meaningful picture of children's development than test scores. They address a much broader definition of intelligence, encourage children to become reflective, self-directed learners, help parents to see their children's progress, and enhance children's parents' and teachers' ability to develop shared meaning and memories. (Novick, 1996, p. 38)

Three characteristics of student assessment deserve mention.

1. Learner Centered educators desire to take the value loading out of evaluation. They want to remove the connotation of good or bad, right or wrong, better or worse, from the actions of learners in order to help them make use of their mistakes, as well as their

successes, to direct their future learning. They believe that mistakes are a natural part of learning, just as successes are, and that both contain important feedback that can contribute to future growth and learning.

2. Learner Centered educators tend to view students (and curricula) as wholes and take a gestalt approach to assessment. The idea of partitioning learners (or curricula) into component parts in order to atomistically evaluate each part, under the assumption that the sum of the atomistic evaluations is equivalent to evaluation of the whole, is avoided. Evaluation "should not be a separate 'technical' issue, conceptualized, analyzed, and implemented independent from the entire educational setting" (Hein, 2005, p. 177). It must "take into account the entire context of schooling" (p. 177), take place over time, and consider students (and curricula) in their wholeness.

3. Student assessment is viewed as an integral part of teaching and learning. It is not something distinct from teaching and learning that needs a special time, place, or materials set aside for it. It occurs whenever a student is learning from a teacher who is teaching. It is an ongoing part of the dynamics of teaching and learning and occurs continuously during instruction.

Curriculum Evaluation

Learner Centered educators tend to have little interest in summative curriculum evaluation. When such is compiled, it tends to be in the form of testimonials, and it tends to measure the degree of student involvement in the curriculum and the degree of learner enthusiasm about the curriculum. Subjective formative evaluation of the curriculum, in contrast, is undertaken with enthusiasm, for it leads to improvement in the curriculum as it is being developed. Such evaluation is usually based on measures such as the degree to which learners get involved with the curriculum, is usually intuitively conducted through developer observation and teacher reports, and is usually based on criteria such as the extent to which the curriculum is believed to be in the best interests of learners as dictated by their nature, needs, and interests.

An important assessment question to ask is, how effective is the Learner Centered ideology in comparison to the traditional approach? Usually this question is phrased in terms of whether students educated and assessed in nontraditional Learner Centered environments do as well as students educated and assessed in traditional classrooms when they go on to higher levels of schooling that operate and assess in more traditional ways. The findings of the Eight-Year Study in the 1930s (Aiken, 1942) and Walberg's research (1984) clearly indicate that children educated in Learner Centered environments do as well as or better than children educated in traditional classrooms in most academic and nonacademic areas at the elementary, secondary, and college levels.

Concluding Perspective

The Learner Centered ideology has done much to humanize education over the last century. Its insistence on putting the learner at the center of the educational process, belief that self-actualizing growth is the goal of education, view that teachers are facilitators of learning, introduction of personal meaning to our vocabulary as a way of speaking about knowledge, bringing to our attention the importance of different learning styles, integration of curricula through the use of projects and learning centers, and broadening of our view of evaluation to include authentic assessment have done much to make schools more humane and vital educational institutions from preschool through adult education.

The Learner Centered ideology first gained influence on education at the end of the 19th century and beginning of the 20th century as it was being introduced by educators such as Parker, Dewey, and Johnson. It gained greater influence as part of the Progressive Education Association when it insisted that education must minister to the needs and nature of the child but fell from prominence when George Counts challenged educators to dare to build a new social order and to attend to the poor and needy in society. It regained its influence in the 1960s with the rise of the open education movement, the rediscovery of developmental and counseling psychology, and the infusion of funds into education by the federal government. The attempts to implement open education by educators who did not fully understand it did much to undermine the movement and decrease its influence in the late 1970s. However, the whole language movement, constructivist philosophy, and the ideology's promotion of authentic assessment maintained Learner Centered influence on education until the end of the 20th century. Attacks by the back-to-the-basics movement, the social justice movement, and the No Child Left Behind mandates did much to decrease its influence at the beginning of the 21st century. Advocates of the Learner Centered ideology now wait for appropriate political and social conditions that will allow them to again assert their influence to humanize and revitalize education. Figure 4.2 provides a rough estimation of those times when advocates of this ideology have been most active, with respect to their own norms, in attempting to influence American education.

❖ **Figure 4.2** Times of relative high and low activity of the Learner Centered ideology.

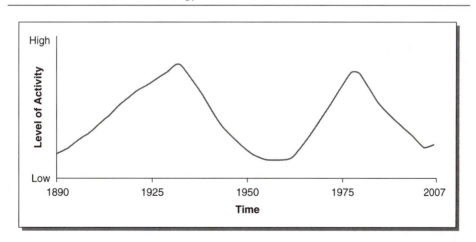

Activities designed to extend what is written here and provide additional insight into the ideology are located on the Sage Web site at www.sagepub .com/schiroextensionactivities.

5

Social Reconstruction Ideology

Educators who promote the Social Reconstruction ideology view curriculum from a social perspective. First, they assume that our society is unhealthy—indeed, that its very survival is threatened—because the traditional mechanisms developed by society to contend with social problems are incapable of doing their job. Second, Social Reconstructionists assume that something can be done to keep society from destroying itself. This assumption necessitates the development of a vision of a society better than the existing one, a society whose problems and conflicts have been resolved. It also requires action directed toward reconstruction of society based on that vision. Finally, Social Reconstruction educators assume that education provides the means of reconstructing society. They have faith in the ability of education, through the medium of curriculum, to educate "the masses of humanity" to critically analyze themselves in relation to their society, understand the ills of their society, develop a vision of a better world based on a conception of social justice, and actualize that vision.

Social Reconstructionists begin with the assumption that the survival of our society is threatened by many problems. These problems include, among others, racism, war, sexism, poverty, pollution, worker exploitation, global warming, crime, political corruption, population explosion, energy shortage, illiteracy, inadequate health care, and unemployment. Underlying many of these problems are deep social structures—many based in Eurocentric conceptions of knowledge, culture, and values—that through the school's hidden curriculum subtly shape student beliefs and behavior in such a way that they, as both students and future adults, will contribute to the continuation and worsening of these problems. If these problems are not resolved, they will threaten the survival of our society.

However, all is not lost. There are actions that can be taken to improve our situation and save society. As George Counts wrote in 1932, during the Great Depression, the point should be emphasized, that the present situation is full of promise, as well as menace. Our age is literally pregnant with possibilities. There lies within our grasp the most humane and majestic civilization ever fashioned by any people. At last men have achieved such a mastery over the forces of nature that wage slavery can follow chattel slavery and take its place among the relics of the past. No longer are there any grounds for the contention that the finer fruits of human culture must be nurtured upon the exploitation of the masses. The limits set by nature have been so extended that for all practical purposes we may say that we are bound merely by our own ideals, by our power of self-discipline, and by our ability to devise social arrangements suited to . . . [our] age. . . . In other words, we hold within our hands the power to usher in an age of plenty, to make secure the lives of all and to banish poverty forever from the land. (1932a, pp. 260–261)

To save society from self-destruction, we must develop a vision of a society better than the existing one, a vision of "the most humane and majestic civilization ever fashioned by any people" in which our present society's problems do not exist and in which social justice for all people prevails. Then we must reconstruct our society into the envisioned one "that extend[s] the principles of liberty, equality, justice, and freedom to the widest possible set of institution[s]" and people (Giroux, 2005, p. 74).

For Social Reconstructionists, education provides the means by which society is to be reconstructed. Counts and Giroux put it this way:

Today, as social institutions crumble and society is shaken by deep convulsions that threaten its very existence, many persons are proclaiming that education provides the only true road to safety. They are even saying that it should be brought into the service of building a new social order. (Counts, 1934, p. 533)*

Educators need to assume the role of leaders in the struggle for social and economic justice. . . . Educators must connect what they teach and write to the dynamics of public life . . . and . . . concern for . . . democracy. (Giroux, 2006, p. 9)

Social Reconstructionists assume that education, *if it is revitalized along the lines they recommend,* has the power to educate people to analyze and understand social problems, envision a world in which those problems do not exist, and act so as to bring that vision into existence. Thus, education of individuals in appropriately revitalized schools can lead to social transformation.

Social Reconstructionists hold diverse beliefs about society, its problems, and the vision for a better society, and therefore the particular beliefs of educators will not be specified here. Rather, the context within which the beliefs are held will be discussed. Whether the curriculum is designed around the oppression of poverty or illiteracy, the destructiveness of war or pollution, the social injustice of racism or sexism, the economic problems of worker exploitation or political corruption, or other such problems, the particular issues and visions will not be our concern. Our concern will be the assumptions that underlie Social Reconstructionists' views. To give the assumptions

---

*Reprinted with the permission of Scribner, an imprint of Simon & Schuster Adult Publishing Group, from *The Social Foundations of Education* by George S. Counts. Copyright © 1934 by Charles Scribner's Sons; copyright renewed 1962 by Charles Scribner's Sons. All rights reserved.

meaning, two Social Reconstruction educational institutions will be described: an adult education school and a middle school mathematics classroom.

Highlander

The Highlander Folk School, founded by Myles Horton in 1932 on Monteagle Mountain in Tennessee, provides an example of the work of a Social Reconstructionist. The school was founded to stop an impending social crisis arising out of the industrial revolution: rich industrialists and landowners were economically exploiting and oppressing poor factory, farm, and mine workers to such an extent that democracy as Americans knew it was threatened. Horton founded the school to provide an educational "means by which all suppressed people in America could challenge their oppressors" (Adams, 1972, p. 516). The school's purpose was to "educat[e] for a revolution that would basically alter economic and political power relationships to the advantage of the poor and powerless" (Horton, 1936, p. 117). To accomplish this, Horton invited potential labor organizers to Highlander, helped them understand the nature of the oppression under which the workers of America were suffering, inspired them with a vision of an ideal society in which laborers were not oppressed, and helped them formulate strategies for organizing oppressed laborers. He then sent the labor organizers back to their factories, farms, and mines to organize the masses of oppressed workers to strike for better living and working conditions, and thus begin the establishment of a new social order. Horton believed "the Highlander Folk School's most important contribution [would] be to help the workers envision their [new] role in society and in so doing, make the labor movement the basis for a fundamental social change" (p. 118). Note that Horton assumed the existence of a social crisis that could be overcome: the economic exploitation of the working class. To overcome the social crisis, he used educational means: he educated labor leaders, who then educated the working class, both to envision a new society lacking economic exploitation and to act in ways that would transform the existing society into the envisioned new society. Crucial to Horton's educational program was his curriculum. Labor leaders educated via Horton's curriculum at Highlander used that same curriculum when they returned to their factories, farms, and mines to educate the masses of oppressed laborers.

The essence of Horton's curriculum consists of labor workshops that last for 6 weeks, during which about 25 potential labor leaders interact under the careful guidance of the Highlander staff. The labor workshops progress through three loosely structured, but carefully guided, stages of group discussion. During the first stage, participants "state and analyze their problems" in terms of their actual experiences and collectively paint a picture of a society in which such problems do not exist (Horton, 1966, p. 492). On the one hand, a feeling of commonality is established among strangers as they share their personal experiences with each other while developing an *understanding* of the social crisis. On the other hand, a feeling of shared hope arises as participants develop *a vision* of an ideal society that they might help construct in order to eradicate the problems of the existing society. At this stage, an understanding of society both "as it is" and "as it ought to be" is generated as Highlander staff help workshop participants reflect on their firsthand experiences with labor problems. This means that workshop participants are required to have had firsthand encounters with labor problems so that they can both contribute to the discussion from their own experienced perspectives and understand the experiences of others. Persons without the required experience are sent to participate in labor strikes and to live alongside exploited workers before they are allowed to join workshops.

During the second stage of workshops, participants discuss alternate strategies that might be used to eradicate society's problems and bring into existence an improved society. On the one hand, participants are guided to engage in "a lot of criticism, a lot of informal discussion . . . about how they've failed" and about "their inability to achieve what they want to achieve" in light of their vision of a better society (Horton, 1966, p. 492). This self-criticism allows for discussion of unsuccessful change strategies, gives workshop participants insight into their shortcomings as leaders, and frees participants from guilt over past failures. On the other hand, participants discuss each other's successes in working to overcome oppression and share possible new methods of acting as social groups to bring into existence the envisioned new society—such as massive strikes and sit-ins. During this workshop stage, Highlander "staff . . . deliberately reinforce talk in the group that points to united social action" versus individual action (Adams & Horton, 1975, p. 213), deliberately draw solutions to social problems out of the experiences and thoughts of workshop participants rather than those of outside experts, and deliberately examine these solutions in terms of participants' firsthand experiences rather than judge them theoretically. Important here is that solutions come from the people and relate to the people, and that

> the search for solutions becomes, itself, a group process. Without saying so, Highlander provides an experience in group problem solving. The group stretches the imagination of every individual in it and becomes the vehicle for introducing the concept of collective power. (Adams & Horton, 1975, p. 214)

(Here the social medium of group process complements the social message of collective power.)

During the third stage of workshops, participants are led to synthesize what they have learned and to commit themselves to action directed toward transforming the existing crisis-ridden society into the future *good society*. Commitment to action, strengthened through vows taken openly in front of colleagues, is central to this workshop stage. Participants commit to what they will do when they return home: both to educating their fellow workers in the same way they were educated at Highlander and to taking action that will help their fellow workers establish the envisioned good society. It is through workshop participants' going home to act that Horton disseminates his curriculum and uses it to educate "the masses," which make up society, to reconstruct society.

Three things occur at all stages of the labor workshops. First, Highlander staff act more as catalysts for and companions to workshop participants than as teachers or authorities. They communicate *with* participants rather than lecture *at* them or *about* them. Second, at no time does Horton present "a clearly defined program of action" for those coming to Highlander to mindlessly learn and then follow when they return home. He does not intend to teach such a program, for he believes that men must solve their problems in the context in which they arise. Horton does provide a value-laden vision of a new society and a method of deep reflection based on critical analysis of social forces that allows people to understand their problems, to have hope that they can be overcome, to plan ways of overcoming them, and to act to overcome them. Crucial here is that the particular action people must take depends on the specific time, place, and situation in which they find themselves—the value-laden vision *guides* their action but does not *dictate* their action. Third, in all three stages of the labor workshops, Highlander staff make heavy use of social media, such as group discussions, singing, storytelling, and drama, as a means of binding people together into social groups, leading them to see their problems clearly, helping them envision a new society, and inspiring them to action directed toward building a new social order. Scores of labor plays and songs, including "We Shall Overcome," were written or rewritten from earlier traditional folk versions at Highlander in its attempt "to develop feelings and will more than memory and logic" (Adams, 1972, p. 501). Education at Highlander is thoroughly social in nature. It uses the means of human interaction during discussion and song to educate and motivate, it promotes social rather than individual ways of acting (advocating massive strikes and sit-ins), and it educates people to improve society as a whole rather than themselves as individuals.

What Myles Horton did as a Social Reconstructionist in the 1930s and 1940s for the labor movement could be done at other times and in other places with different social crises. For example, during the 1950s and 1960s, Horton devoted his efforts to the civil rights movement. The Citizenship Schools that sprang up throughout the South and the sit-ins of the Student Nonviolent Coordinating Committee (SNCC) were programs that originated at Highlander. Although the issues and times were different, the method, vision, and purpose were the same: using interactional workshops as a social means of "educating for a revolution that would basically alter economic and political power relationships to the advantage of the poor and powerless."

Sixth-Grade Social Reconstruction Mathematics

The mathematics instruction described here took place in middle school classrooms in a large urban public school and was reported in *Rethinking Mathematics* (Gutstein & Peterson, 2005). The goal was to teach mathematics in a way that would allow students—many of them poor or members of minorities—to use mathematics to help them notice social injustices in their world, analyze and understand these injustices, plan ways of righting the injustices, and take action to bring about a more just world.

Projects

Students worked on numerous projects, including the following (Gutstein, 2005, pp. 117–120):

- Saving Morningstar Park (save a park from a condo developer who wants to build a parking lot in its place)
- Environmental Hazards (clean up a neighborhood toxic waste site after exploring EPA data)
- School Overcrowding (measure school size and population and compare the results with the size and population of other schools and state recommendations for space per student)

- Liquor Store Distribution (compare the density of liquor stores in your urban neighborhood to the density of liquor stores in the suburbs)
- World Wealth Distribution (compare world wealth distribution to continental population)
- Cost of the Iraq War (compare war costs to the costs of providing shelter for everyone, removing land mines, eliminating illiteracy, and providing safe drinking water worldwide)
- Random Traffic Stops (analyze police data for racial profiling)

Instructional Procedures

The procedures used in teaching each project were similar. Issues to be explored arose from student concerns. Students participated in an initial discussion, during which issues and values were highlighted and concerns to be explored were identified. Students went on a field trip, engaged in a simulation, listened to a speaker, exchanged personal experiences, role-played, watched a movie, or in some way experienced the issue they were exploring in a manner that personally involved them in it and touched them intellectually and emotionally. The teacher introduced the mathematics that would help students collect and examine data related to the issue being investigated, and then students gathered and analyzed data using the mathematics introduced by the teacher. Referring to the results of their mathematical analyses, students held further discussion in an attempt to better understand the issues and to clarify their stance on them. As part of the discussion, students also attempted to understand themselves, the ways social institutions and issues liberated or enslaved them, and how they could become more powerful and influential in their world. Related problems were raised, and, where appropriate, explored, with discussion following. If possible, class consensus about the issue was formed. Students discussed the types of action that could be taken to improve their world and worked to construct a collective vision of a more just society. If they could, they took social action in their community to get its members to support their social agendas and improve their world.

Examining these procedures gives insight into the Social Reconstruction ideology.

Start Where Students Are

All the middle school projects began as a result of problems that students brought to school from experiences in their community, that the teacher identified based on personal familiarity with the community, or that newspapers reported about events that touched students' lives. Saving Morningstar Park, Environmental Hazards, School Overcrowding, Random Traffic Stops, and Liquor Store Distribution (students frequently encountered drunks in front of liquor stores on their way to and from school) resulted from student experiences in their neighborhood. World Wealth Distribution was explored when discussions of poverty and hunger arose after UNICEF collections at Halloween and Thanksgiving. Cost of the Iraq War arose from newspaper articles the teacher brought to class in response to student concerns.

Personal Experience

An experience that intellectually and emotionally involved the children in an issue and its related mathematics was part of each project. The experience set the stage for the mathematical activities and discussions that followed. Children took field trips in coordination with the Morningstar Park, Environmental Hazards, and School Overcrowding projects. They shared personal experiences during the Liquor Store Distribution project, participated in a simulation during the World Wealth Distribution project, and did both during the Random Traffic Stops project.

Examining one of these experiences gives insight into classroom instructional dynamics. The simulation used during World Wealth Distribution provides an example. "The purpose of this activity is to . . . demonstrate . . . differences in wealth between different areas of the world" (Hersh & Peterson, 2005, p. 64).

To begin the World Wealth Distribution simulation, students are paired. Each pair is given a world map and asked to identify the continents. Students are also asked to estimate the number of people in the world. After they make their estimate, they are shown a current estimate in an almanac. Students are then given 24 chips (one for each of the 24 students in the class) and asked, "How many people is each chip worth?" (Hersh & Peterson, 2005, p. 64). (Students do the calculations: since there are about 6 billion people in the world, each chip represents about 250 million people.) Each pair of students is now given 24 red chips and asked to stack them on continents based on where they believe people reside. Next, student estimates are discussed, and then the accurate figures are disclosed. Students do calculations, rearrange their chips to reflect the data, and discuss what the stacks of chips tell them about the distribution of the world's population. Students are now given 24 blue chips, which "represent all the wealth produced in the world," and asked "to put the chips on the continents to indicate their estimate of who gets this wealth" (p. 65). Student estimates are discussed, as are the comparative sizes of the two stacks of chips on each continent.

The direction of the activity now changes. Each student chooses "an 'I was born in . . . ' slip from a container labeled 'chance of birth'" (Hersh & Peterson, 2005, p. 65). Students are now taken to the playground, where a large map of the world has been drawn with chalk, and are asked to stand on the continent in which their slip of paper says they were born. The students on each continent designate one student as a negotiator. Students are now told that the world's wealth is going to be distributed. They are also told that once the wealth is distributed, each group needs to discuss their situation. Twenty-four chocolate chip cookies (each representing one twenty-fourth of the world's wealth) are now distributed to the continents in proportion to the way in which wealth is distributed in the world. After group discussions, negotiators from each continent visit other continents to try to find out what others received and to negotiate for a more equitable distribution of resources. Negotiators return to their respective continents for discussion, and then another round of negotiation begins— with some students pleading for a more equitable distribution of cookies. Negotiators then return to their continents and discuss the results of their negotiations; trading and donation of resources take place; students begin eating cookies; and, while eating, they begin to discuss (with a great deal of emotion) what they think of the way the world's resources are distributed. Students then fill out a work sheet in which percentages need to be calculated: the work sheet contains seven columns for continents, population, percentage of world population per continent, number of students in class (24) on each continent, wealth (GNP) of each continent, percentage of world GNP per continent, and number of cookies (out of 24) each continent received. Students also construct graphs that depict different aspects of their data using percentages, fractions, and decimals.

Intense Discussion

Group discussion is an important Social Reconstruction instructional method. In exploring an issue such as world wealth distribution, a discussion allows students to expose their thoughts and values to each other, have their thoughts and values challenged, and reconstruct their thoughts and values in light of insights obtained from the discussion and any group consensus that might arise from it. Students' personal experiences with an issue and their mathematical analyses of it provide the substance for the discussion. For example, when students finish the World Wealth Distribution simulation and complete their calculations and graphs, the teacher leads a whole-class discussion during which students discuss the following types of questions: How do you feel about the unequal distribution of world wealth? How does the inequality of wealth affect the kinds of lives people lead? "Should wealth be distributed equally?" "How does the unequal distribution of wealth affect the power that groups of people hold?" and "What can be done about the unequal way wealth is distributed?" (Hersh & Peterson, 2005, p. 66). During the discussion, information is exchanged, injustices are highlighted, values are clarified, feelings are expressed, solutions to problems are suggested, and alternative solutions are assessed. After the discussion, "students write an essay about their feelings, what they learned, what questions they continue to have, and what they might want to do about world poverty" (p. 66). Media other than the written word—such as sociodrama, singing, painting, and dance—are frequently used to express student thoughts and feelings.

Follow-Up

Follow-up activities examine related problems that can be analyzed using the mathematics introduced in the initial activity. These activities provide practice for both social analysis and mathematical development, and they allow students to explore even more deeply their meanings, their values, the ways in which social institutions and events liberate or enslave them, and how they might become more powerful actors in their world. For example, World Wealth Distribution was followed up using newspaper data about the unequal distribution of wealth in America, unemployment trends in the U.S., and the hiring of 10,000 workers by a new company in the students' neighborhood (students compared the racial distribution of company workers and their neighborhood population; Peterson, 2005, p. 13).

Teaching mathematics using simulations, discussion, and follow-up activities that foster continuing discussion at ever deeper levels can be powerful. The teacher comments about World Wealth Distribution as follows:

Not only does such a lesson connect math to human beings and social reality, it does so in a way that goes beyond paper and pencil exercises; it truly brings math to life. I could simply tell my students about the world's unequal distribution of wealth, but that wouldn't have the same emotional impact as seeing classmates in the North American and European sections of the map get so many more cookies even though they have so many fewer people. (Peterson, 2005, p. 13)

I have found that as a result of [using activities such as World Wealth Distribution that] . . . my students' interest and skill in math have increased, both in terms of their understanding of basic concepts and their ability to solve problems. Furthermore, they can better clarify social issues, understand the structures of society, and offer options for better social policies. . . . Kids need every tool they can get to make this world—their world—a better place. Mathematics is one very important tool. (p. 15)

Vision and Social Action

In all of the above projects, students not only experienced, analyzed, and discussed social situations, but they also discussed how they could improve their world and, where feasible, took action to do so. Discussing how to improve one's world involved understanding a problem, examining options for improvement, clarifying values, taking a value stance, making a commitment, forming a group vision (or several visions, if differing opinions existed) of what a more just world might look like, and deciding what social action or actions should be taken to correct the problem. As part of this process, students wrote reports on their opinions about the social justice issues involved in each project and how these injustices might be rectified. Students' discussion of how they might improve their world was paralleled by discussion of how they might improve themselves; their meanings, thoughts, and values; and their ability to act with power, effectiveness, and wisdom in their world.

Social action directed toward making the world a better place included students' attempts to convince their families and community to support their endeavors and take the action necessary to mitigate existing problems. For some projects, students shared their opinions about the issues with family and friends, collected data on their family and friends' opinions before and after sharing their own opinions, and then, back in the classroom, aggregated the data they had collected using graphs and data analysis in such a way that they could see the results of sharing their opinions.

Student social action during the Environmental Hazards project created such a community uproar that it resulted in the elimination of neighborhood toxic waste. When students discovered that their school was overcrowded, they created and distributed flyers, made a poster displaying their findings, shared their findings with the school district, and gave a presentation to their school advisory council. Letters and reports were delivered to newspapers and city offices on issues such as liquor store licenses, racial profiling, and the number of college scholarships that could be given for the cost of one B-2 bomber used in the Iraq War. Students shared with children in earlier grades the results of their mathematical inquiries (including their graphs and data analysis) regarding world wealth distribution and other social concerns—which involved teaching younger children mathematics and showing them how it could help them better understand their world. Action taken to reconstruct society followed and reflected action students took to reconstruct themselves as part of class discussions and experiences.

Academics

All the projects involved mathematics presented in the school curriculum: calculation with integers, decimals, and percents; graphing and algebra; probability and statistics; measurement and data analysis; mathematical reasoning, problem solving, communication, and representation; and the formation of mathematical connections. The teacher reported that students learned the mathematics faster and with greater understanding because it was relevant to their lives and because they saw how it gave them insight into their world and power to influence events.

When asked whether it is appropriate to interject social or political issues into mathematics instruction or whether mathematics teachers and curriculum should remain neutral, the teacher's response was that "teaching math in a neutral manner is not possible. No math teaching—no teaching of any kind, for that matter—is actually 'neutral'" (Gutstein & Peterson, 2005, p. 6). For example, compare these two word problems:

> A 14-year-old girl goes into a store and purchases 12 candy bars. Each candy bar costs 43 cents. How much does she spend?

> A 14-year-old factory worker in Central America makes children's clothing for Wal-Mart. She earns 43 cents an hour and works 12 hours each day. How much money does she make in one day?

The teacher continued,

> While both problems are valid examples of applying multi-digit multiplication, each has more to say as well. The first example has a subtext of consumerism and unhealthy eating habits; the second has an explicit text of global awareness and empathy. Both are political, in that each highlights important social relations.
>
> When teachers fail to include math problems that help students confront important global issues, or when they don't bring out the underlying implications of problems like the first example here, these are political choices, whether the teachers recognize them as such or not. These choices teach students three things:
>
> They suggest that politics are not relevant to everyday situations.
>
> They cast mathematics as having no role in understanding social injustice and power imbalances.
>
> They provide students with no experience using math to make sense of, and try to change, unjust situations.
>
> These all contribute to disempowering students and are objectively political acts, though not necessarily conscious ones. (Gutstein & Peterson, p. 6)

It is important to note that the "reconstruction of the curriculum" required for teaching courses such as the mathematics class just described

> would not call for the addition of new subjects. Indeed, to superficial observation, perhaps no important changes would be discernible. The same disciplines would be taught. . . . Children would learn to read and write and figure; they would work and play together. But the . . . orientation would be different. . . . [T]he emphasis everywhere would be placed on the social and co-operative. . . . [S]ubject matter composing the curriculum would be given a social meaning. (Counts, 1934, pp. 544–546)

In addition to being given social meaning and being placed in a value-laden social context, academic content is treated in an interdisciplinary manner, with content from different disciplines being integrated together rather than being held apart.

Society and Reconstruction

Social Perspective

Social Reconstructionists view their world from a social perspective. The nature of society as it has been, as it is, and as it should be determines most of their concepts and assumptions. For example, *human experience, education, truth*, and *knowledge* are socially defined. Human experience is believed to be fundamentally shaped by cultural factors; meaning in people's lives is defined in terms of their relationship to society. Education is viewed as a function of the society that supports it and is defined in the context of a particular culture. Truth and knowledge are defined by cultural assumptions; they are idiosyncratic to each society and testable according to criteria based in social consensus rather than empiricism or logic.

As a result, Social Reconstructionists believe that "there is no good individual apart from some conception of the nature of the good society. Man without human society and human culture is not man" (Counts, 1932a, p. 258). They believe that "there is also no good education apart from some conception of the nature of the good society. Education is not some pure and mystical essence that remains unchanged from everlasting to everlasting" (p. 258). They believe that there is no truth or knowledge apart from some conception of the nature of the good society; "and the good society is not something that is given by nature: it must be fashioned by the hand and brain of man" (Counts, 1932b, p. 15). Important here is the belief in cultural relativity. The "good individual," the "good education," and "truth and knowledge" are defined by a particular culture, and the only thing that gives them either meaning or value is the existence of that culture in a particular time and place. Counts affirms this:

> The historical record shows that education is always a function of time, place, and circumstance. In its basic philosophy, its social objective, and its program of instruction, it inevitably reflects . . . the experiences, the condition, and the hopes, fears, and aspirations of a particular people . . . at a particular point in history. . . . [I]t is never organized and conducted with sole reference to absolute and universal terms. . . . [E]ducation as a whole is always relative. . . . There can be no all-embracing educational philosophy, policy, or program suited to all cultures and all ages. (1934, p. 1)

Since society is considered to be currently undergoing a crisis, it follows that its conception of the good man, the good education, and truth and knowledge are also undergoing a crisis. For stability to return, a vision of a good society must be developed. Conceptions of the good man, the good education, and truth and knowledge will be derived from that vision. As individuals reconstruct themselves based on their vision, they act on society so as to bring into existence new conceptions of the good man, the good education, and truth and knowledge; and from the reconstruction of society in accordance with the vision comes the actualization of these conceptions.

Deep Social Structures

Underlying the dynamics of society and schools are deep social structures that shape and determine human behavior.

When examining, analyzing, and comprehending society, Social Reconstructionists often connect social phenomena to concepts such as colonial Eurocentric conceptions of knowledge, culture, social class, and values. For example, when dealing with social problems, these educators are frequently concerned about how such things as "inequalities, power, and human suffering are rooted in basic institutional structures" (Giroux, 2005, p. 21).

When looking at schools, Social Reconstructionists frequently focus on hidden aspects of the curriculum that invisibly shape human relationships and behavior. Here their perspective might lead them to, for example, examine "schools . . . as part of the existing social and political fabric that characterizes the class-driven dominant society" (McLaren, 2007, p. 18); view "schooling as a resolutely political and cultural enterprise" (p. 187); analyze "schools . . . as sorting mechanisms in which select groups of students are favored on the basis of race, class, and gender" (p. 187); or discuss schools as institutions that "perpetuate or reproduce the social relationships and attitudes needed to sustain the existing dominant economic and class relations of the larger society" (pp. 214–215). As McLaren emphasizes,

> the traditional view of classroom instruction and learning as a neutral process antiseptically removed from the concepts of power, politics, history, and context can no longer be credibly endorsed. . . . [R]esearchers have given primacy to the social, the cultural, the political, and the economic, in order to better understand the workings of contemporary schooling. (2007, p. 187)

The Individual in Society

Social Reconstructionists' concern is primarily the forces at work in society that shape human experience and secondarily the individuals at work who shape society (although both function together). They focus on economic, political, social, and educational forces that control the impact on individuals in society of such varied things as social class, cultural and linguistic heritage, moral trends, and aesthetic movements. Causal explanations proceed from the dynamics of society as a whole to the dynamics of social subgroups to the individual. In this context, individuals are viewed as fulfilling their potential in relationship to social groups, in interaction with other individuals, and as part of human communities. This does not mean that man is a creature of social determinism. Man is shaped by society and man can shape society. In fact, individuals must first reconstruct themselves before they can reconstruct society. However, interpretations and intentions are expressed with respect to social groups rather than individuals.

Society, Change, and Crisis

The Social Reconstruction view of society is one of historical evolution: societies pass through periods of evolution, stability, and degeneration. One of the prime characteristics of our society is that it is undergoing change that threatens its survival. Whether because of technological, economic, political, cultural, racial, or psychological factors, many of our society's problem solving strategies and institutions are dysfunctional. If society fails to detect that its problem solving strategies and institutions are dysfunctional, these strategies and institutions will become threats to its survival.

The situation of society, however, is full of promise as well as menace. The changes wrought on society by its internal dynamics have extended the limits previously set by its structure so that, as Counts said, "there lies within our grasp the most humane, the most beautiful, and the most majestic civilization ever fashioned by any people." The possibility to significantly improve the total human condition lies within reach.

Hope exists, for it is believed that there is no deterministic, metaphysical design that prescribes the history of a society, even though societies are largely formed and limited by the characteristics of the period in which they exist. Society hammers out its own history through the thoughts and struggles of its members: "The course it takes and the goals it attains depend wholly upon the choice made and the failures and successes experienced by man" (Brameld, 1956, pp. 60–61). As a result, the evolution of society is "bound merely by our ideals, our power of self discipline, and by our ability to devise social arrangements suited to" our situation (Counts, 1932a, p. 260).

Reconstruction and Vision

Faced with the crises of society, Social Reconstructionists devise a vision of a new, better society that lacks its existing problems. They then develop educational programs that allow people to see the differences between the crisis-ridden present society and the future "good" society in such a way that it motivates them to transform the current society into the future one.

Social Reconstructionists do not accept current societal conditions as unalterable "givens." Nor do they accept present social conditions as factors to be improved through simple tinkering. They reject certain aspects of the present crisis-ridden society, and they attempt to build a new society out of the existing one rather than attempt to perfect the best aspects of the existing society in hopes that this will make the present society more just and equitable. They seek to provide "for qualitatively better life for all through the construction of a society based on nonexploitative relations and social justice" (McLaren, 2007, p. 195).

In assuming that the way to overcome the present social crisis is to envision and implement a future better society, Social Reconstructionists assume that people need a "compelling and challenging vision of human destiny" (Counts, 1932a, p. 259) that points the way to better social conditions:

> The times are literally crying for a new vision of American destiny. . . . Such a vision of what America might become . . . I would introduce into our schools as the supreme imposition . . . one to which our children are entitled—a priceless legacy which . . . should be the first concern of our [educational] profession to fashion and bequeath. . . . To refuse to face the task of creating a vision of a future America immeasurably more just and noble and beautiful than the America of today is to evade the most crucial, difficult, and important educational task. (Counts, 1932b, pp. 54–55)

The Social Reconstruction vision of the future good society has several character-istics. First, it is not a finished vision that portrays in precise detail a utopia in its ulti-mate state, but rather a vision of direction that points to the way society must move toward reconstruction. It is "a vision of the possibilities which lie ahead" (Counts, 1932b, p. 37) rather than the endpoint that society should reach in order to achieve perfection (Freire, 1992, p. 175).

Second, the vision does not prescribe a specific program of action that dictates how it is to be achieved. The situations in which people find themselves determine this. The vision is a general one that provides values and directions, not a blueprint that specifies exactly how to build the future good society. This is as it should be, given the Social Reconstruction belief in social relativity and the uniqueness of the particular "time, place, and circumstances" in which people find themselves (Counts, 1934, p. 1).

Third, the vision of the future good society is created in response to existing social conditions. As such, it embodies both a picture of reality as it is and a vision of reality as it ought to be. Its power lies in its ability both to offer people salvation from an intolerable reality, reality as it is, and to offer them a vision of life as it should be. Understanding the vision requires that one understand society as it is in order to fully appreciate society as it ought to be.

Fourth, the Social Reconstruction vision is a social rather than individual vision. It is a "public vision of self- and social empowerment," a "vision . . . that extend[s] the principles of liberty, equality, justice, and freedom to the widest possible set of institu-tional and lived relations" (Giroux, 2005, p. 74). It is a vision that allows the masses, which comprise society, to overcome their problems together and to collectively achieve the good life. It is not a vision that allows certain individuals to achieve the good life and escape from their problems at the expense of others.

The Social Reconstruction vision of the future good society helps people recon-struct society in several ways.

- The vision allows people from diverse situations to rise above their particular circum-stances to see social crises as a whole (as, for example, when African Americans, Mexican Americans, and Native Americans see that they are all oppressed), allows them to share a common vision of a better life, and allows them to act together to meet common needs and to collectively better themselves and improve society as a whole (Apple, 1996, pp. 14–15).
- The vision offers people an alternative to and the possibility of escape from their crisis-ridden society through "a language of possibility . . . [that] goes beyond critique," "a positive language of human empowerment" (Giroux, 1992, p. 10). Without the percep-tion that their oppression can be overcome and without a language that allows them to speak about overcoming their oppression, people would not be able to wage the strug-gle to reconstruct their society.
- The vision has inherent values that enable people to see their problems as solvable rather than to simply accept them as innate characteristics of their world. For example, someone who places no value on freedom would not see the lack of it as a problem. Educating people to value freedom prepares the way for dissatisfaction that can lead to action. The vision educates people to see problems and to see them as solvable.
- The vision offers people the hope of something better, hope that can motivate them to act in ways not normal for them. As Freire says, "without a vision for tomorrow, hope

is impossible" (1997, p. 45), and any "attempt to do without hope, in the struggle to improve the world, as if that struggle could be reduced to calculated acts alone, or a purely scientific approach, is a frivolous illusion" (1992, p. 2). Giving people hope and courage that allow them to step outside their normal social roles is crucial in motivating them to overcome their social problems, problems that so frequently trap them in hopelessness and ignorance (Greene, 1988, p.25).

- The vision gives people clear long-range goals that offer direction to their thinking so that they do not become distracted from their reconstruction endeavors by the immediacies of daily life. Short-range and vaguely defined goals will not suffice, for "it is now imperative that we know where we want to go . . . because, so long as we do not know we shall be unprepared to go there" (Brameld, 1956, p. 76).
- The vision of the future good society defines the nature of the good individual, the good education, and worthwhile truth and knowledge. Without the ability to identify these, people would not be able to cultivate them and make them multiply in ways that help reconstruct society.

The emphasis on developing a vision of a good society leads Social Reconstructionists to utopianism. Here the distinction must be made between utopias of escape and utopias of social reconstruction. The first leaves society the way it is as small groups or individuals escape from it; the second seeks to change society so that people can live in it and interact with it on their own terms (Mumford, 1933, p. 15). Social Reconstruction visions are utopias of social reconstruction.

Social Dynamics

In viewing society in its stark reality, Social Reconstructionists usually identify three social subgroups: the "bad guys," the "good guys," and the "masses." Freire calls the good guys and the bad guys the "oppressed" and the "oppressors" (Freire, 1970). McLaren calls them the "subordinate" and the "dominant" social classes (McLaren, 2007, pp. 211–212). Both the bad guys and the good guys are smaller groups who attempt to control the masses. The bad guys perpetuate the status quo by supporting ideas and institutions suited to a bygone age in order to selfishly exploit the masses. The good guys are future-oriented forces attempting to bring into existence a better and more just society run for the benefit of the masses. In 1956, Brameld made explicit this view of social dynamics:

> If the reconstructionist is prepared to argue that he is the minority spokesman for values that are already cherished by the majority, whether consciously or not, he is equally prepared to show that another minority actually dominates the majority. This is the minority that now so largely controls the instruments of power and that has succeeded in persuading the majority that their own interests are best served by perpetuating those controls . . . in behalf of continued scarcity, chronic insecurity, frustration, and war. In this sense, indeed, one may say that the great political struggle that goes on in our democracy is not, after all, one between the majority and a minority . . . it is between at least two organized minorities. One minority is concerned with widening. . . . The opposing minority works to narrow . . . (1956, pp. 129–130)

Note several assumptions in this statement. First, the good guys are out of power and the bad guys are in control of the masses. Responsibility for the ills of society falls solely upon the shoulders of the bad guys.

Second, the good guys are "the minority spokesmen for *values* that are *already cherished* by the *majority, whether consciously or not*" (italics added). This assumption leads to belief in a hierarchical set of values—where some values are better than others—and to several other beliefs: that the good guys possess the truth as represented in their better values; that those values are good for the masses whether they are conscious of it or not; that it is permissible to educate the masses as one chooses, since one knows what is really good for them; and that it is permissible to control and manipulate the masses so long as it is for their own good.

Third, society is engaged in a "great political struggle," with the good and bad guys waging war over the masses. As McLaren and Giroux exclaim, "educators need to wage nothing less than war in the interest of the sacredness of human life, collective dignity for the wretched of the earth, and the right to live in peace and harmony" (1997, p. 13). This is a holy war, a great crusade in which good battles evil over value-laden issues. Further, education and the school are weapons to be used in the war.

Fourth, the war's emphasis is on forming a single, unified "group mind" that agrees upon what the true values of society are and what the vision of the future good society should be (Brameld, 1956, p. 247).

Underlying this view of social dynamics are several other suppositions. Only the "oppressed" are the ones who can find within themselves the strength and vision to rectify the problems of society. They do so because of the pain of the social injustices they feel and their innate impulse to be recognized as fully human and to be treated as such. The powerful and privileged of society cannot find the strength to transform society into a more just and egalitarian institution because they cannot see human equality to be in their vested interest. In improving their social conditions, the oppressed correct some of the problems of society, and in so doing make society a better place for everyone to live in (Freire, 1970). (For example, in the U.S. a century ago, only a few women struggled for equal rights because they felt the pain of inequality, but now that conditions have improved for women, we all benefit.)

Reconstruction Through Education

Education takes place in many locations, including the family, community, and school. Social Reconstructionists want to influence how education takes place in all of these locations and believe that it is the job of educators to do so. However, it is in the school where educators focus their endeavors—whether the school is located in a school building, home, factory, or park.

The School as the Institution of Change

Social Reconstructionists dedicate themselves to the reconstruction of society. Their approach consists of analyzing and understanding society, constructing a vision of an improved society, and acting to transform the existing society into a better one. This approach is embedded in school curricula that are taught to students. Schools then become the social institution through which leadership is provided and action is initiated to reconstruct society.

Education, thus, has the role of preparing people to transform society. To accomplish this, educators

> should deliberately reach for power and then make the most of their conquest. . . . To the extent that they are permitted to fashion the curriculum and the procedures of the school they will definitely and positively influence the social attitudes, ideals, and behaviors of the coming generation (Counts, 1932b, pp. 28–29)

and through them enable the masses of society to reconstruct themselves. By doing so, they will reconstruct society.

This requires educators to assume new roles and functions, for at present they are meek followers of social consensus rather than dynamic leaders who mold social beliefs and values. This means that "instead of shunning power, the profession [of education] should rather seek power and then strive to use that power fully and wisely and in the interests of the great masses of the people" (Counts, 1932b, pp. 29–30), for "if the schools are to be really effective, they must become centers for the building, and not merely for the contemplation of our civilization" (p. 37). Schools must

> face squarely and courageously every social issue, come to grips with life in all of its stark reality, establish an organic relation with the community, develop a realistic and comprehensive theory of welfare, fashion a compelling and challenging vision of human destiny, and become somewhat less frightened than . . . [they are] today of the bogeys of imposition and indoctrination. (Counts, 1932a, p. 259)

For this to be accomplished, current conceptions of education (which view schools as transmitters of established disciplinary knowledge and social values) must be reconceptualized so that they are in phase with a vision of the future based in concepts of social justice and human empowerment and so that they prepare students to live in and to transform our current society into the envisioned future society. Schools will then be catalysts that stimulate the reconstruction of society.

Education as a Social Process

Social Reconstructionists want to reconstruct society through social processes. Their first concern is the education of the group and their second the education of the individual. From this perspective, learning experiences are construed to be group experiences that take place through human interaction, and the focus is on the "group mind" rather than the "individual mind." As Freire writes, "in this theory of action one cannot speak of *an actor*, nor simply of *actors*, but rather of *actors in intercommunication*" (1970, p. 123). Individuals are critical to the ideology, for it is through the reconstruction of individuals that one reconstructs society. However, the education of individuals is viewed as achievable primarily through group-centered, social processes.

Here one speaks of social self-realization for both the society and individuals, not of individual self-realization. Here social consensus plays a central role, for it is believed that once social consensus is reached about the nature of current society and the vision for the future society, it will be possible for the masses to reconstruct society. The aim is to fashion, through education, a social consensus among the masses that will by majority rule force society to align itself with the vision of the future good society and eradicate current social ills. It is through the creation of social consensus that educators hope to achieve social reconstruction both by and for society.

Educational Methods: Group Discussion and Experience

Two of the primary instructional methods used by Social Reconstructionists are the discussion and experience methods. Both depend on having students learn indirectly through social media.

The discussion method involves engaging students in conversations with their peers, during which teachers elicit from them their thoughts and feelings. The discussion process allows teachers to get students to expose their meanings to the group so that the group—under the guidance of the teacher—can help them reconstruct their meanings. During discussions, the teacher provides the rules for discussion, the desired social perspective and values, and the model for the modes of thinking in which students are to engage. The instructive function is embedded in the language, questions, evidence, value judgments, modes of argumentation, and criteria of relevance the teacher uses during discussion and urges students to use by example. Here, it is primarily through the medium of the discussion process rather than through the message (or topic) of discussion that instruction takes place.

Many forms of the discussion method exist. Values clarification was popular during the 1970s. By the end of the 20th century, critical analysis, which includes both a "language of critique" and a "language of possibility" and is part of critical pedagogy (Giroux, 2006, pp. 4–5), had become popular.

The experience method involves placing students in an environment where they encounter a social crisis. Students learn about the social crisis both from those who usually function in that environment and from their teacher. The people who normally function in the environment share with students their attitudes, values, modes of perception and interpretation, and worldview regarding the social crisis being examined. The teacher acts as a counselor and discussion leader who provides instructional opportunities during which students can share, discuss, reflect on, and construct meaning about their experiences. This instructional method uses something like a combination of group therapy and an apprenticeship system to introduce students to an educator's view of a social crisis and vision of a future utopia. During the experience method, the teacher is not an imparter of information but a colleague who can be trusted and confided in as a friend. This puts the teacher and students on the same side of the experience and facilitates the sharing of experiences, knowledge, meanings, feelings, values, and visions.

Students can be provided with many types of experiences with social crises. They can participate in public protests or demonstrations, paint a school in a depressed urban or rural community, clean up trash-ridden parks or streams, visit elderly adults in nursing homes, work in shelters for battered women or the homeless, or help the poor in food pantries or soup kitchens.

Education and Language

Underlying both the discussion and experience methods is a belief in the crucial role that language plays in education and social reconstruction. As McLaren and Giroux emphasize, "knowledge . . . is a social construction" that takes place largely through language, "which means that the world we inhabit as individuals is constructed symbolically by the mind (and body) through social interaction" (1997, p. 27). Further, "the nature of the language we use determines how we make sense of our experiences and the type of social action we choose to engage in as a result of interpreting our experiences" (p. 21). In addition, "language . . . is always situated within ideology and power/ knowledge relations," which means that "meanings of any event or experience are only available through the language selected by the particular interpretive community wishing to render such event intelligible" (p. 22). As a result, "the struggle over how to name and transform experience [through language] is one of the most critical issues in . . . the fight for social change" (p. 26), for

> the purpose of developing a critical language . . . is not to describe the world more objectively, but to create a more ethically empowering world which encourages a greater awareness of the way in which power can be mobilized for the purposes of human liberation. (p. 21)

Education and Social Change

The question of how Social Reconstructionists—whose views are held by a minority within society—are to convince society what is best for it and thus bring into existence the desired social consensus raises questions about the civic responsibility of educators to the society they serve, educators' engagement in politics, and the socialization, acculturation, or indoctrination of a social majority by a minority. These questions arise because Social Reconstructionists believe that their insight into the nature of society and what is good for the masses is superior to and different from that of the masses, and because they believe that it is their job to transform society's knowledge base and values so that they agree with theirs.

Civic Responsibility

Do educators have the right to attempt to change the social patterns of a culture without the permission of its members? Do educators have the right to teach children to live in a world that might be different from that of their parents, and of which their parents might not approve? What responsibility do educators have to the society they serve?

In other words, "are schools to uncritically serve and reproduce the existing society or challenge the social order to develop and advance its democratic imperatives?" (Giroux, 1992, p. 18). Giroux's answer to this question is simple: "I opt for the latter. . . . I believe that schools should function to provide students with the knowledge, character, and moral vision that build civic courage" (p. 18) in a manner that leads to the reconstruction of society in accordance with "the principles and practices of human dignity, liberty, and social justice" (p. 8).

From the Social Reconstruction perspective, educators have the responsibility to go beyond simply reflecting the wishes of society and to do what is best for society. In fact, "representing as they do, not the interests of the moment or of any special class, but rather the common and abiding interests of the people, [educators and] teachers are under heavy social obligation to protect and further those interests" (Counts, 1932b, p. 29). If this involves educating a culture's children in such a way that they will reject parts of the existing culture, then it is necessary to do so for the good of the culture. The role of educators in this time of crisis is different from the roles they have had in the past. No longer are educators simply charged with the responsibility of inculcating in children the myths of their society or developing in children their ability to dispassionately analyze social history. They must take a stance with respect to the current social crisis and educate students in such a way that they, too, work to reconstruct society. This means that education must be

> a form of social action.... [T]he educator fails ... if he refuses to step out of academic cloisters, ... reject the role of a disinterested spectator, take an active part in shaping events, make selections among social values, and adopt, however tentatively and broadly, some conception of social welfare. (Counts, 1934, pp. 2–3)

Education and Politics

As actors within a "form of social action," Social Reconstructionists engage in political action with a clearly defined set of values and an ethical stance. A Social Reconstruction educator "makes no claim to political neutrality" (McLaren, 2007, p. 31) and unabashedly accepts that "no curriculum, policy, or program is ideologically or politically innocent, and that the concept of the curriculum is inextricably related to issues of social class, culture, gender, and power" (p. 213). This is because it is assumed that

> schooling always represents an introduction to, preparation for, and legitimization of particular forms of social life. It is always implicated in relations of power, social practices, and the favoring of forms of knowledge that support a specific vision of past, present, and future. (p. 188)

This is a surprise to many educators. As Freire exclaims, "this is a great discovery, education is politics!" (1987, p. 46). Social Reconstruction education is political for numerous reasons, including the following, which Giroux describes:

> At best it teaches students to think critically about the knowledge they gain, and what it means to recognize antidemocratic forms of power and to fight substantive injustices in a world marked by deep inequalities. (2006, p. 8)

> [It] create[s] new forms of knowledge through its emphasis on breaking down disciplinary boundaries.... This is ... an ... issue ... of power, ethics, and politics.... At stake here is ... [the provision of] knowledge, skills, and habits for students ... [that allow them] to read history in ways that enable them to reclaim their identities in the interests of constructing more democratic and just forms of life. (2005, p. 69)

> [It emphasizes] the intellectual, emotional, and ethical investments we make as part of our attempt to negotiate, accommodate, and transform the world in which we find ourselves. The purpose and vision that drives such a pedagogy must be based on a politics and view of authority, that links teaching and learning to forms of self- and social empowerment . . . that extend the principles of liberty, equality, justice, and freedom to the widest possible set of institution[s and people]. (2005, p. 74).

While embracing their political agendas, Social Reconstructionists emphasize that all educators promote one political agenda or another. If educators' instructional efforts are not directed toward social reconstruction, then they are directed toward social maintenance—which is simply the opposite side of the political agenda.

Education and Socialization

To accomplish what they believe is best for society, Social Reconstructionists use whatever means that they require, that society will tolerate, and that their visions will support. But the means one uses to accomplish preconceived ends—as inherent in the educator's vision of the future good society—raises the question of social acculturation and imposition.

Many educators are fearful of the phrase "social acculturation" (or "imposition") because they believe that it implies changing people's values and social perspectives in a manner that they are not fully conscious of and without their prior agreement through the use of subconscious educational processes. This is not its meaning for Social Reconstructionists. For them, socially acculturating students means deliberately socializing them, accepting the biased values that underlie all socialization and educational processes. Those who are afraid of the phrase "social acculturation" or "social imposition" often wish to replace it with either "socialize" or "educate."

Do educators have the right to convince students of their values, views of current day social crises, and visions of the future good society, either with or without their consent? The answer for early Social Reconstruction educators during the 1930s was "Yes!" Education must "become less frightened than it is today of the bogies of imposition and indoctrination" and deliberately use them openly and forthrightly during instruction (Counts, 1932b, pp. 9–10).

There are many reasons why Social Reconstructionists condone the use of social acculturation (or imposition). Central to them all is the belief that social acculturation is unavoidable and that education cannot avoid being biased. Social Reconstructionists believe that social acculturation is an inevitable consequence of living in social groups. As Counts (1932b, p. 13) phrases it,

> the most crucial of all circumstances conditioning human life is birth into a particular culture. By birth one becomes a Chinese, an Englishman, a Hottentot, a Sioux Indian, a Turk, or a[n] . . . American. . . . By being nurtured on a body of culture, however . . . the individual is at once imposed upon

and acculturated. To grow from infancy to adulthood in a culture is to become socialized into and by that culture. In fact, "the induction of the immature individual into the life of the group" through the process of socialization is the traditional role of the school (Counts, 1934, p. 536). In inducting "the immature individual into the life of the group," education "stands at the focal point in the process of cultural evolution—at the point of contact between the older and the younger generation where values are selected and rejected" (p. 532). As such, the school necessarily acts as an agent of society in acculturating the child into society:

> 1 am prepared to defend the thesis that all education contains a large element of imposition, that in the very nature of the case this is inevitable, that the existence and evolution of society depend upon it, that it is consequently eminently desirable, and that the frank acceptance of this fact by the educator is a major professional obligation. I even contend that the failure to do this involves the clothing of one's own deepest prejudices in the garb of universal truth. (Counts, 1932b, p. 12)

From the Social Reconstruction perspective, bias and partiality are inherent in the very nature of education. The questions teachers ask, the language teachers use, the social interactions acceptable in school (respect for teachers, for example), and the hidden curricula of schools (for example, expectations for work-related behavior of children from different economic classes; Anyon, 1980) all have social biases embedded in them. Questions of what to teach, what to expect of students, where to teach, and how to teach all involve value decisions that make impartiality impossible. Social Reconstructionists believe educators who consider themselves impartial and neutral transmitters of instruction to be ignorant of the nature of their endeavors.

What is really at issue is not whether social acculturation or imposition will take place in schools or whether schools will be biased. The question is whether a social minority should use education for purposes other than those of simply getting the individual to fit into and adjust to society as it is. The Social Reconstructionists' answer is clear: "Neutrality with respect to the great issues that agitate society, while perhaps theoretically possible, is practically tantamount to giving support to the forces of conservatism" (Counts, 1932b, p. 54). And to give support to the forces of conservatism is to perpetuate the existing social crisis that threatens society's very existence. The following statement by George Counts gives the flavor of one way in which social bias could be introduced into the school:

> The several divisions of subject matter composing the curriculum would all be given a social meaning. . . . [For example, g]eography would be taught and studied, not merely as a body of information useful and interesting to the individual, but as the physical basis for the building of a finer civilization and culture. The natural resources of the nation would actually be regarded as possessions of the nation—as the source of a richer and more abundant common life, rather than as fields for the operation of profit-seeking enterprise and the accumulation of great private fortunes. . . . All of the subjects of study would be integrated by the might and challenging conception of the building of a great . . . civilization conceived in terms of the widest interests of the masses. (1934, p. 546)

Note that school subjects are still taught, but for purposes of understanding and reconstructing society rather than for purposes inherent in the school subjects themselves.

What needs to be explicitly stated is that Social Reconstructionists do not want to simply program learners' minds or fill them with a specific collection of facts and concepts. Because such an approach would prepare learners to deal with only the crises of the past and not the crises of the future, it is inconsistent with the Social Reconstruction belief in social relativity. It is the unknown crises of the future that children must be prepared to encounter, understand, and act to resolve. Social Reconstructionists want to have children construct a specific social orientation and social perspective along with a specific set of social values and problem solving skills that will allow them to confront, analyze, understand, react to, and rectify whatever social problems might arise in the future—in a manner consistent with the social perspective and values of the educator. Providing learners with such a social perspective and set of social values—which are by definition biased—is what Social Reconstructionists call social acculturation (or imposition).

Historical Context

One could say that the origins of the Social Reconstruction ideology in the U.S. are as old as the founding of the nation. Cremin claims that the American Revolution was "essentially a matter of popular education" and that "teachers used the lectern to nurture ideas of independency, while students organized symbolic actions ranging from burning in effigy to boycotts of tea," as much of the population of the countryside opposed British political, economic, and social practices (1977, p. 38).

Lester Frank Ward began the discussion of the Social Reconstruction agenda in the 1880s and 1890s with the publication of *Dynamic Sociology* (1883) and *The Psychic Factors of Civilization* (1893). He asserted that men had the ability to influence the social world in which they lived through their application of intelligence to the problems of their society and suggested that education through the development of intelligence could influence society to be a more just and equitable place for people.

John Dewey prepared the way for the Social Reconstruction ideology in *Reconstruction in Philosophy* (1948), where he described education as a crucial ingredient in social and moral development, and in *Democracy and Education,* where he described education as "that reconstruction or reorganization of experience which adds to the meaning of experience, and which increases ability to direct the course of subsequent experience" (1916, p. 76).

The ideology was formally brought to life for educators in 1932 when George Counts gave a rousing presentation at the Progressive Education Association annual meeting in which he asked, "Dare the school build a new social order?" This speech led to a deep split in the Progressive Education Association between those who advocated the Social Reconstruction ideology and proponents of the Learner Centered ideology. It also led to the publication, beginning in 1934, of *The Social Frontier: A Journal of Criticism and Reconstruction.*

The Social Reconstruction ideology flourished during the Great Depression of the 1930s, during which many educators questioned the American way of life. Myles

Horton started Highlander in 1932 to help labor deal with the oppression of industry. A bit later, Harold Rugg published a popular social studies textbook series in which he introduced students to controversial economic, social, and political issues (1936–1938).

World War II dimmed the flame of the ideology, but during the 1950s Theodore Brameld wrote books such as *Toward a Reconstructed Philosophy of Education* (1956) advocating the Social Reconstruction ideology. During the 1960s and 1970s, the civil rights movement, the women's movement, and the protest against the Vietnam War were stimulated and supported by adherents of the Social Reconstruction ideology. Neil Postman and Charles Weingartner wrote *Teaching as a Subversive Activity* (1969) and other such books to promote the ideology.

In the last quarter of the 20th century and the first years of the 21st century, critical theory began to flourish in academia in a variety of highly competitive forms, including postmodernism, poststructuralism, radical feminism, and critical constructivism (McLaren, 2007, p. 13). These forms of critical theory revolted against traditional ways of viewing and conceptualizing our world; against powerful (oppressive, exploitative, and/or dominant) social groups who made economic, cultural, and educational decisions affecting the lives of those less powerful; and against rationalist, Eurocentric cultural traditions that privileged those who were white, educated, rich, and male in comparison to those who were nonwhite, uneducated, poor, or female. They focused on the subjective and social construction of knowledge rather than on objective knowledge. Critical theory is concerned with emancipation through the questioning of political, economic, social, and psychological conventions that have been previously taken for granted. It is critical of these conventions, using a value system based on social justice and equity, and it promotes action to improve society and the individual through education. Advocates of critical theory sought to do research like that of Jean Anyon, who demonstrated how the hidden curriculum of education influenced the work expectations, aspirations, and perspectives of children of different economic classes (1980). Advocates of critical pedagogy also sought to engage in practical educational endeavors like those of Brazilian educator Paulo Freire, who in *Pedagogy of the Oppressed* (1970) described how poor people with little political, economic, or social power could take control of their lives and education by critically examining the social, political, economic, and psychological forces that enslaved them. And advocates of critical pedagogy sought to write social analyses like those by Michael Apple, who in *Ideology and Curriculum* (2004) and *Education and Power* (1995) described how schools are reproductive agents of society that maintain social power relationships by socializing students to society's conception of appropriate class, gender, race, political, cultural, and economic relationships among people through the hidden curriculum of the school.

During the last decade of the 20th century and the first years of the 21st century, aspects of the Social Reconstruction ideology have become fashionable among university faculty in departments of education. Some of the slogans they frequently use include "social [cultural, economic, and political] justice," "empowerment," "critical analysis," and "praxis."

We now turn from an examination of beliefs affecting the general context in which Social Reconstructionists work to an examination of their aims and their views of children, learning, teaching, knowledge, and evaluation.

Aims

The aim of Social Reconstructionists is to eliminate from their culture those aspects they believe undesirable, to substitute in their place social practices and values they believe more desirable, and in so doing to reconstruct their culture so that its members attain maximum satisfaction of their material, social, cultural, and spiritual needs. They wish to redirect the growth of their society to reconstruct it into a more just, satisfying, democratic, egalitarian, and humane society than the current one.

To accomplish this, Social Reconstructionists attempt to create a social consensus that rejects the faults of the existing society and affirms the virtues of a future good society. To develop the social consensus, educators manipulate society at the point where it inducts children into the life of the culture: society's educational system. Their intent is to educate youth to reconstruct our current society and to live in a society superior to the existing one. To do this, they build a social, political, economic, and cultural educational program—a curriculum.

Different visions of the future good society and different strategies that suggest how to transform today's society into the future good society exist. The overall Social Reconstruction orientation, however, begins with analysis of society, moves to the creation of a vision of a subjective future good society, and then moves back to manipulation of the existing social reality to transform it into the future good society that will provide its members with the maximum possible social, cultural, economic, and political equality, satisfaction, and justice. In the process, as new social problems and crises arise, members of society become empowered to continually reconstruct themselves and society.

The Child

Children as Social Agents

Children are not viewed primarily as children. Rather, children are viewed as products of society, as social actors, and as potential contributing members of society who can aid in its reconstruction (McLaren, 2007, p. 94). As Giroux indicates, "social betterment must be the necessary consequence of individual flourishing" (1992, p. 11).

Children carry within themselves unique collections of individual meanings that result from experiences they encounter. They bring to school not only their potential to act in the future but also their past histories from family, peer group, and community interactions as well as their personal meanings and ways of thinking that result from such interactions.

At birth, a child is by nature "neither good nor bad; he is merely a bundle of potentialities which may be developed in manifold directions" (Counts, 1932b, p. 15). Throughout their lives, children are "unfinished, uncompleted beings" (Freire, 1970, p. 72) in the process of "becoming [ever] more fully human" (p. 52). It is the role of education to guide the development of the child's potentialities so that they contribute to the functioning of the good society, which will in turn give value to the developed potentialities.

Children are "born helpless" (Counts, 1932b, p. 13). As they grow they develop the power and freedom to mold their world. It is the role of education to guide the development of children's growth so that they use their freedom and power to mold today's society into the best possible future one.

At birth, children are viewed as meaning-making organisms who contain little meaning. As they grow, children construct meaning by actively interpreting the world to themselves. It is the role of education to shape the meaning created by children and the ways in which children make meaning so that they can act to support appropriate visions of a future good society.

Children are not viewed primarily from a developmental context that emphasizes their living fully in each stage through which they pass. As they grow, children progress toward an educated state from which they can contribute to society's reconstruction. It is the role of education to speed children toward this educated state.

Children as Meaning Makers

Children are viewed as meaning makers. They make meaning for themselves as the result of being stimulated by the environment in which they live:

> We now know that each man creates his own unique world, that he, and he alone, generates whatever reality he can ever know. . . . [W]e do not "get" meaning from things, we assign meaning. . . . In other words, whatever is out there [in our environment] isn't anything until we make it something, and then it "is" whatever we make it. (Postman & Weingartner, 1969, pp. 98–99)

There are several corollaries to the assumption that people are meaning makers:

- Subjective reality within learners is distinguished from objective reality outside of learners.
- Meaning is assumed to reside in individuals' subjective realities and not outside of individuals in objective reality.
- Children are believed to make meaning as a result of being stimulated by their environment (which includes teachers, other children, the community, and any other experiences they might encounter in their world).
- It is assumed that children actively make meaning for themselves; they are not passive absorbers of meaning conveyed by agents external to themselves.

This view of the child as a meaning maker is portrayed in Figure 5.1.

❖ **Figure 5.1** The child as a meaning maker.

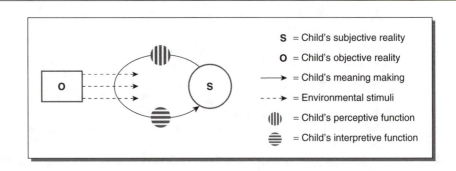

In viewing children as meaning makers, four aspects of children's minds are distinguished:

1. Children's minds have contents, called "meanings," that include such things as their knowledge, beliefs, facts, theories, affiliations, fears, and hopes.

2. The contents of children's minds are stored in a "meaning structure" that contains, among other things, the organization of meaning in children's minds and the functions governing the intake, output, and redistribution of their meanings.

3. Children have perceptual filters and functions that control the types of stimuli they perceive from the many sensations that impinge on them. These filters and functions control the manner in which children perceive reality. (The vertical crosshatching on the meaning making arrow in Figure 5.1 portrays them.)

4. Children's minds have "interpretive functions" that control how they give meaning to the sensations they perceive and thus how they interpret reality. (They are portrayed by the horizontal crosshatching on the meaning making arrow in Figure 5.1.)

Children's perceptive functions, interpretive functions, and meaning structures are important to Social Reconstructionists because they affect the manner in which children perceive, interpret, and organize reality. They affect, for example, whether or not children hear certain overtones in peoples' complaints about society, how they interpret the overtones they hear, and how they give meaning to that information by fitting it into their meaning structure. While creating or teaching curricula, educators design and use instructional strategies to influence these structures and functions as well as children's meanings.

Children in Society

Children are viewed primarily as members of a social group, not as individuals. They realize their potential in social interaction with others, are educated in a social community, and act as part of a social group to bring into existence the future good society.

Two types of communities to which children belong are of interest to Social Reconstructionists: the community outside the school, in which children spend most of their life and on which they must act to reconstruct society; and the community in the school, over which the educator exercises control. Social Reconstructionists have the task of figuring out how to both (1) bring aspects of society that function outside the school into the school so that they can be used to educate children while they are in school, and (2) bring endeavors that take place during school time outside the school so that children can have firsthand experiences in their community. Bringing children's lives from outside the school into school involves dealing with all aspects of their lives, including their experiences, thoughts, feelings, dreams, and ways of relating, valuing, and acting, which are relevant both inside and outside the school.

Learning

Social Reconstructionists view learning from the perspective of constructivism. They regard learning as active assimilation of new experiences into learners' meaning structures in such a way as to force those meaning structures to accommodate to the new experiences (McLaren & Giroux, 1997, p. 34). There are two significant components of this view of learning. The first hinges on the phrase "meaning making": learning occurs when learners construct meaning out of their sensations. Learning is a process of actively assimilating and accommodating experience in such a way that it makes sense to the learner. The second component of this view of learning depends on the concept of "meaning structure": learning is based on what one already knows about the world, and it is meaningful only when it can be accommodated to one's overall conception of reality. As a result, learning must happen in the context in which what is learned occurs and in terms of what one already knows. Thus, educators

> should construct curricula that draw upon the cultural resources that students bring with them to school. This suggests not only taking the languages, histories, experiences, and voices of students seriously, but also integrating what is taught in schools with the dynamics of everyday life. This points to developing curricula that . . . address the real problems and concerns that students face on a local, societal, and global level. (Giroux, 2006, p. 6)

Meaning Making

Learners are viewed as active agents in their learning. Learning is not a passive process of incorporating objective reality into the mind by simple absorption. Learners actively choose from among their many sensory experiences those that they will become cognizant of (the perceptive function) and interpret those sensations into perceptions that have meaning in relation to their existing meaning structures (the interpretive function). As Postman and Weingartner wrote in 1969:

> We do not get our perceptions from the "things" around us. Our perceptions come from us. This does not mean that there is nothing outside of our skins. It does mean that whatever is "out there" can never be known except as it is filtered through a human nervous system. We can never get outside of our own skins. "Reality" is a perception, located somewhere behind the eyes. . . . What we perceive is largely a function of our previous experiences, our assumptions, and our purposes (i.e., needs). In other words, the perceiver decides what an object is, where it is, and why it is according to his purpose and the assumptions that he makes at any given time. You tend to perceive what you want and need to perceive, and what your past experience has led you to assume will "work" for you. . . . If rain is falling from the sky, some people will head for shelter, others will enjoy walking in it. Their perceptions of "what is happening" are different as reflected in the fact that they "do" different things. The fact that both groups will agree to the sentence "It is raining" does not mean they will perceive the "event" in the same ways. (pp. 90–91)

Both choosing which sensations to perceive and choosing how to interpret those perceptions are active functions on the part of learners and uniquely determined by their meaning structures. The subjective reality learners come to know results from their personally impressing meaning onto objective reality.

It is important to note that what learners come to know is not nature itself but nature actively interpreted through such things as the structure and lexicon of their language. Learners incorporate into themselves the stimuli impinging on them by passing them through their perceptive and interpretive functions while applying meaning-giving filters to them such as their language and modes of thinking. In McLuhanesque terms, the medium (the mind) is the message (what one knows) in the sense that the operators governing the working of the mind actively mold psychological sensations into mental perceptions.

Meaning Structure

One learns things in terms of what one already knows and in the context in which they occur.

First, it is believed that learning can take place *only* in relation to what one already knows. For experiences to make sense to a learner, they must be capable of being accommodated into the learner's meaning structure. This means that they must be of a form and contain a content that relates to both the learner's meaning structure and the totality of his or her past learning experiences. The mere occurrence of a "psychological fact" does not result in learning. It is only when the occurrence is related to other phases of the learner's experience and capable of being related to and incorporated into the learner's meaning structure that learning occurs.

It is, in fact, learners' meaning structures that give import to what they perceive. That is, whatever learners hear or see will be meaningful to them only on their own terms and not on the terms of the emitter of the information: what they learn will be a function of their past experiences, their assumptions, and their purposes—and not those of the stimulator of their sensations. This means that

> one cannot expect positive results from an educational . . . program which fails to respect the particular view of the world held by the people. . . . The starting point for organizing the program content of education . . . must be the present, existential, concrete situation, reflecting the aspiration of the people. Utilizing certain basic contradictions, we must pose this existential, concrete, present situation to the people as a problem which challenges them and requires a response, not just at the intellectual level, but at the level of action. (Freire, 1970, pp. 84–85)

Second, it is believed that, for valid meaning to be infused into anything, it must be learned in the context in which it occurs and in the context of a total pattern of events. The Social Reconstructionist's concern is not the acquisition and then organization of unrelated atomistic facts but rather the learning of gestalts of occurrences in organic relatedness. To be considered worthwhile, learning must be the product of insight into the patterns that relate the parts of an event to the total occurrence of the event.

The Nature of Learning

Learning has a number of important interrelated characteristics.

- Learning is primarily a social act rather than an individual act. In both process and product, in both means and ends, it aims mainly at "social self-realization" (Brameld, 1950). Learning requires not only that a social group acquire knowledge but also that it reach a consensus concerning both the nature and truth of that knowledge. Learning is always directed toward the achievement of social consensus or agreement. In fact, "the objective of the entire [learning] process is to attain a consensus upon which the group can depend and from which it can act" to reconstruct society (p. 546).

- Learning takes place in both classrooms and communities. It requires immersion in and interaction with a social group that "extends beyond the school proper into the community" (Brameld, 1950, p. 533). This means that curricula require two separate social settings for learning: inside and outside the school.

- Learning takes place through language and communication, which include such things as group discussion, talking, singing, acting, sociodrama, sculpture, group processing, and value clarification. From a practical point of view, learning through communication transforms the traditional classroom:

  Instead of communication being limited to the imparting of indirect evidence from textbooks, pictures, or lectures, learning takes place by the reciprocal expression among students and teachers alike. The effort to *articulate* interests [feelings or thoughts] is encouraged and respected. Likewise the effort to *interpret* all evidence provided by science, art, or history replaces the passive recitation, which does virtually nothing to bring such evidence into vital relationship with one's own experience. The more that genuine back-and-forth communication takes place, the more spontaneous it becomes, and the more facile and precise the meanings that emerge. (Brameld, 1950, p. 542)

- Learning involves some form of direct experience:

  Fundamental to learning is the kind of evidence about our wants which springs from our own experience, and of which we ourselves become directly aware. Education that fails to provide generous opportunity for such experience . . . cannot hope to reach successful practice of social consensus. (Brameld, 1950, p. 540)

- Learning is not limited to firsthand experiences, but Social Reconstructionists try to keep learning as close to firsthand experience as possible. Thus, if a group is to learn something like history, of which they cannot have firsthand experiences, educators attempt to do such things as provide firsthand accounts of occurrences or engage students in simulations that approximate experiences.

- Valuable learning requires not just thought, but also an emotional response to what is understood that includes commitment to a social position and action directed toward reconstructing society. Counts, writing in 1932, hints that learning has this tripartite nature of thought, commitment, and action when he writes that society requires learners who, while "capable of gathering and digesting facts, are at the same time able to think in terms of life, make decisions, and act" (1932b, p. 22). In the language of the last quarter of the 20th century, learning requires praxis: "reflection and action, in such radical interaction that if one is sacrificed—even in part—the other immediately suffers" (Freire, 1970, p. 75).

- Learning requires interaction of learners with the environment outside themselves. The learner must actively interact with someone or some situation to make meaning. In terms of Figure 5.1, the learner (S) does not learn in isolation from stimuli coming from an outside reality (0). Rather, the learner learns as a result of his or her meaning making endeavors by engaging and interacting with stimuli from an outside source. That is, there must be a learner (S) actively interacting with an outside reality (0) for meaning to be made and learning to take place within the learner. Interactive learning best occurs in social groups where both the group affects the learner and the learner affects the group. Here it is important that "children . . . continually share in a social environment which they enrich by that sharing, and which enriches them" (Brameld, 1950, p. 533).

Teaching

At one level, the intent of teaching is to reconstruct society. At another level the intent of teaching is to stimulate students to reconstruct themselves so that they can contribute to the reconstruction of society. At still another level the intent of teaching is to stimulate students to learn *how* to reconstruct society. Stimulating students to learn how to reconstruct society involves helping them construct a set of meanings, meaning structures, perceptive functions, and interpretive functions so that when they encounter social problems they can analyze and understand them, formulate a vision of better society where those problems do not exist, and act in such a way as to eliminate those social problems.

It is important to note that it is not just students' meanings that Social Reconstructionists want to have an impact on. They want to stimulate students to construct a *method* of perceiving and interpreting social events, developing a social vision, and acting that will allow them to confront as yet unknown future social crises. Providing students with a method is critical. Given the Social Reconstruction belief in social relativity, it is important that students be taught an *approach* to confronting social problems rather than a fixed formula that has proved useful in confronting past or present social problems. Society's past and present condition is not the only consideration here—at stake is society's future.

Social Reconstructionists use a variety of instructional methods. The two discussed here are the discussion and experience methods. Both depend on having students learn indirectly through the media they encounter while engaging in educational activities, media whose overt messages may not be their most important ones.

The Discussion Method

Group discussion is a social means of educating a group of persons. It requires both a social context and social interactions. It is considered an ideal educational medium because it uses language to help groups and individuals construct and reconstruct their knowledge of themselves, their knowledge of society and its strengths and weaknesses, a vision of a future good society, and a strategy for transforming the current society into the future good society. Here language is viewed broadly as a primary mediator of human perception, learning, knowing, feeling, and acting.

The discussion method of teaching involves engaging a group of students in a conversation while the teacher elicits "from students the meanings that they have already stored up so that they may subject those meanings to a testing and verifying, reordering and reclassifying, modifying and extending process" (Postman & Weingartner, 1969, p. 62). The assumption underlying this mode of teaching is that for students to reconstruct their already established knowledge and ways of knowing, they must regurgitate them so that they can be examined and reconstructed during the discussion process. Group discussion accomplishes this transformation and reconstruction of knowledge by getting participants to disclose to the group their social understanding so that the group can help them reconstruct their social knowledge in light of the knowledge of the group as a whole. Knowledge can thus be reaffirmed and elaborated by the group to give greater insight into it; shown to be inaccurate or incorrect, so that it can be made accurate or correct by the group's pointing out of its errors; shown to be inadequate because it lacks connection to appropriate social values, so that it can be made more adequate through group processes; or shown to be deficient because it lacks the necessary commitment and inspiration, so that the group can help develop such in the participant. The process involves getting participants to expose their knowledge to the group so that the group can comment on that knowledge in such a way as to allow participants to reconstruct their knowledge in light of the group's comments and peer pressure—all under the careful guidance of teachers who differentially reinforce group understandings and values to guide the group to acquire understandings and values consistent with those of the teacher.

The content for a discussion comes from those involved in the discussion. It is a re-presentation to the group by its members of things they have experienced or already understood and now want to understand more or in a new way. Thus, the actual social experiences and knowledge of those involved in the dialogue are crucial. The discussion is defined by those experiences and that knowledge and must take into account those experiences and that knowledge as the persons who have had them perceive them. Although the discussion is defined by the perceived experiences and knowledge of its participants, it is not limited by those experiences and that knowledge, because the social interactions that take place during a discussion can expand on the experiences of its participants (as when two people's thoughts are joined together to generate a new thought neither would have been capable of generating alone) and because the group can re-present the experiences of participants back to them so that they can see them in a new way and thus perceive, experience, or construct them anew (as when one person's interpretation of the meaning of a particular experience allows another person who has had a similar experience to understand that experience in a new way).

Important here is "starting where the people are" and participants' prior social experiences and knowledge (Adams, 1972, p. 516). Social Reconstructionists believe that a discussion (and a person's education) must start where the participants are; must start with what people have experienced and what they understand, as they themselves perceive them; and must relate to their prior experiences and knowledge. As a result, Social Reconstructionists must either find a way to tap into the prior experiences and knowledge of those who will experience a curriculum or find a way to provide them with the experiences and knowledge the curriculum will build on. Important here is the centrality of the social experiences and knowledge of those participating in the discussion. Anything said during the discussion as well as any input into the discussion from sources such as outside experts, books, movies, or the like must relate to the prior experiences and knowledge of participants if they are to benefit from them.

At their best, group discussions have three crucial components: thought, commitment, and action. The potential for all three must be present in a group discussion for it to be vital. If a group discussion lacks the potential for action, then the thinking that takes place during it degenerates into useless verbalism. If a group discussion lacks the potential for thought, then the action that takes place as a result of it degenerates into meaningless activism (Freire, 1970, pp. 75–77). If a group discussion lacks the potential for commitment, then the thinking that takes place during it will lack the power to be transformed into action. If a group discussion does not carry the potential for thought about society as it is and as it ought to be, the potential for commitment to transforming current society as it is into society as it ought to be, and the potential for action directed toward such, then the discussion is not vital within the context of the Social Reconstruction ideology.

Social Reconstruction group discussions take place at two levels: (1) an "explicit" level at which students are openly challenged by analysis of the present social crisis and vision of the future good society, and (2) a "hidden" level at which students are subconsciously conditioned by group norms to have a particular social perspective and set of social values. At the explicit level of discussion, students are aware of the messages being communicated to them and they consciously and with understanding construct their concepts and conceptual structures. At this level, they are aware of their decisions and choices and what is happening to them while they are being educated. At the hidden level, educators manipulate the "hidden curriculum" to subconsciously condition students to a way of viewing, valuing, and judging what they experience by subtly socializing them to the educators' perspectives on the world. At this level, the rules and norms of the group discussion educate members without their understanding what is occurring.

When operating at the explicit level, discussion tends to proceed by having students learn about society, verbally analyze society, explicitly formulate a vision of a future society, develop a social conscience that impels them to commit themselves to transform the existing society into the future better society, and decide how to act to implement the future good society. At this level, instruction depends on the power of ideas to move students to reconstruct themselves and society. The belief is that if people think about and understand the reasons for a reconstructed society, they will act in such a manner as to bring it into existence.

When operating at the hidden level, the discussion process and the social environment in which the discussion takes place mold students to think and act in accordance with an educator's beliefs. During discussions, teachers provide the rules for discussion, the desired social perspective and values, and the model for the modes of thinking in which students are to engage. The instructive function is embedded in the language, questions, evidence, value judgments, modes of argumentation, and criteria of relevance the teacher uses during discussion and urges students to use by example. Thus, if "sharing" (as compared to competing) is valued, sharing (and the belief that sharing is good) will be directly conditioned into students during the discussion by their being required to conform to discussion norms that demand sharing behavior and censor competitive behavior. Similarly, if "critical analysis" of social forces is valued, critical analysis will be demonstrated by teachers, students' engagement in critical analysis will be rewarded by teachers, and students will learn critical analysis by conforming to discussion norms that value and reward critical analysis. In these cases, the norms of the discussion and the behaviors expected during the discussion become forces that mold students. Here it is the medium (the discussion itself) more than the message (the topic of discussion) that is designed to provide the teaching.

The Experience Method

Social Reconstructionists believe that it is from one's experiences *with* (and knowledge of) an existing social crisis and in response to a perceived difficulty that one has experienced *within* that social crisis that one is motivated to understand the nature of society, envision a better society, and act to reconstruct society. This means that one's experiences (and related knowledge) play a crucial role in the Social Reconstruction ideology. It also means that *if* Social Reconstructionists want group participants to acquire a particular understanding of a social crisis *and* they have not already experienced that crisis, *then* they must provide for those participants appropriate experiences that will result in the corresponding appropriate understandings. This is why Myles Horton insisted that participants at Highlander have experiences with exploited laborers before attending Highlander. This is also why the teacher in the sixth-grade mathematics classroom described earlier referred to well-defined student experiences in the community, took students on field trips, and had them engage in simulations.

Important here is that students obtain more than knowledge from a social experience. They also acquire feelings (including feelings about such things as their self-concept and their power to act and make a difference in their world), a social perspective, and a set of values about what is socially just or unjust, good or bad, fair or unfair, right or wrong.

The experience method involves placing students in an environment where they encounter a social crisis and learn from those who usually function in that environment. Experiences that students might participate in include public protests, recycling, visiting the elderly in nursing homes, rehabilitating public places in depressed urban or rural areas, and working with battered women, the homeless, or the poor in shelters. The environments in which students are placed and those with whom they work are specially chosen to educate students about particular social problems. It is assumed that students will absorb the attitudes and values, modes of perception and interpretation, and worldview of those normally engaged in the environment—because they will experience firsthand the reasons for these perspectives and because they will get carried away by the immediacy of the experience in such a manner that they will reconstruct themselves to be like the people who normally function in the environment. Here teaching involves the provision of firsthand experience with social crises; counseling sessions designed to help students adjust to the environment in which they find themselves; and discussion sessions intended to help them construct meaning from their experiences. Counseling and discussion sessions are a crucial part of the experience method, for in these sessions students are debriefed and reconstruct their previously held beliefs.

The Teacher as Colleague

Social Reconstructionists view the teacher as a colleague or companion whom students can look up to rather than as an authority who has control over them. The teacher and the students are considered to be on the same side of both the discussion and the experience. They are allied against the evils of the world. They complement each other rather than combat each other. They teach and learn from each other: "There are not teachers and students, but teacher-students, and student-teachers" (Freire, 1970, p. 67).

The teacher is not viewed as knowing everything and the students as knowing nothing; rather, both bring experiences to share with each other during instruction. It is not that the teacher actively thinks and the students passively absorb; rather, both actively engage in meaning making in the presence of each other. It is not that the teacher talks and the students listen; rather, both talk and listen as partners in a mutual endeavor. It is not that the teacher chooses content and the students accept it; rather, both have experiences that contribute to the content of instruction. It is not that only students reveal their inner meanings to the group for analysis; rather, both students and teachers contribute their inner meanings to the group for scrutiny for both their own and the group's educational benefit. It is not that teachers teach and the students learn; rather, both teach each other and learn from each other. It is not that teachers are emotionally disengaged and detached from discussions and experiences; rather, both teachers and students become emotionally engaged in learning and present to each other their thoughts and values—and these responses are considered interconnected. As Freire writes, "authentic education is not carried on by 'A' *for* 'B' or by 'A' *about* 'B,' but rather by 'A' *with* 'B,' mediated by the world" (1970, p. 82).

Characteristics of Teaching

Several characteristics of what Social Reconstructionists consider good teaching are common to both the discussion and experience methods.

- Both are group methods and make use of group pressures to teach students. Not only are the messages often social, but also the medium used to convey the messages is a social medium.
- Both methods depend on the relevance of their message in students' lives. In the experience method, relevance comes from the immediacy of the situation in which students find themselves. In the discussion method, topics often come from the expressed concerns of students.
- In both methods, teachers find out what students know, draw it out of them, and help them reflect, analyze, and reconstruct their meanings in a value-laden context—where values shape much of what and how students learn.
- The important messages in both methods are often subliminal ones conveyed through the learning medium—such as the rules of proper discussion or the proper values (for instance, social justice) with which to view and interpret experiences.

Characteristics of Teachers

Three characteristics of teachers deserve mention, beyond those implied in the above discussion.

Social Reconstructionists view the attitudes, interpretations, and visions of teachers to be of crucial importance:

> There can be no significant innovation in education that does not have at its center the attitude of teachers. . . . The beliefs, feelings, and assumptions of teachers are the air of a learning environment; they determine the quality of life within it. (Postman & Weingartner, 1969, p. 33)

Teachers must be capable of reflecting on themselves and on their society and of using critical analysis to "raise fundamental questions about the social, economic, and political forces shaping their lives and the lives of their students so that they can all be better prepared for participating in—and changing—the larger world" (McLaren, 2007, p. 192). That is, they must be "able to critically analyze the ideologies, values, and interests that inform their role as teachers and the cultural politics they promote in the classroom" (Giroux, 2006, p. 7); "able to analyze their relationship with the larger society in order to critically apprehend themselves as social agents capable of recognizing how they might be complicitous with forms of oppression and human suffering" (Giroux, 2006, p. 7); able to analyze the deep cultural, social, political, and economic forces that contribute to injustice and inequality in their society; and able to envision a future better society and act to bring it into existence. Giroux sums this up when he says that teachers are

> transformative intellectuals. . . . They understand the nature of their own self-formation, [understand the nature of their society,] have some vision of the future, see the importance of education as a public discourse, and have a sense of mission in providing students with what they need to become critical citizens. . . . They believe something, say what they believe, and offer their belief to others in a framework that always makes it debatable and open to critical inquiry. . . . Above all, [they are] . . . able to exercise power. Pedagogy is always related to power . . . to shaping public life and school relationships. (1992, p. 15)

Social Reconstructionists believe that teachers should be "qualified to provide . . . vigorous, enlightened, and public-spirited . . . leadership, ready and competent to challenge the power of selfish interests and to champion the cause of the masses of the people" (Counts, 1934, p. 558). This means both that teachers must be "people on fire with an awareness of injustice and the determination to correct it" (Adams & Horton, 1975, p. 501) and that "teachers should deliberately reach for power and then make the most of their conquest" (Counts, 1932b, p. 28)—that teachers should be leaders rather than followers.

Knowledge

The Social Construction of Knowledge

Social Reconstructionists view worthwhile knowledge to be a social construction. Here, "knowledge (truth) is socially constructed, culturally mediated, and historically situated . . . [and] dominant [social] discourses determine what counts as true, important, and relevant" (McLaren, 2007, p. 210). In addition, worthwhile knowledge is viewed as being constructed out of social interactions for social, political, economic, or cultural purposes:

> Knowledge is a *social construction* deeply rooted in a nexus of power relations[;] . . . it is a product of agreement or consent between individuals who live out particular social relations (e.g., of class, race, and gender) and who live in particular junctures in time. . . . [T]he world we live in is constructed symbolically by the mind through social interaction with others and is heavily dependent on culture, context, custom, and historical specificity. . . . [S]ome constructions of reality are legitimated and celebrated by the dominant culture while others clearly are not. . . . [S]ome forms of knowledge have more power and legitimacy than

others. For instance, in many schools . . . science and math . . . are favored over the liberal arts. This can be explained by the link between the needs of big business to compete in world markets and the [social] imperative . . . to bring "excellence" back to the schools. (pp. 196–197)

Knowledge and Value

Knowledge is a "value-laden social construction" (Joseph, Bravmann, Windschitl, Mikel, & Green, 2000, p. 146). It embodies both truth and value. It embraces both intelligence and a corresponding moral stance with respect to that intelligence (whether in the form of meaning, functions, or structures). Knowledge and values are interconnected. This interconnection has its origin in Social Reconstructionists' view of reality from the perspective of current social crisis and a future good society. By processing reality through a vision of a future good society, intelligence becomes good or bad, worthwhile or worthless, moral or immoral, ethical or unethical (Giroux, 2005, pp. 29, 67), emancipatory or oppressive (McLaren, 2007, p. 198) as it supports or refutes an educator's utopian vision. Values and intelligence are considered real in the same way, and little differentiation is made between the questions "Is *x* real?" and "Is *x* moral?" A scientific fact (political interpretation, religious hope, or affiliative emotion) is judged by the question, "Is it worthwhile intelligence with respect to the analysis of the existing society and projection of the future society?" Knowledge is not an impartial quantity and knowing is not a neutral affair. Knowledge is of worth because it contributes to the attainment of a future good society, and the construction of knowledge is a moral activity inseparable from the cultural activity of searching for and implementing a satisfactory vision for the future good society.

Knowledge and Reality

Social Reconstructionists distinguish between subjective reality and objective reality. They believe that worthwhile knowledge resides within the subjective reality of both individuals and society. For them,

> there is no such thing as "subject matter" in the abstract. "Subject matter" exists in the minds of perceivers. And what each one thinks it is, is what it is. We have been acting in schools as if knowledge lies outside the learner, which is why we have the kinds of curricula . . . we have. But knowledge . . . is what *we* know *after* we have learned. It is an outcome of perception and is as unique and subjective as any other perception. (Postman & Weingartner, 1969, p. 92)

Worthwhile knowledge does not reside outside of people in such things as books or magazines. It does not reside in "words" separate from people. It resides in the meanings people create for themselves. Knowledge is defined in terms of the subjective meaning it has to its possessors. For Social Reconstructionists, what society and people believe to be true and valuable is more important than what might be true or valuable in any absolute sense.

Knowledge resides in its possessor, originates in that possessor's environmental interactions, and is what each person interprets knowledge to be within the context of a relativistic social consensus. This is a crucial assumption. Knowledge's truth and worth are verifiable through social consensus. What the majority of the members of a society believe to be true is true for those persons:

> The truth of those experiences most vital in the social life of any culture are determined . . . by the extent to which they are *agreed upon* by the largest possible number of the group concerned. Without this factor of agreement or consensus, the experience simply is not "true." (Brameld, 1950, p. 456)

Knowledge is relativistic in nature, and its truth and value depend upon the society within which it exists. For Social Reconstructionists, there is no such thing as absolute knowledge that is true for all peoples under all circumstances in all cultures.

This does not mean that some knowledge is not better for certain purposes and certain peoples than other knowledge. That knowledge which supports educators' analysis of our past and current society and vision of the future good society is the knowledge of most worth to them. It is that knowledge which educators desire their society to accept and acquire through social consensus.

The Creation of Knowledge

In discussing the creation of knowledge, two cases need to be distinguished: the creation of knowledge by members of society and the creation of curriculum knowledge.

Members of society create the knowledge they possess. Knowledge does not come into existence by itself and passively reside in objective reality. It comes into existence when someone actively impresses meaning on sensory data, and it resides within the subjective consciousness of its possessor. The process by which a person actively loads meaning and value onto sensory data is the process by which knowledge is created. Sensory data or objective information without meaning and value loaded onto it by a person is not called knowledge. As such, the meaning structure, the perceptive functions, and the interpretive functions of a person are crucial to Social Reconstructionists. They are the operators that give meaning and value to the knowledge a person creates. In many ways, it is these meaning-giving operators that educators wish to orient toward their future good society. In so doing, educators bring the knower to share their vision of the future rather than simply cause him or her to be informed about that vision.

The knowledge curriculum developers embed in their curricula has its origin in their subjective interpretation of the nature of society in the past, present, and future. It derives from educators' personal analysis of their world. It is chosen for inclusion in curriculum because it acts to convert the child into a participant in the developers' visions of the future good society. It is embedded in curriculum with the intention of aligning children's knowledge and ways of knowing with those of developers and of activating children to reconstruct society. This view of the source of curriculum knowledge is portrayed in Figure 5.2. Note here that curriculum knowledge has its origin in educators' subjective view of society and that it is specifically directed toward affecting the subjective consciousness of children so as to make them into change agents who swell the social consensus that will in turn hopefully align society with educators' visions. Objective information, such as that possessed by the academic disciplines, is of little use to these educators, except as value can be loaded onto it so that it supports their vision of the future good society. Academic skills are also of little use except as they can be used as analytical tools for the purpose of reconstructing the knowledge base of individuals and their societies. This leads some Reconstructionists to even believe that the "enlightenment notion of reason needs to be reformulated . . . because [it denies] . . . its own historical construction and ideological principals" (Giroux, 2005, p. 70).

❖ **Figure 5.2** The Social Reconstruction view of the source of curriculum knowledge.

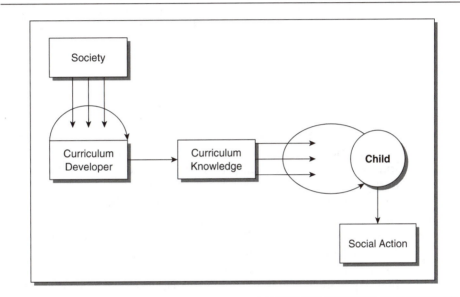

Characteristics of Knowledge

Six other attributes of knowledge need mention.

1. Knowledge is not viewed as a purely intellectual quantity. Both people's "gut" knowledge and their "intellectual" knowledge are important and interdependent. Both their "unrational" (subconscious) and their "rational" (conscious) knowledge are valued.

2. Knowledge is both cognitive and experiential in nature. Knowledge is not just "information about" but also "experience with" a subject. Knowledge is based both in people's experiences and in their ability to understand those experiences.

3. Although knowledge is a personal attribute of the perceiver, Social Reconstructionists are concerned with the knowledge possessed by society. Educators wish to reconstruct society by reconstructing the social consensus of the masses—the summative total of the knowledge held by the many individuals who make up society.

4. Social Reconstructionists take a gestalt approach to knowledge, viewing it in relation to other knowledge. Knowledge has meaning and value because it fits into a structure or pattern. Individual bits of information, atomistically unrelated to any organizing theme or vision, have little value.

5. Social Reconstructionism views knowledge as "interdisciplinary in nature" and questions "the fundamental categories of all disciplines" (Giroux, 1992, p. 10). It creates "new forms of knowledge through its emphasis on breaking down disciplinary boundaries and creating new spheres in which knowledge can be produced" (Giroux, 2005, p. 69). As Giroux emphasizes, "the struggle over the production and creation of knowledge" is "an . . . issue . . . of power, ethics, and politics" (p. 69).

6. Social Reconstructionists highlight the ethical and political dimensions of knowledge and its use by emphasizing that schools "must be seen as places where culture, power, and knowledge come together to produce . . . a vision of the future," a vision that determines what knowledge we consider to be true, ethical, emancipatory, and worthwhile (Giroux, 2006, pp. 4–5).

Evaluation

Social Reconstructionists do not usually use formal objective evaluation during curriculum development. They primarily use subjective evaluation.

They recommend a gestalt field theory approach to the evaluation of both curricula and students. Questions asked are not of the form "How does curriculum z or student y measure up to standard m?" but rather of the form "How does curriculum z or student y measure up to standard m in a particular circumstance?" This is necessary because the particular time, place, and setting in which social crises are confronted are constantly changing, as are the students confronting them, and it is believed that the only valid assessments are those made under real-world circumstances.

Evaluation is not a simple comparison of expected outcomes to achieved outcomes, but rather a comparison of the evaluee—whether curriculum or student—to both expectations and to the field in which the evaluee functions. In the case of curriculum evaluation, this involves taking account of the social environment in which the curriculum is examined. In the case of student evaluation, this involves taking account of both the student's performance and the student's ability to perform. For example, in evaluating a child's self-concept with respect to the variable "power over environment," one would use a function including the following parameters: the power the child exhibits, the power the child is capable of possessing, the power the child thinks other children have, and the power the child thinks he or she has. Here the relation is between (1) the power the child possesses compared to the power available to him, and (2) the power the child thinks he has compared to the power he thinks he is capable of possessing.

For Social Reconstructionists, summative student evaluation and curriculum evaluation are inextricably tied together in the particular social environment in which students live. As Horton says, the measure of a curriculum's "effectiveness—perhaps the only valid one—comes when a workshop participant returns home. Many never become active. Others become devoted to fundamental social change" (Adams & Horton, 1975, pp. 215–216). Here curriculum is evaluated through student performance outside of school. The same holds true for student evaluation. What students learn is thought to be testable only in their everyday life outside of school as they work to reconstruct themselves and society in light of the curriculum's vision of the future good society.

During instruction, and particularly during group discussions, teachers provide students with feedback about their meanings, meaning structures, perceptive functions, and interpretive functions—for the purpose of helping students gain insight that will enable them to reconstruct and transform those meanings, meaning structures, perceptive functions, and interpretive functions and become more insightful and powerful in analyzing, understanding, envisioning, and acting in social situations. Evaluation and feedback are for the purpose of aiding students in reconstructing themselves so that they can in turn aid in the reconstruction of society.

Concluding Perspective

The Social Reconstruction ideology has done much to introduce knowledge of the social dimensions of education to our schools, helping us comprehend that education is a social process, that the hidden curriculum has enormous influence on learners, and that all knowledge carries with it social values. It has brought to the attention of educators the realization that they must take value stances themselves and that they must attend to the social, political, and moral values of the children they teach. Social Reconstructionism's insistence that schools consider the problems of our society and the injustices done to its members has had a powerful effect on schools and added an important dimension to their academic and vocational concerns. This ideology laid the seeds for the ways of thinking, feeling, and acting that help children deal with issues such as civil rights, racial and gender bias, and environmental pollution.

The ideology's influence on education formally began in 1932 when George Counts attacked the Learner Centered ideology for not attending to our society's problems and the injustices done to its members, asking, "Dare the school build a new social order?" This led to a split in the Progressive Education Association between advocates of the Social Reconstruction and Learner Centered ideologies—and was the blow that initiated the decline of the Learner Centered ideology's influence on education. Members of the ideology published numerous social justice textbooks during the Great Depression that deeply influenced schools. The ideology's influence declined during World War II and the McCarthy era. Social Reconstructionism regained its influence in the 1960s and 1970s through its involvement in educational programs supporting the civil rights movement, the women's movement, desegregation, Vietnam War protests, nuclear weapons and energy protests, and the early environmental pollution (recycling) movement. Its influence on schools lessened in the 1980s but began to grow again as the World War II generation of faculty began to retire and be replaced by critical theorists, postmodernists, social constructivists, and social justice advocates. At the beginning of the 21st century, large numbers of Social Reconstructionists were found on the faculties of schools of education promoting a social justice agenda and attempting to influence the next generation of teachers. By 2007 the ideology had begun to come under attack for its social justice agenda; however, environmental pollution and the energy crisis are possible prime issues for a newly reconfigured Social Reconstruction agenda. Figure 5.3 provides a rough estimation of those times when advocates of this ideology have been most active, with respect to their own norms, in attempting to influence American education.

❖ **Figure 5.3** Times of relative high and low activity of the Social Reconstruction ideology.

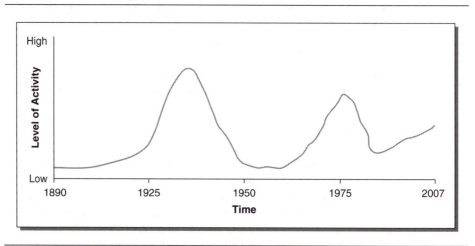

Activities that extend the ideas in this chapter are located on the Sage Web site at www.sagepub.com/schiroextensionactivities.

6

A Comparative Overview of the Curriculum Ideologies

❖

In the preceding four chapters of this book, I have described four curriculum ideologies: the Scholar Academic ideology, the Social Efficiency ideology, the Learner Centered ideology, and the Social Reconstruction ideology. In exploring each ideology, I have examined several essential aspects of its conceptual framework. These include educators' professional aims, conceptions of knowledge, views of learning, postures toward childhood, conceptions of teaching, and beliefs about evaluation. Thus far, these topics have been separately investigated in the context of each ideology. They will now be compared. Afterward, several as yet unmentioned aspects of the ideologies will be briefly examined.

Comparative Summary

Aims

Educators have professional aims that give meaning to their endeavors. The following questions allow their aims to be compared:

- What do educators conceive their professional aims to be?
- For what kind of clients or ideals do educators believe they work?
- Where do educators' vested interests lie?
- Do educators see themselves as responsible to a client whose vested interests are other than their own?

The aim of Scholar Academics is to perpetuate the existence of their discipline both by guaranteeing that future members of the discipline will exist (who will in turn carry on its traditions and further its epistemic development) and by building literacy for the discipline in the general public (so the public will support its endeavors and benefit from its discovered truths). This aim usually takes the form of extending the discipline by transmitting its essence to students. Educators conceive of themselves as working within their academic disciplines in such a way that their own curriculum construction endeavors coincide with those of their academic community.

The aim of Social Efficiency educators is to efficiently and scientifically carry out a task for a client (often society). Educators conceive of themselves as unbiased agents of their client whose vested interests are other than their own. Social Efficiency educators consider their vested interests to lie in how efficiently and scientifically they accomplish their task rather than in which task they accomplish.

The aim of Learner Centered educators is to stimulate the growth of people by designing experiences from which people can make meaning, fulfill their needs, and pursue their interests. This aim includes within it secondary aims of stimulating curriculum developers' own growth and the growth of teachers (both of whom support the growth of students). Learner Centered educators do not view themselves as responsible to a client but as serving the ideal of learners' growth. They believe their vested interests are identical to those of learners.

The aim of Social Reconstructionists is to eliminate undesirable aspects of their culture. They try to reconstruct their culture in such a way that its members will attain maximum satisfaction of their material and spiritual needs. Social Reconstructionists frequently conceive of themselves as working for downtrodden members of society whose material and spiritual needs are not being met. However, they view themselves as responsible primarily to their vision of the future better society. As such, Social Reconstructionists' vested interests (their vision of the future good society) are often different from those of the members of society for whom they work. Educators try to change this difference of opinion through education.

Knowledge

Educators' conceptions of the types of knowledge that are most valuable and most worthy of inclusion in curriculum are of great importance. The positions educators hold with respect to knowledge will be reviewed by examining the following questions:

- What is the nature of knowledge?
- What kinds of abilities does knowledge give to a person?
- What is the source of knowledge?
- From where does knowledge derive its authority?
- How is knowledge's truth verified?

Scholar Academics believe that worthwhile curriculum knowledge has the nature of didactic statements and modes of thinking that correspond to the intellectual traditions of academic disciplines. Knowledge gives the child the ability to understand. It has its source in objective reality as interpreted by the academic disciplines. It derives its authority from the academic discipline to which it belongs. Its truth is verified through a congruence method that evaluates the degree to which it reflects the essence of the academic discipline to which it belongs.

Social Efficiency educators believe that worthwhile curriculum knowledge has the nature of a capability for action. Knowledge gives children the ability to do things. It has its source in normative objective reality as interpreted by the members of society. It derives its authority from the impact it has in perpetuating society by providing individuals with the skills that they need to function within society. Its truth is verified through a congruence method that evaluates its correspondence to empirical reality as interpreted by members of society.

Learner Centered educators believe that worthwhile knowledge takes the form of personal meanings. Knowledge gives learners the ability to be themselves at their highest level of self-actualization. It has its source in individuals' direct experience with their world and their personal creative self-expression in response to experience as directed by their felt needs and personality structure. It derives its authority from the meaning it has to its possessor. Its truth is verifiable through the personal insight of individuals who possess it. Acquisition of knowledge is not a primary concern of Learner Centered educators—it is a first derivative of learning and a second derivative of growth, both of which are respectively more important than knowledge.

Social Reconstructionists believe that worthwhile curriculum knowledge takes a form that expresses both truth and value: both intelligence and a moral stance. Knowledge gives children the ability to interpret and reconstruct their society. It has its source in educators' interpretations (and, through educators' interpretations, children's interpretations) of the past, present, and future society. It derives its authority from educators' visions (and, through educators' visions, children's visions) of the future good society. Its truth is verified through educators' convictions regarding its ability to improve the existing society as it relates to their visions of the future good society.

Table 6.1 sets forth the answers given by each of the ideologies to these questions.

Educators' views about the nature of knowledge can be further examined by clarifying their answers to these two questions:

- Where does worthwhile knowledge reside: within the individual or outside the individual?
- What is more important about knowledge: the source from which it originates or the use to which it can be put?

Underlying these two questions is an implicit distinction between objective reality and subjective reality. Objective reality refers to things in the real world whose existence and nature can be impartially perceived and verified. Subjective reality refers to things in the minds of individuals that are constructed from their own unique observations, thoughts, feelings, temperaments, etc. Objective reality refers to those things (that is, objects) independent of the mind of the perceiver. Subjective reality refers to meanings or perceptions within people's (that is, subjects') minds.

Educators believe that worthwhile curriculum knowledge has its origins in either objective or subjective reality. Scholar Academic and Social Efficiency educators believe that knowledge originates and has a separate existence outside the individual—that is, they believe it exists in the objective, publicly accessible world of reality. In contrast, Learner Centered and Social Reconstruction educators believe that knowledge originates and exists in the subjective minds of individuals and is dependent on the

❖ **Table 6.1**   A comparison of the ideologies' views regarding knowledge.

Knowledge	Scholar Academic	Social Efficiency	Learner Centered	Social Reconstruction
The nature of knowledge is . . .	didactic statements	capabilities for action	personal meanings	intelligence and a moral stance
Knowledge gives the ability . . .	to understand	to do	to actualize oneself	to interpret and reconstruct society
The source of knowledge is . . .	objective reality as interpreted by the academic disciplines	normative objective reality as socially interpreted	individuals' personal creative response to experience	individuals' interpretation of society's past, present, and future
Knowledge derives its authority from . . .	the academic disciplines	its ability to perpetuate society through skills provided to its members	the meaning it has to its possessor	individuals' visions of the future good society
The truth of knowledge is verified by . . .	finding the degree to which it reflects the essence of an academic discipline	seeing if it corresponds to society's view of the nature of empirical reality	the personal insights of its possessor	individuals' beliefs in its ability to improve society

subjective meanings of those individuals. As a result, Scholar Academic and Social Efficiency educators believe that knowledge is universal and that anyone can come to understand it in its true form. In contrast, Learner Centered and Social Reconstruction educators consider knowledge to be idiosyncratic to the individuals who possess it in that each individual understands knowledge in his or her own unique way, which is not easily accessible or comprehensible to anyone other than that individual. Thus, even though Scholar Academic educators believe that knowledge has its origins in the objective interpretations of the academic disciplines and Social Efficiency educators believe that knowledge has its origins in the normative reality of society, they both act on the belief that knowledge originates outside the individual. Similarly, even though Learner Centered educators believe that knowledge has its origins in individuals' creative response to their personal experiences and Social Reconstruction educators believe that knowledge has its origins in individuals' interpretations of social events, they both act on the belief that knowledge is created by the individual who possesses it and that it has its origins in subjective reality.

Educators can also be differentiated according to whether they value knowledge primarily because of the source from which it originates or because of the uses to which it can be put. Scholar Academics believe that knowledge's value comes primarily from the fact that it has its origins in the academic disciplines, while Learner Centered educators believe that knowledge is valuable primarily because it is created by the individual who possesses it. In both cases, knowledge is believed to be valuable because of its origins and not because of its uses. In contrast, Social Efficiency and Social Reconstruction educators value knowledge primarily for the uses to which it can be put. Social Efficiency educators believe that knowledge is useful and thus important because of its ability to sustain and perpetuate the best of our present society. Social Reconstruction educators believe that knowledge is useful and thus important because it allows individuals to act to bring into existence a society better than the present one.

If we correlate the questions "Are the origins of knowledge in objective or subjective reality?" and "Does knowledge's importance come from its source or its use?" we obtain a four-cell matrix that illustrates the relationship among the ideologies (see Figure 6.1). In this matrix, the ideologies can be compared according to whether their position is to the right or left of the vertical axis and whether it is above or below the horizontal axis. Figure 6.2 substitutes in the place of the name of each ideology a visual model of the essence of its views of the relationship between subjective and objective reality. In each visual model, the relation between object (0) and subject (S), the origin of the source of knowledge (plain arrow), and the existence and direction of the uses of knowledge (slashed arrow) reflect the dynamic relationships among these elements as conceived by each ideology.

❖ **Figure 6.1**   The relationship of the ideologies' views regarding the origins and importance of knowledge.

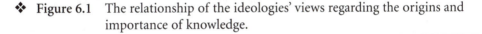

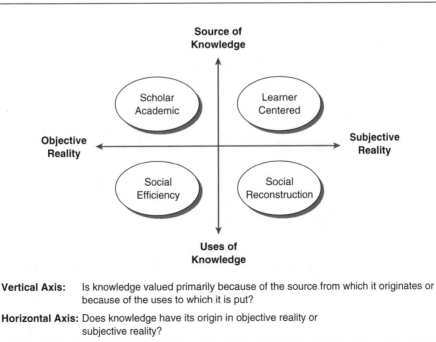

Vertical Axis: Is knowledge valued primarily because of the source from which it originates or because of the uses to which it is put?

Horizontal Axis: Does knowledge have its origin in objective reality or subjective reality?

❖ **Figure 6.2**   Visual models of the ideologies' views of the relationship between the origins and importance of knowledge.

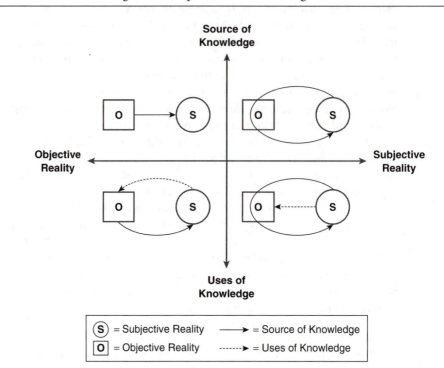

Learning

Educators within each ideology have different views about learning.

Scholar Academics view learning from the perspective of the transmitter of what is to be learned—who is the primary active agent during learning—rather than from the perspective of the receiver of learning.

Social Efficiency educators view learning as a process by which learners' behaviors are shaped by an agent outside themselves. They believe that learning takes place when a change in organization of mind manifests itself as a change in behavior.

Learner Centered educators view learning as a by-product of growth, during which learners make meaning through creative self-expression as a result of organically interacting with their environment in a mode congruent with their inner nature.

Social Reconstructionists view learning as children's having inculcated into them a way of viewing events in their environment through an intelligence oriented around a vision of a future good society. This intelligence allows them to learn things both in relation to what they already know and within the context in which they occur.

The answers to the following questions (presented in Table 6.2) make explicit some of the differences among the ideologies with respect to their views of learning.

- Is learning viewed from the perspective of the receiver or from the perspective of the transmitter of what is to be learned? That is, do educators view learning through the eyes of the teacher (adult) or through the eyes of the learner (child)?
- Is learning viewed primarily as a function of natural growth or as a function of societal transmission? Here the question is whether educators believe that the type of learning their curriculum provides is the same as or different from the type of learning children can naturally acquire while growing up outside of formal schooling.
- Is learning treated as an integrated or as an atomistic process? That is, can one break learning down into individual and disjoint (atomistic) acts, or must one treat the learning process in a holistic (integrated) manner?
- Is learning primarily a process of changing mind or a process of changing behavior?
- Is the desired result of learning a change of mind or a change of behavior?
- Is the primary actor during learning the learner or an agent outside the learner who does something to the learner?
- Is there a concern for formal learning theory? What type of learning theory is used?
- How is the issue of readiness for learning addressed?
- How is the issue of individualized instruction handled?

The Child

The way educators perceive children and childhood and the way they embed these perceptions in their curriculum tells us much about their conception of education.

Scholar Academics view children as neophytes in the hierarchical community of the academic disciplines. Children are viewed as lacking something that exists outside of their minds in the educators' discipline, something that is capable of being transmitted into their minds by the discipline. Educators focus on two qualities of children's minds: memory (which can be filled) and reason (which can be trained).

Social Efficiency educators view childhood as a stage of learning that has meaning because it leads to adulthood. It is in adulthood that people are seen as constructive members of society. Children are viewed as raw materials to be shaped into finished products that will possess well-developed behavioral capabilities. Educators focus on the action capabilities of children rather than on children as actors in their world.

Learner Centered educators view the whole person as an integrated organism possessing natural goodness, as a self-propelled agent of his or her own growth, and as a self-activated maker of meaning. They focus on people rather than on the acts or attributes of people, and on the uniqueness of individuals as they are in the present rather than as they might be in the future. These educators are concerned about processes internal to people, such as mental health and self-esteem, and talk as though they can visualize the inner workings of people's minds during their intellectual, social, and emotional development.

Social Reconstructionists view people as social beings whose nature is defined by the society in which they live. Thus, they are concerned about children as maturing members of society who can act upon society to redefine their own nature and the nature of their society.

The following questions allow the ideologies' concepts of the child and childhood to be compared.

❖ **Table 6.2** A comparison of the ideologies' views regarding learning.

Learning	Scholar Academic	Social Efficiency	Learner Centered	Social Reconstruction
Is learning viewed from the perspective of the receiver or the transmitter?	transmitter	transmitter	receiver	transmitter
Is learning seen primarily as a function of natural growth or as a function of societal transmission?	transmission	transmission	growth	transmission
Is learning an integrated or an atomistic process?	atomistic	atomistic	integrated	integrated
Is learning viewed as changing primarily mind or behavior?	mind	behavior	mind	mind
Is the desired result of learning a change of mind or a change in behavior?	mind	behavior	mind	behavior
Is the primary actor during learning the learner or another agent?	agent	agent/learner	learner	agent/learner
Is there a concern for formal learning theory? (What type?)	no (discipline)	yes (behaviorism)	yes (developmental and constructivist)	yes (social constructivist)
How is the issue of readiness addressed?	by simplification of difficult topics	by providing prerequisite behavioral capabilities	stages of growth	gestalts of prior experience
How is the issue of individualized instruction handled?	it is ignored (children are grouped in terms of achievement)	by providing a standard task for all and varying learning rates and styles	by facilitating individual development	by using individual interests to mold a consensus

- Are children treated as active or passive agents in their world?
- Are children viewed as having something of worth or as missing something of worth?
- Are educators concerned about processes internal or external to children?
- Do educators focus primarily on children's minds or their behavior?
- Are children viewed as integrated organisms or as atomizable organisms?
- Do educators focus their efforts on children themselves or on the acts or attributes of children?
- Are educators concerned about children as they are or as they ought to be?
- Are children thought to exist for themselves or to further ends external to themselves?
- Are children viewed as unique individuals or in relation to standardized norms?
- Are children viewed within a social context (and if so, what type?) or outside and independent of a social context?

Answers to these questions are presented in Table 6.3.

❖ **Table 6.3**   A comparison of the ideologies' views regarding children.

Children	Scholar Academic	Social Efficiency	Learner Centered	Social Reconstruction
Are children treated as active or passive agents in their world?	passive	active	active	active
Are children viewed as having or missing something of worth?	missing	missing	having	having
Are educators concerned about processes internal or external to children?	internal	external	internal	external
Are educators focused primarily on children's minds or their behavior?	mind	behavior	mind	behavior
Are children viewed as integrated organisms or as atomizable organisms?	atomizable	atomizable	integrated	integrated
Do educators focus their efforts on children themselves or on the acts or attributes of children?	attributes	attributes	children themselves	attributes
Are educators concerned about children as they are or as they ought to be?	as they ought to be	as they ought to be	as they are	as they ought to be
Are children thought to exist for themselves or to further ends external to themselves?	for external ends	for external ends	for themselves	for external ends
Are children viewed as unique individuals or in relation to standardized norms?	norms	norms	individuals	norms
Are children viewed in a social context (and if so, what type?) or outside of a social context?	in the context of the discipline	in the context of the present society	out of context	in the context of the future society

Answers to two of these questions deserve comment. The questions are "Are children viewed as having something of worth (that gives them value as children) or as missing something of worth (which they must acquire in order to have value)?" and "Are educators concerned about processes internal or external to children?" If we correlate these questions, we obtain a matrix that illustrates the relationships among the ideologies (see Figure 6.3). The position of the ideologies in this matrix can be compared with the position of the ideologies in Figure 6.1 (which relates to knowledge). Although the definitions of the axes have been changed, the relative positions of the ideologies remain the same. This constancy offers hints about how educators' views of children relate to their beliefs about knowledge. For example, the variables on the horizontal axes of Figures 6.1 and 6.3 ("Does knowledge have its origin in objective reality or subjective reality?" and "Are children viewed as having or missing something of worth?") are closely related. The belief that children have something of worth corresponds to the belief that the origin of knowledge resides in children's subjective reality, while the view that children are missing something of worth corresponds to the belief that the origin of knowledge lies outside children in objective reality. The questions defining the vertical axes are similarly related.

❖ **Figure 6.3** The relationship of the ideologies' views regarding two aspects of children.

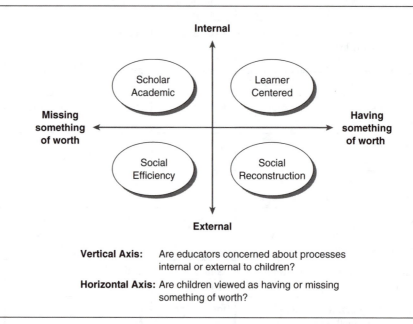

Vertical Axis: Are educators concerned about processes internal or external to children?

Horizontal Axis: Are children viewed as having or missing something of worth?

Teaching

Educators have different views about teachers and teaching.

Scholar Academics view teaching as that function of their discipline responsible for initiating novices into the discipline by transmitting that which is known to those who do not know it. Teachers are considered authorities who are to get the knowledge of a discipline into children's minds in the manner prescribed by the curriculum.

Social Efficiency educators view the teacher as a manager or supervisor of children as they encounter the learning conditions and materials designed by a curriculum developer. Teachers are to act in strict accordance with directions provided by the curriculum. Teachers both prepare the environment in which children learn and supervise children as they learn.

Learner Centered educators view teachers as aids to growing individuals. Their task is twofold: to facilitate students' growth by presenting them with experience from which they can make meaning, and to intervene between students and their experience in order to facilitate their growth. Teachers choose the experience and modes of intervention from among those within the curriculum to match students' individual needs.

Social Reconstructionists believe teaching involves guiding children's learning in such a way that they become acculturated into the modes of knowing and acting that belong to the educator's vision of the future good society. Teachers are to act as companions to children while using group pressures and the medium through which children learn to mold them.

The following questions allow these views of teaching to be compared.

- What are teachers' roles during instruction?
- Is a teacher's job primarily transmitting knowledge or preparing and supervising a learning environment?
- What standards are used to measure teacher effectiveness?
- Are teachers to stimulate student diversity or uniformity?
- Are teachers to implement curricula without changing them or to creatively adapt curricula to their own situation? The question here is whether or not curriculum developers try to create "teacher proof" curricula.
- Is it the job of teachers or curriculum developers to plan for children's individual differences?
- What types of media are usually employed during teaching?
- What is the intent of teaching?
- Are teachers to be concerned about the whole child or only a single dimension of the child (such as his or her cognitive, affective, social, or physical attributes)?
- Are teachers' attitudes, beliefs, interpretations, and visions considered crucial?
- Do educators believe teachers should do research into such things as the nature of children and how to best teach children?

Answers to these questions are presented in Table 6.4.

Evaluation

Educators have differing views about evaluation.

Scholar Academics evaluate student success through the use of objective statistical instruments designed to measure the extent to which students can re-present that which has been transmitted to them. Students are evaluated with respect to a posteriori standards so that they may be ranked in the discipline's hierarchy. Scholars evaluate curricula to determine how well they reflect their discipline's essence and prepare students to pursue future work in the discipline.

Social Efficiency educators atomistically evaluate curricula and students with respect to an a priori standard based in normative values. They evaluate in order to

❖ **Table 6.4** A comparison of the ideologies' views regarding teaching.

Teaching	Scholar Academic	Social Efficiency	Learner Centered	Social Reconstruction
What is the teacher's role during instruction?	transmitter	manager	facilitator	colleague
Are teachers transmitters of knowledge or preparers and supervisors of classrooms?	transmitters	preparers and supervisors	preparers and supervisors	preparers and supervisors
What standards are used to measure teacher effectiveness?	accurate presentation of the discipline	efficiency of student learning	facilitation of child growth	effective transference of the vision
Are teachers to stimulate student diversity or uniformity?	uniformity	uniformity	diversity	uniformity
Are teachers to directly implement curricula unchanged or creatively adapt curricula to their situations?	directly implement	directly implement	adapt (based on children's needs)	adapt (based on social concerns)
Do teachers or developers plan for children's individual differences?	neither	teacher	both	teacher
What types of media are usually employed during teaching?	didactic discourse	programmed instruction	child-environment interaction	group dynamics
What is the intent of teaching?	to advance students in a discipline	to prepare children to perform skills	to stimulate child growth	to acculturate students into the educators' vision
Are teachers to be concerned about the whole child? (If not, what aspect of the child should they be concerned about?)	no (cognitive)	no (skills)	whole child	whole child
Are teachers' attitudes, beliefs, and visions considered important?	no	no	yes	yes
Are teachers expected to do classroom research?	no	no	yes	yes

scientifically determine quality control. In doing so, they use a binary criterion that determines acceptance or rejection (pass or fail) of what they evaluate.

Learner Centered educators attempt to use evaluation solely for the benefit of the person or curriculum being evaluated. Evaluation takes on a reflective quality devoid of "moral loading." The intent is to enable the evaluees, be they students, teachers, or curriculum developers, to learn from their mistakes. It is believed that evaluative feedback should come directly from materials with which the evaluees are interacting rather than from an outside authority.

Social Reconstructionists take a subjective and holistic approach to evaluating curricula and students in relation to the social situations in which they exist.

To compare educators' views about evaluation, the distinction must be made between student evaluation and curriculum evaluation.

The following questions allow different views of student evaluation to be compared.

- What is the purpose of student evaluation as it relates to the person who receives the results of the evaluation?
- What is the intent of student evaluation as it relates to the evaluee?
- Is the development of formal evaluative measures for student evaluation considered to be an integral part of the curriculum development process?
- What is the nature of the evaluative instruments used in evaluating students?
- Are subjective or objective instruments used to evaluate students?
- Is student evaluation viewed from an atomistic or holistic perspective?
- To whom are the results of student evaluation to be directed or beneficial?
- During student evaluation, is the focus on the individual, group norms, or a fixed criterion?
- Does student evaluation take place during the instructional process or after the instructional process?
- When are the criteria for successful student work defined?

Answers to these questions are presented in Table 6.5.

A further distinction needs to be made between evaluation that takes place during the curriculum development process, which is designed to give curriculum developers information that will help them improve their curriculum, and evaluation designed to give potential curriculum users information on either the curriculum's overall worth and effectiveness with respect to its own goals or the curriculum's comparative worth and effectiveness with respect to the goals of several different competing programs. The former is called formative evaluation and the latter summative evaluation.

The following questions allow different views of formative curriculum evaluation to be compared.

- Is formative curriculum evaluation considered important enough to engage in?
- Why is formative evaluation considered important?
- Is accountability a central issue during formative evaluation? If yes, accountability to whom?
- Are subjective or objective instruments used during formative curriculum evaluation?
- Are the norms for formative curriculum evaluation determined before, during, or after evaluation takes place?
- Is formative evaluation primarily conducted in an atomistic or a holistic manner?

❖ **Table 6.5** A comparison of the ideologies' views regarding knowledge.

Student Evaluation	Scholar Academic	Social Efficiency	Learner Centered	Social Reconstruction
What is the purpose of student evaluation for the evaluator?	to rank evaluees for a future in the discipline	to certify to a client that a student has certain skills	to diagnose student abilities to facilitate growth	to measure student progress with respect to ability
What is the purpose of student evaluation for the evaluee?	to test ability to represent what has been transmitted	to test ability to perform a specific task	to reflect to evaluees their progress	to allow students to demonstrate their values to others
Is designing assessment part of curriculum development?	no	yes	no	no
What is the nature of evaluative instruments?	norm reinforced	criterion reinforced	informal subjective diagnosis	informal subjective diagnosis
Are assessments subjective or objective?	objective	objective	subjective	subjective
Is evaluation atomistic or holistic?	atomistic	atomistic	holistic	holistic
Who gets or benefits from the results of student evaluation?	academic disciplines (academicians, administrators)	educators' client (society, parents, administrators)	child	teacher
During evaluation, is the focus on the individual, group norms, or a fixed criterion?	group norms	criterion	individual	individual with respect to criterion
Are students evaluated during or after instruction?	after	after	during	during
When are criteria for good student work defined?	after evaluation	before evaluation	never	never

- What type of information results from formative evaluation: binary information ("it's OK" or "it needs revision") or specific information on the individual successes and failures of each component of the curriculum?
- What methodology or criteria are used to determine a curriculum's success or failure during formative evaluation?

Answers to these questions are presented in Table 6.6.

❖ **Table 6.6**   A comparison of the ideologies' views regarding formative curriculum evaluation.

Formative Curriculum Evaluation	Scholar Academic	Social Efficiency	Learner Centered	Social Reconstruction
Is formative evaluation engaged in?	yes	yes	yes	no
Why is formative evaluation considered important?	to ensure that curriculum reflects its discipline and is teachable	to ensure conformity to scientific procedures and to demonstrate accountability	to allow the best curricula to be designed	
Is accountability a central issue? If yes, accountability to whom?	yes, to the discipline	yes, to the client	yes, to educators	
Are subjective or objective instruments used?	subjective teacher and scholar reports	objective	subjective educator observations	
When are the norms for evaluation determined?	after evaluation	before evaluation	during evaluation	
Is evaluation primarily atomistic or holistic?	holistic	atomistic	holistic	
What type of information does evaluation provide?	binary ("OK" or "needs revision")	binary ("OK" or "needs revision")	data regarding what to improve and how to do so	
What methods and criteria are used to determine a curriculum's success?	logical analysis by scholars and teacher reports on teachability	objective criterion-referenced data on student achievement	observational data on student interest and growth	

The following questions allow different views of summative curriculum evaluation to be compared.

- Is summative curriculum evaluation considered important enough to engage in?
- Why is summative evaluation considered important?
- Are subjective or objective instruments used during summative curriculum evaluation?
- Is accountability a central issue during summative curriculum evaluation?

Answers to these questions are presented in Table 6.7.

❖ **Table 6.7**   A comparison of the ideologies' views regarding summative curriculum evaluation.

Summative Curriculum Evaluation	Scholar Academic	Social Efficiency	Child Centered	Social Reconstruction
Is summative evaluation engaged in?	yes (necessary but not important)	yes	no	no
Why is summative evaluation considered important?	to sell curriculum	to ensure conformity to scientific procedures and to demonstrate accountability		
Are subjective or objective instruments used?	objective	objective		
Is accountability a central issue?	no (to the discipline)	yes (to the client)		

Other Parameters

Freedom

Educators like to use the word freedom, but educators can mean many different things when they speak of giving children freedom.

Scholar Academics wish to give children *freedom from* the restrictions of society and nature by giving them knowledge that will allow them to understand society and nature and thus avoid the ways in which they are influenced by them.

Social Efficiency educators wish to give children *freedom to* constructively contribute to and function within adult society in the manner they desire by providing them with the variety of social behaviors and technical skills they will need to do so.

Learner Centered educators wish to provide children with *freedom from* the influences and controls of society so that they can develop naturally in accordance with their organic selves.

Social Reconstructionists wish to give children *freedom to* control the destiny of society.

Time

Educators orient their efforts within different temporal frameworks, even though each in some way considers the past, present, and future.

As Scholar Academics create curricula, they look to knowledge that has already been accepted by their discipline—they look to the past for guidance.

Social Efficiency educators look to the present needs of society (or some other client) to guide them in their endeavors to create curricula to meet those present needs in the very near future.

Learner Centered educators attempt to focus on only the present as seen through the eyes of learners.

Social Reconstructionists make use of the past and present to analyze the nature of society while intently focusing on the future.

Social Improvement

Educators within each ideology have their own ideas of how to improve society.

Scholar Academics wish to improve society by educating an intellectual elite so that scholar-kings can rule society through knowledge.

Social Efficiency educators wish to accentuate the best of the past and present in training people to perpetuate the existing social order.

Learner Centered educators are concerned about the development of individuals under the assumption that better people will make a better society.

Social Reconstructionists wish to break with the past and present and reconstruct society according to their vision of a future better society.

Multicultural Education

As the 21st century began and the "melting pot" view of America faded, issues of multicultural education arose.

Educators in all four ideologies accept the assumption that cultural diversity exists: that people speak different languages, have different views of causality, and have different ways of perceiving, conceptualizing, and interpreting events that occur in their world. Educators in all four ideologies also accept the assumption that children from different cultural backgrounds approach learning and knowledge with different knowledge bases (including different conceptual frameworks, learned ways of making meaning, and understandings) that reflect the accumulated knowledge and ways of knowing of their cultures. Further, they accept that differences in the structure of languages influence how children comprehend, that thinking and learning styles children acquire from early family interactions influence the way they learn, and that cultural interpretations of the nature of knowledge that children learn in their families influence the way they interpret, make meaning from, and understand what they are taught in school (Schiro, 2004). However, just because educators agree that cultural diversity exists and that the cultures in which children are brought up influence how and what they learn in school does not mean that all educators view the education of children from different cultural, ethnic, and socioeconomic backgrounds in the same way.

The Scholar Academic posture toward multicultural education emphasizes two types of equity. First, these educators focus on determining the true nature of the contributions of different cultures to our intellectual knowledge base and helping children understand and appreciate the intellectual knowledge that has been created by different world cultures. Their intent is to present an accurate picture of the historical and cultural foundations of each discipline. This type of equity includes the belief that the school curriculum should provide all students with the understanding that most cultures engage in disciplined intellectual activity and that "no single culture has a monopoly" on intellectual endeavors (Nelson, Joseph, & Williams, 1993, p. 19). Children learn about the content discovered by many different peoples as well as the wide range of methods of disciplined thinking they employed. This is intended to contribute to children's understanding and appreciation of the knowledge of their own culture (or cultures) under the assumption that "an understanding of one's own culture depends upon a knowledge of other cultures, with which it can be compared and through which we can see what is often taken for granted" (p. 3).

The second type of equity involves providing all learners—independent of race, cultural background, and socioeconomic status—with equal access to the knowledge of the academic disciplines and the chance to excel in learning that knowledge. This includes making sure that "disadvantaged" groups and individuals are not deprived of equal access to knowledge because of the way instructional practices might be biased against them. Here it is assumed that children must be presented with rigorous authentic instruction in the academic disciplines and that high standards for excellence must be insisted upon, for "equity for all requires excellence for all, both thrive when expectations are high" (National Research Council, 1989). Adler (1982) emphasizes different dimensions of this belief:

> We should have a one-track system of schooling, not a system with two or more tracks, only one of which goes straight ahead while the others shunt the young off onto sidetracks not headed toward the goals our society opens to all. The innermost meaning of social equality is: *substantially the same quality of life for all.* That calls for: *the same quality of schooling for all.* . . . The best education for the best . . . is the best education for all. (p. 6)
>
> With the exception of a few suffering from irremediable brain damage, every child is educable up to his or her capacity. Educable—not just trainable for jobs! As John Dewey said almost a century ago, vocational training, training for particular jobs, is not the education of free men and women. . . . True, children are educable in varying degrees, but the variation in degree must be of the same kind and quality of education. (p. 7)

What this means is that educators often focus their endeavors on "the best education for the best" students. As Keynes writes,

> the overall goal is to provide an intense . . . challenging, and dynamic academic program . . . in order to reflect the best current ideas about all subjects. . . . [T]he content, teaching styles, and support activities available to the students are designed to enable virtually *all* students . . . to be highly successful. (1995, p. 59)

The Social Efficiency approach to multicultural issues involves two initiatives. First, these educators believe that to efficiently teach skills to children one must synchronize the skills that children will need as adults to the variety of different culturally based conceptual frameworks with which children come to school. Here it is considered necessary to determine the nature of children's knowledge bases (acquired from their families and communities) so that curricula can be constructed that take into account, accommodate, and compensate for those knowledge bases. In this way, skills required for future adult life can be efficiently taught and learned.

Second, Social Efficiency educators consider the multicultural world in which all children will have to live as adults and seek to provide children with the skills necessary to productively function in those environments. Here instruction is "seen as part of a broader set of efforts to create a society that offers opportunity to each of its members to be successful and to contribute to the social and economic good" (Silver, Smith, & Nelson, 1995, p. 10).

For Social Efficiency educators, equity issues relate to helping children—particularly children of cultural, ethnic, and racial groups different from those in control of the political, economic, and social functions of the society in which they are located, and children of the poor and working classes—obtain access to social positions of power and success by learning appropriate skills. This is important because "the potential of this country's cultural diversity has not been fully developed, because all children have not been given reasonable opportunity to learn . . . school subjects that would open the doors to employment and further education" (Silver, Smith, & Nelson, 1995, p. 9). Here the emphasis is on learning socially useful skills because they are tools that will provide children with access to good jobs, social prestige, and the ability to productively participate in society.

The Learner Centered approach to multicultural education emphasizes that the purpose of instruction is to help children grow—intellectually, socially, and emotionally—in accordance with their own innate natures and the innate nature of their culture. To accomplish this, educators must make sure that powerful social and economic forces within society—which want to keep certain social, racial, cultural, economic, and sexual groups in their "subservient places" through the "hidden curriculum" of schools—do not inhibit, limit, or pervert children's natural growth.

Here educators recognize and value the heritage of cultural and social groups, including minorities within a larger nation and nations within a larger world culture. They want to help members of those groups recognize, participate in, value, and use their indigenous cultural heritages. In so doing, educators allow individuals to make meaning and develop their thinking styles in accordance with their cultural orientation and conceptual frameworks. This not only builds children's confidence and pride in their cultural background, but also allows children to develop unique meanings and ways of making meaning that are consistent with their cultural heritage, which in turn produces a more integrated, holistic, coherent, and powerful view of knowledge within the child and a more holistic and integrated approach to teaching, curriculum, and knowledge within the instructional arena.

From an equity perspective, this approach encourages children to find their own unique ways of making meaning that are consistent with their innate and culturally acquired intellectual, social, and emotional natures and their knowledge bases. Here the concern is not about accessibility to the knowledge of the dominant culture or accessibility to skills that will allow one to be a productive member of society, but about allowing all children to develop in their own unique manner in ways that are consistent with their individual nature and cultural background.

Social Reconstructionists have been very active in their opposition to social, economic, ethnic, cultural, linguistic, and racial inequities of instruction, and as one means of attaining a more fair, just, and egalitarian society they have urged teachers to work to transform their instruction and society to eliminate these inequities so that all children will have equal opportunity to succeed in learning. Advocates of this ideology have given particular attention to multicultural education in urban centers under the rallying call of social justice and the elimination of Eurocentric views of educational content. Anderson and Ladson-Billings highlight this when they write,

> Those of us who are genuinely concerned with educating students for liberation rather than training them for the job market must attack, critique, and dismantle the Eurocentric educational construct while simultaneously planting the seeds for more holistic, in-tune-with-nature, popular, and egalitarian forms of learning. We cannot wait any longer . . . to offer an alternative that is genuinely egalitarian. (Anderson, 1997, pp. 305–306)

> The underlying assumption of multicultural education is that the nation's educational system promotes the status quo and that the status quo is rife with inequity along race, class, gender, and ability lines. . . . multicultural education assumes that students are social, political, and cultural actors and that through experiences with schoolwide change they an promote social change . . . [that will] ensure . . . that students of diverse race, social class, and gender groups experience equal educational opportunity. (Ladson-Billings, 1995, p. 126)

From this perspective, equity issues relate to helping children acquire academic skills, knowledge, and social values that will allow them to analyze and reconstruct society in such a way that all of its members have an equal chance for success in a society that does not discriminate among people because of their cultural background, racial origins, linguistic background, economic status, or social class. This goes considerably beyond the goals of helping children acquire academic knowledge, become productive members of the existing social structure, or develop in accordance with their own unique personal and cultural potentialities.

Concluding Perspective

This chapter compares the conceptual structures and language of the Scholar Academic, Social Efficiency, Learner Centered, and Social Reconstruction ideologies. There are significant differences in the ways in which educators think about curriculum, instruction, and schooling, and significant differences in the meaning they give to such common terms as learning, teaching, and knowledge. If one desires to have constructive interactions with the wide range of educators (and the general public) who are interested in our schools, it is necessary to know both how they conceptualize education and what meaning they give to common educational words. In addition, it is necessary to be able to quickly assess their educational ideologies and to use words in the same way they do. Clarity on the differences that exist will help with this task.

Figure 6.4 combines earlier graphs that provide rough estimates of when the four ideologies have been most active, with respect to their own norms, in attempting to influence American education. Notice that the graph indicates two time periods during which the four ideologies were simultaneously active in their endeavors. The first was between about 1890 and 1940, the second between about 1955 and 1995. Many questions can be asked about what has happened in the past and what might occur in the future. They include the following: Have the past endeavors of the Scholar Academic ideology to influence schools resulted in a counter-response by other ideologies, motivating them to initiate efforts to improve education? How will the excesses of the No Child Left Behind Act influence educators to begin new curriculum initiatives? Are we now at the beginning of a new time period when all four ideologies might simultaneously attempt to improve American education? What sorts of events might initiate a new surge of effort by all of the ideologies to improve education? (Possibilities include the federal government's decision to devote more money to educational improvement, more terrorist attacks such as those that occurred on September 11, 2001, and fear that America might no longer have such great economic and military influence in the world.) Questions such as these should be asked, as well as speculative answers offered, as we attempt to understand what is occurring now and what might occur in the future in American education.

Activities that extend the ideas in this chapter are located on the Sage Web site at www.sagepub.com/schiroextensionactivities.

❖ **Figure 6.4** Times of relative high and low activity of the four ideologies.

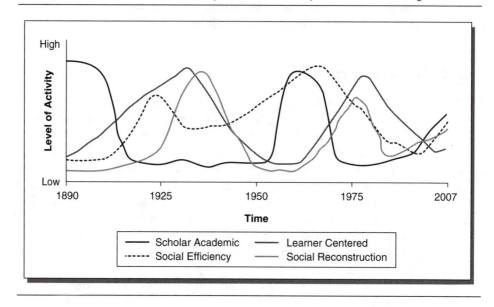

7

Individual Perspectives on the Curriculum Ideologies

After studying the four curriculum ideologies presented in this book and reflecting deeply on their beliefs about curriculum, educators frequently ask at least one of the following two very personal questions: "My beliefs are a combination of two different ideologies; is that OK?" and "I have changed my philosophy of education since I first began teaching; is that acceptable?" This chapter addresses these types of personal questions as this book turns its attention from describing the field of curriculum as a whole to describing events in the lives of individual educators. The intent of this chapter is to help educators obtain perspective on how the study presented in this book is relevant to their individual lives over the span of their professional careers.

In this book, the four curriculum ideologies have been discussed as ideal types. The ideal types were chosen because they represent the range of viable ideological alternatives available to American educators over the last hundred years that have exerted the greatest influence on educators' practices and aspirations. Educators' beliefs cluster around the ideal types that describe each ideological position, with the density of all educators' beliefs being the greatest around each ideology. However, most educators' beliefs deviate from the ideal types described in this book in one way or another.

As a consequence of using this type of category system, a number of important questions arise for educators as they attempt to relate their personal belief systems to the ideal types that have been described. The most important questions include the following: Can people simultaneously believe in more than one ideology? Over time, do people change their curriculum ideologies? What forces influence educators to change their ideologies? How do educators conceptualize the way in which they change their beliefs about curriculum over time? Answers to these questions will now be presented. The intent is to introduce educators to some of the complexities of the field of curriculum and life. Insight into these complexities should help educators obtain perspective on how the discussion within this book relates to their present and future lives.

Briefly, research indicates that educators can believe in more than one ideology at a time, that they change their ideological orientation about once every 4 years, and that the most frequently noted events associated with ideological shifts are changes in the school or grade in which an educator works, the noting of and responding to previously unknown needs of children or communities, and changing jobs.

It is strongly suggested that readers now turn to the Appendix and complete and score the curriculum ideologies inventory. If you did so before reading this book, please complete and score the inventory a second time and then compare the graph of the curriculum beliefs you had before reading this book with the graph of the beliefs you have after completing it.

The research results that follow are based on two studies of 100 experienced educators, all of whom studied the ideologies described in this book, completed the ideology inventory before and after studying the ideologies as part of a graduate course, and reflected on and wrote about the changes in their curriculum beliefs over the span of their careers (Schiro, 1992).

Curriculum Life Histories

It is possible to study the manner in which educators conceptualize their ideologies, and the way in which they view their ideologies as changing over time, by using the biographical method (Denzin, 1989). This involves having educators describe their ideologies at different times during their careers and make drawings that illustrate any changes that have taken place. Descriptions and drawings note any critical events that caused or coincided with a change in ideology. These descriptions and drawings are called curriculum ideology life histories.

Five types of drawings that educators use to describe their curriculum ideology life histories have been identified. A sample drawing of each type, along with a brief description of what is occurring in each, is presented below. They are presented in a "cleaned up" format that maintains the structural integrity of the originals while altering such things as uneven line quality, spatial orientation, and particular life events or comments that might identify their authors.

Figure 7.1 portrays a "life history as a trip." The educator who created this drawing began teaching at the first-grade level with a close affiliation to the Scholar Academic ideology (position 1). Experience teaching children gave this educator an increased desire to nurture children's individual needs, and he moved away from the Scholar Academic ideology toward the Learner Centered ideology (position 2). When he began teaching fifth grade instead of first grade, the increased emphasis on academics and classroom control caused him to move to a combination of the Scholar Academic and Social Efficiency ideologies (position 3). Another change of grade level that accompanied a change of school and community placed him in a situation where he vacillated between the Scholar Academic and Social Efficiency ideologies before subscribing to the Social Efficiency position, a position supported by the parents of the children he

❖ **Figure 7.1**   Life history as a trip.

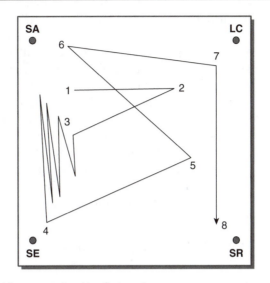

1. First three years teaching first grade

2. Fourth to seventh years teaching first grade

3. Three years teaching fifth grade

4. Four years teaching junior high in a large urban school

5. Five years teaching junior high in a small rural school

6. Five years as principal in an affluent suburban junior high

7. First year as principal at the Native American reservation

8. Second to fifth years as principal at the Native American reservation

SOURCE: From "Educators' Perceptions of the Changes in Their Curriculum Belief Systems Over Time" by Michael Schiro, in *Journal of Curriculum and Supervision,* Vol. 7, No. 3, pp. 250–286, copyright © 1992. Reprinted with permission from Association of Supervision and Curriculum Development via Copyright Clearance Center.

taught (position 4). When he moved again, from an urban to a rural community, he found himself working in a school and for a principal who believed in open education and the progressive approach; as a result he moved his ideology toward the Learner Centered position (position 5). When his job changed from teacher to school principal and he moved from a rural to a suburban school, he moved toward the Scholar Academic ideology, which reflected the desires of upwardly mobile suburbanites who wanted their children to attend the "best" colleges (position 6). Another relocation allowed this educator to serve as the principal of a school on a Native American reservation, where he saw how problems of alcoholism, drugs, and unemployment were daily concerns of the children. Because most children and parents on the reservation did not possess high self-esteem, the Learner Centered ideology became primary for this educator during his first year at this location (position 7). Upon learning more about the needs of the Native Americans, he moved toward the Social Reconstruction ideology, for he felt he needed to help the Native Americans reconstruct the social conditions under which they lived rather than to simply nurture them. He realized that these children had to do something for their people. They had to become the leaders of their people to combat the serious problems on the reservation (position 8).

Figure 7.2 portrays a "life history as a set of influences." As a teacher of a single academic subject to seventh- and eighth-grade students between 1965 and 1970, this educator was most heavily influenced by the Scholar Academic ideology. In 1970, after becoming a fifth-grade teacher, this educator became increasingly influenced by the Learner Centered ideology as he became aware of the needs of the "whole child" across all academic subjects and within the context of peers and family. This ideology contin-ued to influence him for another 8 years, although the sociopolitical events associated with the Vietnam War also resulted in the Social Reconstruction ideology's influenc-ing him for a short time during the early 1970s. With a change of job from regular classroom teacher to special education teacher in the mid 1970s, this educator had to

❖ **Figure 7.2** Life history as a set of influences.

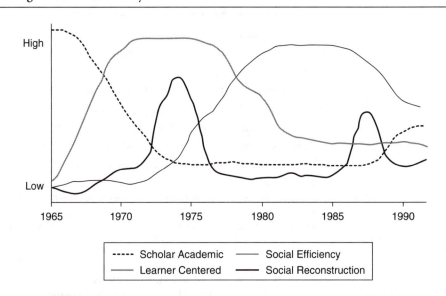

1965–1970: Seventh- and eighth-grade teacher

1970–1972: Fifth-grade teacher

1972–1976: Second-grade teacher

1974–1976: Special education training

1976–1984: Special education teacher

1984–1987: Assistant principal

1987–1989: Principal

SOURCE: From "Educators' Perceptions of the Changes in Their Curriculum Belief Systems Over Time" by Michael Schiro, in *Journal of Curriculum and Supervision*, Vol. 7, No. 3, pp. 250–286, copyright © 1992. Reprinted with permission from Association of Supervision and Curriculum Development via Copyright Clearance Center.

follow state and federal mandates and create behaviorally oriented individual education programs (IEPs) for children. As he did so, he began to subscribe to the Social Efficiency ideology. Upon becoming a school principal in the mid 1980s, being freed from the constraints of conceptualizing education through the lenses of IEPs, and being pressured by veteran teachers to reevaluate the importance of imparting knowledge to children, this educator gradually came under greater influence from the Scholar Academic ideology while the Social Efficiency ideology exerted increasingly less influence over him.

Figure 7.3 portrays a "life history as a composite of ideologies." In 1971, as a student teacher, this educator's ideological orientation was primarily Learner Centered. (From her drawings, her orientation was determined to be 70% Learner Centered, 19% Social

❖ **Figure 7.3**   Life history as a composite of ideologies.

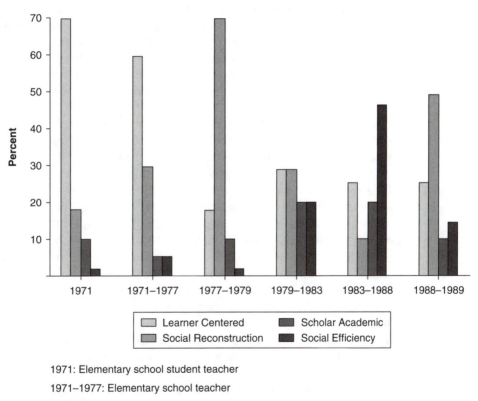

1971: Elementary school student teacher

1971–1977: Elementary school teacher

1977–1979: Economics master's student

1979–1983: Junior college teacher

1983–1988: College dean

1988–1989: Doctoral student and college dean

SOURCE: From "Educators' Perceptions of the Changes in Their Curriculum Belief Systems Over Time" by Michael Schiro, in *Journal of Curriculum and Supervision*, Vol. 7, No. 3, pp. 250–286, copyright © 1992. Reprinted with permission from Association of Supervision and Curriculum Development via Copyright Clearance Center.

Reconstruction, 10% Scholar Academic, and 1% Social Efficiency.) During her first full-time job as an elementary school teacher, she modified her views slightly (60% Learner Centered, 30% Social Reconstruction, 5% Scholar Academic, and 5% Social Efficiency). Between 1977 and 1979, she left teaching to obtain a master's degree in sociology. The academic atmosphere of the university, which she resented, and the social and political contexts she found herself in as a student influenced her to alter her ideology dramatically (19% Learner Centered, 70% Social Reconstruction, 10% Scholar Academic, and 1% Social Efficiency). Returning to teaching and changing grade levels from elementary school to junior college equalized the influence of the four ideologies (30% Learner Centered, 30% Social Reconstruction, 20% Scholar Academic, and 20% Social Efficiency). When she became a college dean in 1983, the managerial demands of her administrative position influenced her to subscribe to the Social Efficiency ideology (25% Learner Centered, 10% Social Reconstruction, 20% Scholar Academic, and 45% Social Efficiency). Upon entering a doctoral program in 1988, while still a college dean, this educator altered her ideological orientation to a position similar to the one she had taken after entering her master's degree program; thus, the influence of the Social Reconstruction ideology increased while that of the Social Efficiency ideology decreased (25% Learner Centered, 50% Social Reconstruction, 10% Scholar Academic, and 15% Social Efficiency). This increase in the Social Reconstruction ideology's influence seemed to come as a reaction to her being a student within the sociopolitical context of a university.

Figure 7.4 represents a "life history as a portrayal of internal change." During the 1960s, as an elementary school special education teacher working with poor children in a poor urban community, this educator adopted the Social Reconstruction and Social Efficiency perspectives. Her students lived in a world of poverty and violence, and she knew that she wanted something better for them. Thus, she worked hard to provide them with the literary tools they would need to escape from their poverty and transform their world into a better place to live. During the 1970s, her life took an interesting turn when she bore two children and adopted two war orphans. Caring for these children, as well as teaching part time, influenced her curriculum and instructional beliefs. While her children were growing up, she worked part time in a Montessori school and learned to enjoy letting youngsters make their own decisions about what they wanted to do. In this context, the Learner Centered ideology had a deep influence on her. At the same time, she worked to establish an alternative school for dropouts. Here, Social Reconstruction was a motivating ideology in her work with adolescents. The Social Efficiency ideology took a position quite peripheral to her life because of her growing dislike of IEPs. The early 1980s took this educator out of the traditional school arena and into church activist work. By the mid 1980s, however, she was back in public education as a high school assistant principal in charge of student services, staff-student relations, and management. The managerial demands of the assistant principal position enabled this educator to readopt components of the Social Efficiency ideology and add it to her acceptance of the Social Reconstruction and Learner Centered ideologies.

❖ **Figure 7.4**   Life history as a portrayal of internal change.

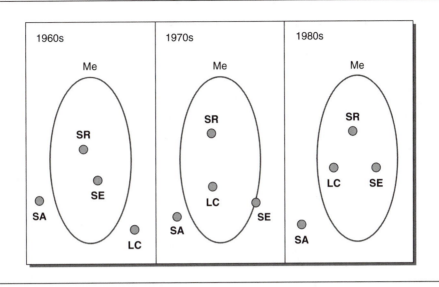

SOURCE: From "Educators' Perceptions of the Changes in Their Curriculum Belief Systems Over Time" by Michael Schiro, in *Journal of Curriculum and Supervision,* Vol. 7, No. 3, pp. 250–286, copyright © 1992. Reprinted with permission from Association of Supervision and Curriculum Development via Copyright Clearance Center.

Figure 7.5 portrays a "life history as a vector analysis of influences on an educator." Between 1962 and 1966, the primary influence on this kindergarten teacher was the Learner Centered ideology (position 1). After changing teaching levels from kindergarten to high school in 1966, the major influences upon her were the Scholar Academic and Learner Centered ideologies, with the Scholar Academic ideology having more influence than the Learner Centered ideology because of the academic orientation of her high school (position 2). In 1968, she became a special education teacher and was heavily influenced by the Social Efficiency ideology (with its accompanying IEPs), even though the Scholar Academic and Learner Centered ideologies continued to assert a minor influence over her (position 3). In 1971, she left teaching for a year to study at a university with a mentor, who influenced her to take a socially active role in addressing the injustices done by schools to special education students. As a result, she became influenced primarily by the Social Reconstruction and Learner Centered ideologies, with a little pull from the Social Efficiency ideology (position 4). Returning to teaching in 1972 and continuing as a special education teacher until 1977, this educator became increasingly influenced by the Learner Centered and Social Efficiency ideologies, and the influence of the Social Reconstruction ideology decreased (position 5). In 1977, she changed her job from teacher to director of special education. She became increasingly influenced by the Social Efficiency ideology as she attended to her management tasks, although the Learner Centered ideology

❖ **Figure 7.5** Life history as a vector analysis of influences on an educator.

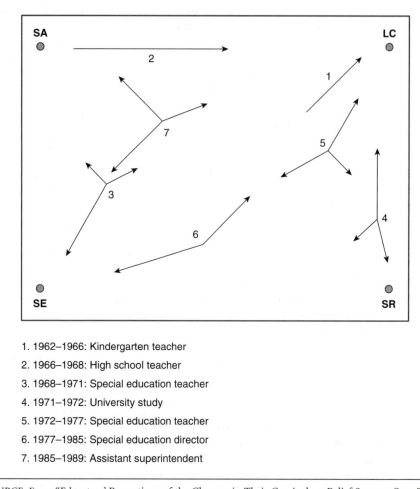

1. 1962–1966: Kindergarten teacher
2. 1966–1968: High school teacher
3. 1968–1971: Special education teacher
4. 1971–1972: University study
5. 1972–1977: Special education teacher
6. 1977–1985: Special education director
7. 1985–1989: Assistant superintendent

SOURCE: From "Educators' Perceptions of the Changes in Their Curriculum Belief Systems Over Time" by Michael Schiro, in *Journal of Curriculum and Supervision*, Vol. 7, No. 3, pp. 250–286, copyright © 1992. Reprinted with permission from Association of Supervision and Curriculum Development via Copyright Clearance Center.

continued to have a large influence over her (position 6). In 1985, she accepted a job as an assistant superintendent, where she had to deal with all students in her school system and not just special education students. Concern for the academic needs of all the children in the school system led her to become increasingly influenced by the Scholar Academic ideology. At the same time the influence of the Social Efficiency ideology decreased, as IEPs mandated by the government for special education students no longer claimed her attention (position 7).

Figures 7.1 through 7.5 illustrate five ways that educators portray how their curriculum ideologies changed during their careers. They have been described as a trip, a set of influences, a composite of ideologies, a portrayal of internal change, and a vector analysis of influences. Inherent in the figures are answers to the following questions: Can people believe in more than one ideology? Do people change their ideologies over time? What forces influence educators to change their ideologies?

Can People Believe in More Than One Ideology?

More Than One Ideology

People would like to believe that they are consistent. However, in everyday life, they frequently hold beliefs that are mutually inconsistent. The inconsistency occurs both at any one point in time and over the span of a career.

During any particular day, the context in which educators find themselves can influence their beliefs. For example, reflect on how a second-grade teacher might instruct the following two children: a second-grader who is having problems learning to read and another second-grader who can read fluently but has problems with comprehension. While dealing with the former, a teacher might believe that phonics is the best instructional approach to reading (with its stress on skills, in the context of the Social Efficiency ideology); in contrast, while dealing with the latter, the teacher might believe whole language instruction provides the best approach to reading (with its stress on meaning construction, from the perspective of the Learner Centered ideology). In this situation, a teacher might rapidly oscillate between the Social Efficiency ideology and the Learner Centered ideology, depending upon his or her assessment of the needs of particular children in the classroom. Consider another example: when teaching mathematics, a teacher might act as a Scholar Academic (and assume that understanding is the most worthwhile type of knowledge), but while teaching history, he or she might act as a Social Reconstructionist (and assume that values are the most worthwhile type of knowledge). In this situation, a teacher might systematically switch ideologies depending on the school subject being taught. A superintendent of schools describes how he rapidly oscillated between ideologies this way:

> In 198[–] I became a superintendent of schools, and my authority, as well as my vision, was broadened. . . . In retrospect, it would seem that any adherence, however temporary, to any curricular ideology was, perhaps, a knee-jerk reaction. When the school committee or community called on me to provide an answer, I moved in the direction of greatest benefit. Some might say that I was a politician in that respect, and I might agree, except that I know that I was running hither and yon just trying to figure out what I was doing. . . . As a budgeter, I heartened to the *Social Efficiency* way of thought; at an elementary PTO meeting, paint me *Learner Centered* with a tinge of *Scholar Academic*; in giving a seminar to high school kids, the *Social Reconstructionist* reigns supreme; and when comforting the high school staff about lack of scholarship in this generation, that old *Scholar Academic* emerges like a taken-for-granted wife. (Schiro, 1992, p. 274).*

---

*From "Educators' Perceptions of the Changes in Their Curriculum Belief Systems Over Time" by Michael Schiro, in *Journal of Curriculum and Supervision*, Vol. 7, No. 3, pp. 250–286, copyright © 1992. Reprinted with permission from Association of Supervision and Curriculum Development via Copyright Clearance Center.

The life history diagrams presented earlier in this chapter illustrate how educators change their beliefs over the span of their careers. Flexible educators usually alter their curriculum beliefs in response to changing social trends and the changing school populations that they serve. One educator expresses his feelings about the beliefs he has held during his career this way:

> I am a chameleon. I often wondered, but I never believed it. . . . I have been called flexible; I have been called adaptable; I have been called a survivor; but I am a chameleon, one who changes (color if one is a lizard) in reaction to situations. . . . I discovered my new self when I traced my life history through the perspective of curriculum ideologies. My span of review encompasses 30 years, and my [life history] diagram reveals more than a few stops at each of the curricular ideologies along the way. . . . I am, perhaps, at this venerable age, understanding for the first time, that there are four (or even more) different approaches to curriculum. More importantly, I, again for the first time, see how each of those approaches, while built of theory, becomes "popular" in response to a societal stance or need. Up to this point, I merely thought that I was altering methodologies in response to student needs, when in fact, I was a victim of society's tugs, my own desire to be continually competent, and a lifelong frustration with sameness. I am a chameleon! (Schiro, 1992, p. 273).

Posture Toward Different Ideologies

Not only do some educators change their curriculum ideologies during a single day or over the span of their careers, but there are also different intellectual postures educators take on the relationships among ideologies that influence both their understanding of their own ideology and how they relate to others who hold different ideologies. Following are brief descriptions of what have been identified as four different positions educators take on the relationships among ideologies:

Dualistic. Educators believe, understand, and value only one ideology, using a dualistic perspective of right versus wrong: those curriculum beliefs that agree with their own are correct and good, and those that are different from their own are incorrect. At one substage, educators see only two sets of curriculum beliefs: those similar to theirs and those that are different. At another substage, educators perceive a variety of different curriculum belief systems, but they still believe, understand, and value only one curriculum belief system from a dualistic perspective.

Relativistic. Educators perceive a variety of curriculum ideologies, and they operate from a relativistic viewpoint that gives equal value to each way of viewing curriculum issues. Here it is held that everyone has a right to his or her own opinion, that no opinion is better than any other, and that curriculum ideologies cannot be measured against any absolute scale of value. From this perspective, educators have the ability to identify and understand the language and images of each curriculum ideology they recognize.

Contextual. Educators perceive a variety of curriculum ideologies, each of which they believe is best for accomplishing certain goals or purposes. Here educators have the ability to express curriculum opinions using the language and images of each ideology they recognize. They switch their ideology depending on the nature of the curriculum task they are engaged in or the ideology of the group or individual with whom they are speaking. Here an ideology is valued because of its utility in accomplishing certain tasks or purposes better than others.

Hierarchical. Educators can differentiate between a variety of well-defined, viable ideologies while making a personal and thoughtful commitment to only one. Educators can use other ideologies to further their endeavors and can hold discourse with other educators who subscribe to different ideologies using their language and images while still advocating their own curriculum beliefs.

Educators who take a relativistic or contextual posture toward the existence of different ideologies can believe in more than one ideology simultaneously and can combine ideologies in unique (and often inconsistent) ways.

Educators who take a hierarchical posture toward the existence of different ideologies can use different ideologies in the service of promoting a single ideology. For example, they might believe primarily in the Social Reconstruction ideology and use the Scholar Academic ideology for certain purposes to promote their ultimate Social Reconstruction ends.

Educators who take a dualistic posture toward the existence of different ideologies tend to hold only one curriculum ideology, and the ideological positions they take correspond fairly closely to the ideological positions presented in this book. Many of the curriculum wars waged by the general public, parents, and politicians—who have no experience as teachers or school administrators—take place because those persons are at the dualistic level of thinking about curriculum issues. The wars over skill-based mathematics versus understanding-based mathematics, and the wars over phonics versus whole language approaches to reading, are usually waged by educators and members of the general public who take a dualistic posture toward the existence of different ideologies.

Why Do Educators Change Ideologies?

Most educators report that they undergo important shifts in their educational philosophies during their careers. Not only do educators report changing their educational beliefs, but they report doing so more frequently than might be expected—on average, about once every 4 years. Despite public opinion to the contrary, most educators are constantly assessing their curriculum beliefs and altering them as a result of their interactions with their world.

Educators report 12 major reasons for ideology change—or 12 types of occurrences that formed turning points in their lives and stimulated a change in curriculum ideology. They are listed here in order of frequency of occurrence:

1. A change in the school in which an educator works

2. A change in the grade level with which an educator works

3. Addressing or responding to the needs of the children or community served

4. A change from one type of administrative job to another (for example, moving from being a school principal to being an assistant superintendent)

5. Attending graduate school

6. Significant life events (such as having a child, confronting the death of a loved one, or divorce)

7. A change in occupation from teaching to administration

8. Confrontation of the realities of teaching or administration

9. Temporary interruption of one's career (to be a full-time mother, work in business, or travel abroad, for example)

10. Responding to social trends or sociopolitical occurrences (these include education-based social trends, such as the popularity of whole language, or sociopolitical events, such as a war)

11. A change from one type of teaching job to another (for example, moving from being a classroom teacher to being a special education teacher)

12. Working with an influential mentor (often for several years)

Other reasons reported for ideology change, with a small percentage of occurrence, include such things as a change in the academic subject taught, becoming comfortable with oneself as a teacher, taking a sabbatical, a change in school principal or superintendent, and a significant religious experience. These reasons for change are interdependent and cannot be treated as independent variables. Several of these reasons for change in ideology need discussion.

The most frequently mentioned event that precipitates a change in ideology is the changing of the school or school system in which an educator works. About 16% of reported ideology changes have been linked to a change in school or school system. While a change in school or school system may not have been the direct cause of an educator's change in ideology in these cases, it was identified as the factor resulting in a change in ideology. This is because a change in school or school system can place an educator in a situation where a new group of children or a new school community must be dealt with, a new grade must be taught, or a new occupational role must be assumed (such as when a teacher becomes an administrator).

The second most frequent reason given for changing curriculum ideology is a change in the grade taught. About 13% of reported ideology changes have been linked to such a change. Examination of ideology life histories seems to indicate that moving from teaching a lower grade to teaching a higher grade pushes teachers to adopt aspects of the Scholar Academic ideology. The reverse (moving from a higher to a lower grade) nudges teachers to adopt aspects of the Learner Centered ideology.

Responding to the needs of the children or community served is the third most frequent reason given for a change in ideology. This includes working in a school that has a changing student population (as has occurred in many urban areas over the last 40 years), changing the type of children one teaches (for example, shifting from regular to special education), visiting children's homes and families, and dealing with parental pressure. About 12% of reported ideology changes have been linked to educators' responding to the needs of the children or community served. Its frequency supports our current understanding of the complex ways that American schools are responsive to, embody, and reflect both the general culture and the local communities in which they are located.

Taken together, these three change factors—school change, grade change, and response to children's or community needs—reportedly account for more than 40% of the reasons why educators change their ideologies. The school system an educator works in (and the beliefs of the superintendent leading that organization), the school environment an educator works in (and the principal heading that school), the grade level an educator teaches (and the other teachers teaching at that grade level), and the children and community with whom an educator works exert powerful social, political, and ideological influences on an educator's curriculum ideology. The normal, everyday curriculum and instructional expectations and atmospheres in which educators work are the "hidden curriculum" of schools for teachers. When a change takes place in these things, the educators confronting the changes frequently face turning points in their lives that leave them open to change in their curriculum and instructional beliefs. Stability of the everyday relationships and expectations in educators' lives enables them to maintain an ideological stance. Changes in ordinary working relationships and expectations that educators confront stimulate change in their curriculum and instructional belief systems.

Three other observations about the events that stimulate educators to change their ideologies deserve mention.

First, most school administrators change their ideology upon moving from teaching to administration. About 80% of school administrators report such a change. In addition, most of the changes in ideology are toward the Social Efficiency ideology, as administrators take on the duties of management.

Second, about 25% of educators report that their first change in ideology was due to their confronting the realities of teaching, which include such things as classroom control issues, appropriate grade level content, the limits on teacher time and energy, the expectations of principals and fellow teachers, and external pressures from such things as state-mandated achievement testing. New teachers need to expect that the realities of teaching will exert pressure on them to change their ideology.

Third, about 10% of educators report that events that occur outside their professional lives stimulate them to change their educational philosophies. These personal events include having children, having children enter school, marriage, divorce, midlife crisis, death of a close relative, and a close call with death. This reason for change in beliefs is particularly important because it points out that educators' personal and professional lives cannot be treated as completely disjoint realities. An educator who is aware of the personal events occurring in an another educator's life can direct the energy generated from personal turmoil toward helping that individual change his or her curriculum and instructional beliefs, if this is desired. Either fortunately or unfortunately, we tend to excuse educators who are undergoing significant changes in their personal lives from professional growth rather than to see changes in personal lives as facilitators of professional growth.

Understanding these influences on ideological change can help educators comprehend some of the pressures they are likely to face as they traverse their professional lives. For example, a change in ideology is likely when one changes the school one works in or the grade one teaches.

Understanding these influences on ideological change can also help educators direct their own careers and facilitate the growth of others. Three examples—one involving a teacher, one involving a school principal, and one involving a school superintendent—illustrate this. Upon learning about these ideologies, one teacher realized that she was unhappy in the school in which she was teaching because the dominant ideology of the school was Social Efficiency while her ideology was Learner Centered. She had the courage to resign from that school, search for a teaching position in a school that was "friendly" to her ideology, and take a teaching position in a school in which the dominant ideology was a combination of Learner Centered and Scholar Academic. She was much happier in her new school than she had been in her old one (Cotti & Schiro, 2004). A school principal reported moving teachers from one grade level to another to facilitate and support their growth. And a school superintendent reported moving a principal from one school to another to stimulate the development of his educational philosophy.

Concluding Perspective

Life span psychology asserts that as most adults confront the realities of their personal lives, they grow through a series of crises. What occurs in the personal lives of adults also occurs in the professional lives of educators.

Most educators who are sensitive and responsive to the professional environment in which they work confront numerous philosophical and ideological crises as they traverse their careers. I hope they will have the courage to deal with the crises with an attitude that allows them to welcome changes in their beliefs about education. There is nothing wrong with learning, growing, and changing in response to the events that we confront as we live our lives. Usually this involves no more than welcoming for ourselves the same things that we hope for our students.

In America today, four visions of what good education involves are actively vying for influence over our educational system, as they have during the last century. As we traverse the future, different visions will surely exert pressure on each of us in different ways at different times in our lives as we interact with different groups of people, as we do different types of jobs, and as social, economic, political, and cultural forces influence the direction of our society.

I hope the discussion in this book will provide readers with an understanding of the philosophical visions they will surely confront in the future, a perspective on the ideological landscape they will need to navigate in the future, and a perspective on the ideological pressures for change to which they will have to respond.

I hope the discussion in this book will provide readers with an understanding of their own visions for education, a perspective on how their visions relate to the other visions that are active in shaping the future of our schools, and a perspective on how their professional thoughts might evolve over time.

I hope the discussion in this book will provide readers with not only an understanding of the multiple languages that educators speak and the ability to speak in each of those languages, but also a perspective on how the visions we have for education influence the meaning we give to words and how the ways in which we use language can influence our actions in the present and our visions for the future.

I also hope the ideas in this book will provide readers with a perspective on both the field of curriculum and their own beliefs, a perspective that will enable them to shape their own visions for the future of American education. And I hope this perspective will provide educators with the personal insights and power they need to make themselves into the people they want to be as they confront the multiple visions for the future of education that compete for their allegiance.

Activities that extend the ideas in this chapter are located on the Sage Web site at www.sagepub.com/schiroextensionactivities.

Appendix

Curriculum Ideologies Inventory

dditional copies of the curriculum ideologies inventory and its graphing sheet can be found on the Sage Web site at www.sagepub.com/schiroextensionactivities.

Instructions

In each of the following sections you will find four statements with a blank in front of each. Read each statement carefully and then rank the statements from 1 to 4, placing:

1 next to the statement that you like most

2 next to the statement that you like second most

3 next to the statement that you like third most

4 next to the statement that you dislike the most

Use each of the numbers (1, 2, 3, and 4) only once in each part of the inventory. Place the numbers on the lines to the left of each statement. This is not a test. There is no one right answer. Take your time.

Part 1

_____ Schools should provide children with the ability to perceive problems in society, envision a better society, and act to change society so that there is social justice and a better life for all people.

_____ Schools should fulfill the needs of society by efficiently training youth to function as mature constructive members of society.

_____ Schools should be communities where the accumulated knowledge of the culture is transmitted to the youth.

_____ Schools should be enjoyable, stimulating, child-centered environments organized around the developmental needs and interests of children as those needs and interests present themselves from day to day.

Part 2

_____ Teachers should be supervisors of student learning, utilizing instructional strategies that will optimize student learning.

_____ Teachers should be companions to students, using the environment within which the student lives to help the student learn.

_____ Teachers should be aids to children, helping them learn by presenting them with experiences from which they can make meaning.

_____ Teachers should be knowledgeable people, transmitting that which is known to those who do not know it.

Part 3

_____ Learning best proceeds when the student is presented with the appropriate stimulus materials and positive reinforcement.

_____ Learning best proceeds when the teacher clearly and accurately presents to the student that knowledge which the student is to acquire.

_____ Learning best takes place when children are motivated to actively engage in experiences which allow them to create their own knowledge and understanding of the world in which they live.

_____ Learning best occurs when a student confronts a real social crisis and participates in the construction of a solution to that crisis.

Part 4

_____ The knowledge of most worth is the structured knowledge and ways of thinking that have come to be valued by the culture over time.

_____ The knowledge of most worth is the personal meaning of oneself and of one's world that comes from one's direct experience in the world and one's personal response to such experience.

_____ The knowledge of most worth is the specific skills and capabilities for action that allow an individual to live a constructive life.

_____ The knowledge of most worth is a set of social ideals, a commitment to those ideals, and an understanding of how to implement those ideals.

Part 5

_____ Childhood is essentially a time of learning in preparation for adulthood, when one will be a constructive, contributing member of society.

_____ Childhood is essentially a period of intellectual development highlighted by growing reasoning ability and capacity for memory that results in ever greater absorption of cultural knowledge.

_____ Childhood is essentially a time when children unfold according to their own innate natures, felt needs, organic impulses, and internal timetables. The focus is on children as they are during childhood rather than as they might be as adults.

_____ Childhood is essentially a time for practice in and preparation for acting upon society to improve both oneself and the nature of society.

Part 6

_____ Evaluation should objectively indicate to others whether or not students can or cannot perform specific skills. Its purpose is to certify students' competence to perform specific tasks.

_____ Evaluation should continuously diagnose children's needs and growth so that further growth can be promoted by appropriate adjustment of their learning environment. It is primarily for the children's benefit, not for comparing children with each other or measuring them against predetermined standards.

_____ Evaluation should be a subjective comparison of students' performance with their capabilities. Its purpose is to indicate to both the students and others the extent to which they are living up to their capabilities.

_____ Evaluation should objectively determine the amount of knowledge students have acquired. It allows students to be ranked from those with the greatest intellectual gain to those with the least.

Graphing the Results of the Inventory

Graphing the results of the inventory involves two steps using the curriculum ideologies inventory graphing sheet (Figure A.1). First, transfer responses from the inventory to the sorting form (found under the graph). Second, transfer the data from the sorting form to the graph.

To transfer responses from the inventory to the sorting form, write the numbers from each part of the inventory on the lines next to the letters in the corresponding part of the sorting form *in the same order* in which they were recorded in each part of the questionnaire. For example, if the numbers next to the statements in Part 1 of the inventory are 3, 2, 4, and 1, reading from top to bottom, record the sequence 3, 2, 4, 1 from top to bottom on the lines next to the letters in Part 1 of the sorting form. The letters and numbers will then be paired thus: C-3, D-2, A-4, and B-1. (See Figure A.2.)

The next step is to transfer data from the sorting form to the graph. First, for each part of the sorting form, place a large dot in the middle of the corresponding cell in the graph; that is, place the dot in the cell that matches the letter-number pair in the sorting form. For example, if Part 1 of the sorting form contains the letter-number pairs C-3, D-2, A-4, and B-1, place large dots in the middle of the following cells under Part 1 of the graph: C-3 (Social Reconstruction), D-2 (Social Efficiency), A-4 (Scholar Academic), and B-1 (Learner Centered). Second, connect the dots within each horizontal section of the graph: those within the Scholar Academic (A) section, the Learner Centered (B) section, the Social Reconstruction (C) section, and the Social Efficiency (D) section. See Figure A.3 for an example.

Interpreting the Results of the Inventory

If the line in a section of the graph is high (mostly 1s and 2s), it means that you favor the ideology corresponding to that line. If the line in a section of the graph is low (mostly 3s and 4s), it means that you do not favor the position corresponding to that line. If a line in a section of the graph zigzags from high to low, it means you have mixed feelings about that position. Figure A.3 provides an example of a graph completed by a person who favors the Learner Centered position, does not favor the Scholar Academic position, and has mixed feeling about the Social Efficiency and Social Reconstruction positions. Note that a person's beliefs do not have to fall entirely within the confines of only one ideological position; the ideological positions described here are ideal types rather than mutually exclusive belief systems.

The inventory presents and contrasts educators' beliefs about instructional purposes, teaching, learning, knowledge, childhood, and evaluation from four ideological positions. To compare beliefs across ideologies in any one of these categories (purposes, teaching, learning, etc.), look at the order of the letters in the sorting form for that category and match them to corresponding statements in the inventory. A's correspond to Scholar Academic, B's to Learner Centered, C's to Social Reconstruction, and D's to Social Efficiency. For example, if the third statement on the sorting form under Part 2 (which has the heading "Teaching") is a B, then the third statement in the inventory (which is about teaching) is the Learner Centered position.

❖ **Figure A.1** Curriculum Ideologies Inventory Graphing Sheet

Graph:

		Part 1 Purpose	Part 2 Teaching	Part 3 Learning	Part 4 Knowledge	Part 5 Childhood	Part 6 Evaluation
Scholar Academic	A-1						
	A-2						
	A-3						
	A-4						
Learner Centered	B-1						
	B-2						
	B-3						
	B-4						
Social Reconstruction	C-1						
	C-2						
	C-3						
	C-4						
Social Efficiency	D-1						
	D-2						
	D-3						
	D-4						

Sorting Form:

Part 1	Part 2	Part 3	Part 4	Part 5	Part 6
C ___	D ___	D ___	A ___	D ___	D ___
D ___	C ___	A ___	B ___	A ___	B ___
A ___	B ___	B ___	D ___	B ___	C ___
B ___	A ___	C ___	C ___	C ___	A ___

❖ **Figure A.2** How to transfer your responses from the inventory to the sorting form.

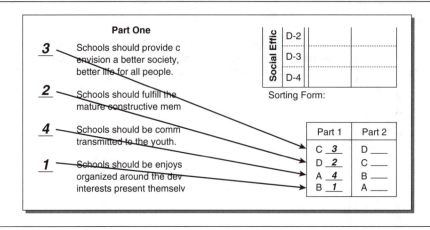

Part One

3
Schools should provide c
envision a better society,
better life for all people.

2
Schools should fulfill the
mature constructive mem

4
Schools should be comm
transmitted to the youth.

1
Schools should be enjoys
organized around the dev
interests present themselv

Social Effic
D-2
D-3
D-4

Sorting Form:

	Part 1	Part 2
C	3	D ___
D	2	C ___
A	4	B ___
B	1	A ___

❖ **Figure A.3** Example of a completed graph for the curriculum ideologies inventory.

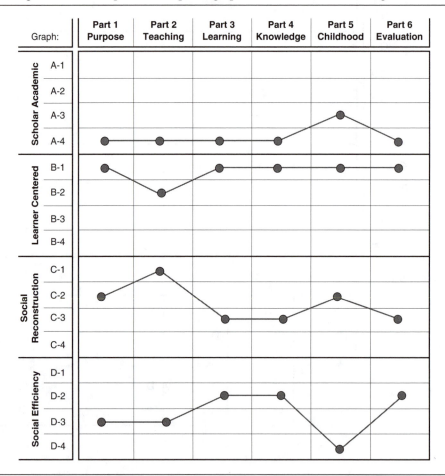

Graph:	Part 1 Purpose	Part 2 Teaching	Part 3 Learning	Part 4 Knowledge	Part 5 Childhood	Part 6 Evaluation

References

Adams, F. (1972). Highlander Folk School: Getting information, going back, and teaching it. *Harvard Educational Review, 42*(4), 497–520.

Adams, F., & Horton, M. (1975). *Unearthing seeds of fire: The idea of Highlander.* Winston-Salem, NC: John F. Wait.

Adler, M. J. (1982). *The paideia proposal: An educational manifesto.* New York: Macmillan.

Aiken, W. M. (1942). *The story of the eight-year study.* New York: Harper.

American Association for the Advancement of Science. (1968). *Science: A process approach.* New York: Xeron.

American Association for the Advancement of Science, Commission on Science Education. (1965). *The psychological bases of science: A process approach.* Washington, DC: American Association for the Advancement of Science.

American Association for the Advancement of Science, Commission on Science Education. (1967a). *Guide for inservice instruction: Science: A process approach* (Miscellaneous Publication 67-9). Washington, DC: American Association for the Advancement of Science.

American Association for the Advancement of Science, Commission on Science Education. (1967b). *Science: A process approach: Purposes, accomplishments, expectations* (Miscellaneous Publication 67-12). Washington, DC: American Association for the Advancement of Science.

American Association for the Advancement of Science, Commission on Science Education. (1968). *Science: A process approach: An evaluation model and its application* (2nd report, Miscellaneous Publication 68-4). Washington, DC: American Association for the Advancement of Science.

Anderson, J. R., Reder, L. M., & Simon, H. A. (1988). Radical constructivism and cognitive psychology. *Brookings papers on education policy: 1988.* Washington, DC: Brookings Institution.

Anderson, J. R., Reder, L. M., & Simon, H. A. (1996). *Applications and misapplications of cognitive psychology to mathematics education.* Retrieved October 22, 2005, from http://act-r.psy.cmu.edu/papers/misapplied.html

Anderson, L. W. (2005). Objectives, evaluation, and the improvement of education. *Studies in Educational Evaluation, 31,* 102–113.

Anderson, L. W., Krathwohl, D. R., Airasian, P. W., Cruikshank, K. A., Mayer, R. E., Pintrich, P. R., et al. (Eds.). (2001). *A taxonomy for learning, teaching, and assessing.* New York: Addison Wesley Longman.

Anderson, S. E. (1997). Worldmath curriculum: Fighting eurocentrism in mathematics. In A. B. Powell & M. Frankenstein (Eds.), *Ethnomathematics: Challenging eurocentrism in mathematics education.* Albany, NY: State University of New York Press.

Anyon, J. (1980). Social class and the hidden curriculum of work [Electronic version]. *Journal of Education, 162*(1), 67–92. Retrieved March 13, 2007, from http://www.scf.usc.edu/~clarkjen/Jean%20Anyon.htm

Apple, M. (1995). *Education and power* (2nd ed.). Boston: Routledge and Kegan Paul.

Apple, M. (1996). *Cultural politics and education.* New York: Teachers College Press.

Apple, M. (2004). *Ideology and curriculum* (3rd ed.). Boston: Routledge and Kegan Paul.

Association for Supervision and Curriculum Development (Ed.). (2005). The whole child. *Educational Leadership, 63*(1).

Atkin, J. M. (1968). Behavioral objectives in curriculum design: A cautionary note. *The Science Teacher, 35,* 27–30.

Baddeley, A. (1986). *Working memory.* Oxford, UK: Clarendon Press.

Barth, R. S. (1972). *Open education and the American school.* New York: Schocken Books and Agathon Press.

Beauchamp, G. A., & Beauchamp, K. E. (1967). *Comparative analysis of curriculum systems.* Wilmette, IL: Kagg Press.

Becker, J., & Jacob, B. (2000). The politics of California school mathematics: The anti-reform of 1997-99. *Phi Delta Kappan, 81*(7), 527–539.

Bell, D. (1966). *The reforming of general education.* New York: Columbia University Press.

Bellack, A. A. (1964). The structure of knowledge and the structure of the curriculum. In D. Huebner (Ed.), *A reassessment of the curriculum.* New York: Teachers College Press.

Bennett, W., Finn, C., & Cribb, J. (1999). *The educated child: A parent's guide from preschool through eighth grade.* New York: Free Press.

Bigelow, B., & Petersen, B. (Eds.). (2005). *Rethinking Columbus.* Milwaukee, WI: Rethinking Schools.

Blackie, J. (1971). *Inside the primary school.* New York: Schocken Books.

Bloom, B. S. (Ed.). (1956). *The taxonomy of educational objectives: Handbook I. Cognitive domain.* New York: McKay.

Bobbitt, F. (1913). Some general principles of management applied to the problems of city school systems. In S. C. Parker (Ed.), *Twelfth yearbook of the National Society for the Study of Education* (Pt. 1). Chicago: University of Chicago Press.

Bobbitt, F. (1918). *The curriculum.* Boston: Riverside Press.

Bobbitt, F. (1920). The objectives of secondary education. *The School Review, 28*(10), 721–749.

Bobbitt, F. (1924a). Education as a social process. *School and Society, 21*(538), 453–459.

Bobbitt, F. (1924b). *How to make a curriculum.* Boston: Houghton Mifflin.

Bobbitt, F. (1924c). The new technique of curriculum making. *The Elementary School Journal, 25*(1), 45–54.

Bobbitt, F. (1924d). What understanding of human society should education develop? *The Elementary School Journal, 25*(4), 292–293.

Bobbitt, F. (1926). *Curriculum investigations.* Chicago: University of Chicago Press.

Bracey, G. W. (2003). *On the death of childhood and the destruction of public schools: The folly of today's education policies and practices.* Portsmouth, NH: Heinemann.

Brameld, T. (1950). *Patterns of educational philosophy.* New York: World Book.

Brameld, T. (1956). *Toward a reconstructed philosophy of education.* New York: Dryden Press.

Bredekamp, S. (Ed.). (1987). *Developmentally appropriate practice in early childhood programs serving children from birth through age 8* [Electronic version retrieved June 15, 2005, from http://www.newhorizons.org/lifelong/childhood/naeyc.html]. Washington, DC: National Association of the Education of Young Children.

Broudy, H. S. (1961). *Building a philosophy of education* (2nd ed.). Englewood Cliffs, NJ: Prentice Hall.

Bruner, J. S. (1960). *The process of education.* Cambridge, MA: Harvard University Press.

Bruner, J. S. (1963). Needed: A theory of instruction. *Educational Leadership, 20*(8), 523–532.

Bruner, J. S. (1966). *Toward a theory of instruction.* Cambridge, MA: Harvard University Press.

Bussis, A., & Cluttenden, E. (1970). *Analysis of an approach to open education.* Princeton, NJ: Educational Testing Service.

Callahan, R. E. (1962). *Education and the cult of efficiency.* Chicago: University of Chicago Press.

Cambridge Conference on School Mathematics. (1963). *Goals for school mathematics: The report of the Cambridge Conference on School Mathematics.* Boston: Houghton Mifflin.

Carini, L. (2005). *The philosophies underlying the prospect descriptive processes.* Retrieved October 25, 2006, from http://www.prospectcenter.org

Carini, P. (2001). *Starting strong: A different look at children, schools, and standards.* New York: Teachers College Press.

Chandler P., Cooper, G., Pollock, E., & Tindall-Ford, S. (1998). *Applying cognitive psychology principles to education and training.* Retrieved October 22, 2005, from http://www.aare.edu.au/98pap/cha98030.htm

Cheney, L. (1988). *American memory: A report on the humanities in the nation's public schools.* Washington, DC: U.S. Government Printing Office.

Coltham, J. B. (1972). Educational accountability: An English experiment and its outcome. *The School Review, 81,* 15–36.

Comenius, J. A. (1896). *The great didactic of John Amos Comenius* (M. W. Keatinge, Trans.). London: Adam and Charles Black. (Original work published 1657)

Connelly, F. M. (1964). Philosophy of science and the science curriculum. *Journal of Research in Science Teaching, 6,* 108–113.

Cotti, R., & Schiro, M. (2004). Connecting teacher beliefs to the use of children's literature in the teaching of mathematics. *Journal of Mathematics Teacher Education, 7*(4), 329–356.

Counts, G. S. (1932a). Dare progressive education be progressive? *Progressive Education, 9*(4), 257–263.

Counts, G. S. (1932b). *Dare the school build a new social order?* New York: John Day.

Counts, G. S. (1934). *The social foundations of education.* New York: Scribner.

Cremin, L. (1961). *Transformation of the school.* New York: Knopf.

Cremin, L. (1977). *Traditions of American education.* New York: Basic Books.

Cruz-Acosta, L. (2006, August). *"Making and Remaking Schools" Comments.* Retrieved March 14, 2007, from http://review.prospectcenter.org/2006/08/louisa_cruzacosta_ making_and_r.html

Davson-Galle, P. (1998). The point of primary education. *Educational Philosophy and Theory, 30*(3), 303–310.

Denzin, N. K. (1989). *Interpretive biography.* Newbury Park, CA: Sage.

Dewey, E., & Dewey, J. (1915). *Schools of tomorrow.* New York: E. P. Dutton.

Dewey, J. (1897). My pedagogic creed. *The School Journal, 54*(3), 77–80.

Dewey, J. (1916). *Democracy and education.* New York: Macmillan.

Dewey, J. (1938/1963). *Experience and education.* New York: Macmillan.

Dewey, J. (1948). *Reconstruction in philosophy.* Boston: Beacon Press.

Duckworth, E. (1987). *"The having of wonderful ideas" and other essays on teaching and learning.* New York: Teachers College Press.

Education Development Center. (1966). *Introduction to the Elementary Science Study.* Newton, MA: Author.

Education Development Center. (1968). *Man: A course of study: Unit 5. Baboons* (Trial teaching ed.). Cambridge, MA: Author.

Education Development Center. (1970). *The ESS reader.* Newton, MA: Author.

Edwards, C. (2002). Three approaches from Europe: Waldorf, Montessori, and Reggio Emilia. *Early Childhood Research & Practice, 4*(1). Retrieved October 22, 2005, from http://www.ecrp.uiuc.edu/v4n1/edwards.html

Eisner, E. (1974). *Conflicting conceptions of curriculum.* Berkeley, CA: McCutchan.

Ellis, A. K. (2004). *Exemplars of curriculum theory.* Larchmont, NY: Eye on Education.

Engel, B. S., & Martin, A. C. (Eds.). (2005). *Holding values: What we mean by progressive education: Essays by members of the North Dakota Study Group.* Portsmouth, NH: Heinemann.

Fayerweather Street School. (n.d.). *Beyond the campus.* Retrieved October 25, 2005, from http://www.fayerweather.org/learning/beyondCampus.asp

Featherstone, J. (1968). A new kind of schooling. *The New Republic, 158*(9), 27–31.

Fenstermacher, G. D. (2001). Educational accountability: Features of the concept. *Theory Into Practice, 18*(5), 330–335.

Fenstermacher, G. D., & Soltis, J. F. (1992). *Approaches to teaching.* New York: Teachers College Press.

Ferris, F. L. (1962). Testing in the new curriculums: Numerology, tyranny, or common sense. *The School Review, 70,* 112–131.

Feuer, M. J., Towne, L., & Shavelson, R. J. (2002). Scientific culture and educational research. *Educational Researcher, 31*(8), 4–14.

Finn, C. (1991). *We must take charge: Our schools and our future.* New York: Free Press.

Finn, C., Julian, L., & Petrilli, M. (2006). *The state of state standards 2006.* Retrieved March 12, 2007, from http://www.edexcellence.net/foundation/publication/publication.cfm?id=358

Foshay, A. W. (1970). How fare the disciplines? *Phi Delta Kappan, 51*(7), 349–352.

Fraser, D. M. (1962). *Current curriculum studies in academic subjects.* Washington, DC: National Education Association.

Freire, P. (1970). *Pedagogy of the oppressed.* New York: Seabury Press.

Freire, P. (1987). *A pedagogy for liberation.* South Hadley, MA: Bergin & Garvey.

Freire, P. (1992). *Pedagogy of hope: Reliving pedagogy of the oppressed.* London: Continuum.

Freire, P. (1997). *Pedagogy of the heart.* New York: Continuum.

Friedrich Froebel time line. (n.d.). Retrieved October 22, 2005 from http://members.tripod.com/~FroebelWeb/webline.html

Gagne, R. M. (1962). The acquisition of knowledge. *Psychological Review, 69*(4), 355–365.

Gagne, R. M. (1963). Learning and proficiency in mathematics. *The Mathematics Teacher, 56*(8), 620–626.

Gagne, R. M. (1965a). The analysis of instructional objectives for the design of instruction. In R. Glaser (Ed.), *Teaching machines and programmed learning: II. Data and directions.* Washington, DC: National Education Association.

Gagne, R. M. (1965b). *The conditions of learning* (1st ed.). New York: Holt, Rinehart &Winston.

Gagne, R. M. (1966). Elementary science: A new scheme of instruction. *Science, 151,* 49–53.

Gagne, R. M. (1967). Curriculum research and the promotion of learning. In R. W. Tyler, R. M. Gagne, & M. Scriven (Eds.), *AERA monograph series on curriculum evaluation: Vol. 1. Perspectives on curriculum evaluation.* Chicago: Rand McNally.

Gagne, R. M. (1970). *The conditions of learning* (2nd ed.). New York: Holt, Rinehart & Winston.

Gandini, L. (2004). Foundations of the Reggio Emilia approach. In J. Hendrick (Ed.), *Next steps toward teaching the Reggio way* (2nd ed.). Upper Saddle River, NJ: Pearson, Merrill, Prentice Hall.

Giroux, H. (1992). *Border crossings: Cultural workers and the politics of education.* New York: Routledge.

Giroux, H. (2005). *Border crossings: Cultural workers and the politics of education* (2nd ed.). New York: Routledge.

Giroux, H. A. (2006). *America on the edge.* New York: Palgrave Macmillan.

Glaser, R. (Ed.). (1965). *Teaching machines and programmed learning: II. Data and directions.* Washington, DC: National Education Association.

Glatthorn, A., Boschee, F., & Whitehead, B. (2005) *Curriculum leadership: Development and implementation.* Thousand Oaks, CA: Sage.

Goodlad, J., Klein, M., & Associates. (1970). *Behind the classroom door.* Worthington, OH: Charles A. Jones.

Greene, M. (1978). *Landscapes of learning.* New York: Teachers College Press.

Greene, M. (1988). *The dialectic of freedom.* New York: Teachers College Press.

Grobman, A. B. (1967). *The changing classroom: The role of the Biological Sciences Curriculum Study.* New York: Teachers College Press.

Gutstein, E. (2005). Real world projects: Seeing math around us. In E. Gutstein & B. Peterson (Eds.), *Rethinking mathematics: Teaching social justice by the numbers.* Milwaukee, WI: Rethinking Schools.

Gutstein, E., & Peterson, B. (Eds.). (2005). *Rethinking mathematics: Teaching social justice by the numbers.* Milwaukee, WI: Rethinking Schools.

Hanson, D., Durton, D., & Guam, G. (2006). Six concepts to help you align with NCLB. *The Technology Teacher, 66*(1), 17–20.

Harvard Project Physics. (1969). *Harvard Project Physics: Newsletter 1.* Cambridge, MA: Author.

Hawkins, D. (1965/1970). Messing about in science. In Education Development Center (Ed.), *The ESS reader* (pp. 37–44). Newton, MA: Education Development Center.

Hein, G. E. (1975). *Open education: An overview.* Newton, MA: Education Development Center.

Hein, G. E. (2005). A progressive education perspective on evaluation. In B. S. Engel & A. C. Martin (Eds.), *Holding values: What we mean by progressive education: Essays by members of the North Dakota Study Group.* Portsmouth, NH: Heinemann.

Hendrick, J. (Ed.). (2004). *Next steps toward teaching the Reggio way* (2nd ed.). Upper Saddle River, NJ: Pearson, Merrill, Prentice Hall.

Hersh, S., & Peterson, B. (2005). Poverty and world health: Recognizing inequality. In E. Gutstein & B. Peterson (Eds.), *Rethinking mathematics: Teaching social justice by the numbers.* Milwaukee, WI: Rethinking Schools.

Hirsch, E. D. (1987). *Cultural literacy.* Boston: Houghton Mifflin.

Holland, J. G. (1960). Teaching machines: An application of principles from the laboratory. *Journal of the Experimental Analysis of Behavior, 3,* 275–287.

Horton, M. (1936, January). The Highlander Folk School. *The Social Frontier,* pp. 117–118.

Horton, M. (1966). An interview with Myles Horton: "It's a miracle—I still don't believe it . . ."*Phi Delta Kappan, 47*(9), 490–497.

Huebner, D. (Ed.). (1964). *A reassessment of the curriculum.* New York: Teachers College Press.

Hutchins, R. M. (1936). *The higher learning in America.* New Brunswick, NJ: Transaction.

Jackson, A. (1997a). The math wars: California battles it out over mathematics education (Pt. I). *Notices of the American Mathematical Society, 44*(6), 695–702.

Jackson, A. (1997b). The math wars: California battles it out over mathematics education (Pt. II). *Notices of the American Mathematical Society, 44*(7), 817–823.

Jacobs, J. (2006). It takes a vision. In C. Finn, L. Julian, & M. Petrilli (Eds.), *The state of state standards 2006.* Retrieved March 12, 2007, from http://www.edexcellence.net/foundation/publication/publication.cfm?id=358

Jersild, A. T. (1946). *Child development and the curriculum.* New York: Teachers College Press.

Johnson, M. (n.d.). *Organic education.* Fairhope, AL: Marietta Johnson Museum of Organic Education.

Johnson, M. (1926). The educational principles of the School of Organic Education, Fairhope, Alabama. In G. M. Whipple (Ed.), *Twenty-sixth yearbook of the National Society for the Study of Education* (Pt. 2). Bloomington, IL: Public School Publishing Company.

Johnson, M. (1974). *Thirty years with an idea: The story of organic education.* University: University of Alabama Press.

Joseph, P., Bravmann, S., Windschitl, M., Mikel, E., & Green, N. (2000). *Cultures of curriculum.* Mahwah, NJ: Lawrence Erlbaum.

Keynes, H. B. (1995). Can equity thrive in a culture of mathematical excellence? In W. G. Secada, E. Fennema, & L. B. Adajian (Eds.), *New direction for equity in mathematics education.* Cambridge, UK: Cambridge University Press.

Kilpatrick, W. H. (1918). *The project method.* New York: Teachers College Press.

Kilpatrick, W. H. (1934). Launching the social frontier. *The Social Frontier, 1*(1), 2.

King, A. R., & Brownell, J. A. (1966). *The curriculum and the disciplines of knowledge.* New York: Wiley.

Kliebard, H. (2004). *The struggle for the American curriculum: 1893–1958.* New York: Taylor & Francis.

Krathwohl, D. R., Bloom, B. S., & Masia, B. B. (1964). *The taxonomy of educational objectives: Handbook II. Affective domain.* New York: McKay.

Krug, E. A. (1969). *The shaping of the American high school: 1880–1920.* Madison: University of Wisconsin Press.

Ladson-Billings, G. (1995). Making mathematics meaningful in multicultural contexts. In W. G. Secada, E. Fennema, & L. B. Adajian (Eds.), *New direction for equity in mathematics education.* Cambridge, UK: Cambridge University Press.

Lauber, E., Robinson, A., Kim, S., & Davis R. (2001). *The World Wide Web cognitive psychology tutor.* Retrieved October 22, 2005, from http://teach.psy.uga.edu/CogPsychTutor

Leeper, R. R. (Ed.). (1966). *Language and meaning.* Washington, DC: Association for Supervision and Curriculum Development.

Leitman, A. (1968). Travel agent. In Association for Childhood Education International (Ed.), *Housing for early childhood education, Bulletin No. 22-A.* Washington, DC: Association for Childhood Education International.

Lessinger, L. (1970). *Every kid a winner: Accountability in education.* Palo Alto, CA: Science Research Associates.

Lessinger, L. (1971). Accountability for results: A basic challenge for America's schools. In L. Lessinger & R. Tyler (Eds.), *Accountability in education.* Worthington, OH: Charles A. Jones.

Lessinger, L., & Salowe, A. (2001). *Healing public schools.* Lanham, MD: Scarecrow Press.

Lindvall, C. M., & Bolvin, J. O. (1967). Programmed instruction in the schools: An application of programming principles in "individually prescribed instruction." In P. C. Lange (Ed.), *Sixty-sixth yearbook of the National Society for the Study of Education: Pt. 2. Programmed instruction.* Chicago: University of Chicago Press.

Locke, J. (1690/1995). *An essay concerning human understanding.* Amherst, NY: Prometheus Books.

Lye, J. (1997). *Ideology: A brief guide.* Retrieved October 22, 2005, from http://www.brocku.ca/english/jlye/ideology.html

MacDonald, J. B., & Leeper, R. R. (Eds.). (1966). *Language and meaning.* Washington, DC: Association for Supervision and Curriculum Development.

Mager, R. F. (1962). *Preparing instructional objectives* (1st ed.). Palo Alto, CA: Fearon.

Marshall, J. D., Sears, J. T., & Schubert, W. H. (2000). *Turning points in curriculum: A contemporary American memoir.* Upper Saddle River, NJ: Merrill.

Martin, D. T., Overholt, G. E., & Urban, W. J. (1976). *Accountability in American education.* Princeton, NJ: Princeton Book Company.

Mayhew, K. C., & Edwards, A. C. (1966). *The Dewey School.* New York: Atherton Press.

McLaren, P. (1997). *Revolutionary multiculturalism: Pedagogies of dissent for the new millennium.* Boulder, CO: Westview Press.

McLaren, P. (2007). *Life in schools: An introduction to critical pedagogy in the foundations of education* (5th ed.). New York: Longman.

McLaren, P., & Giroux, H. (1997). Writing from the margins: Geographies of identity, pedagogy, and power. In P. McLaren, *Revolutionary multiculturalism: Pedagogies of dissent for the new millennium.* Boulder, CO: Westview Press.

McNeil, J. D. (1977). *Curriculum: A comprehensive introduction.* Boston: Little, Brown.

Monroe, P., & Thorndike, E. L. (1911). Research within the field of education: Its organization and encouragement. *The School Review Monographs: No. I.* Chicago: University of Chicago Press.

Morrison, P. (1964/1970). The curricular triangle and its style. In Education Development Center (Ed.), *The ESS reader* (pp. 99–112). Newton, MA: Education Development Center.

Mumford, L. (1933). *The story of utopias.* London: Liveright.

National Commission on Excellence in Education. (1983). *A nation at risk.* Washington, DC: U.S. Government Printing Office.

National Education Association. (1893). *Report of the committee of ten on secondary schools* [Electronic version retrieved October 22, 2005, from http://tmh.floonet.net/books/commoften/mainrpt.html]. New York: American Book Company.

National Research Council. (1989). *Everybody counts: A report to the nation on the future of mathematics education.* Washington, DC: National Academy Press.

Nelson, D., Joseph, G. G., & Williams, J. (1993). *Multicultural mathematics.* Oxford, UK: Oxford University Press.

Noddings, N. (2003). *Happiness and education.* Cambridge, UK: Cambridge University Press.

Noddings, N. (2005a). Identifying and responding to needs in education. *Cambridge Journal of Education, 35*(2), 147–159.

Noddings, N. (2005b). What does it mean to educate the whole child? *Educational Leadership, 63*(1), 8–13.

Novick, R. (1996). *Developmentally appropriate and culturally responsive education: Theory in practice.* Retrieved October 22, 2005, from www.nwrel.org/cfc/publications/DAP2.html

Null, J., & Ravitch, D. (2006). *Forgotten heroes of American Education.* Greenwich, CT: Information Age.

Parker, C. S. (1912). The present status of education as a science. *The School Review Monographs: No. II.* Chicago: University of Chicago Press.

Parker, F. W. (1894/1964). *Talks on pedagogics.* New York: John Day.

Patty, W. L. (1938). *A study of mechanism in education: An examination of the curriculum-making devices of Franklin Bobbitt, W. W. Charters, and C. C. Peters, from the point of view of relativistic pragmatism.* New York: Teachers College Press.

Pearson, P. D. (2004). The reading wars. *Educational Policy, 18*(1), 216–253.

Peddiwell, J. A. (1939). *The saber-tooth curriculum.* New York: McGraw-Hill.

Pestalozzi, J. H. (1801/1898). *How Gertrude teaches her children.* Syracuse, NY: C. W. Bardeen.

Peters, C. C. (1930a). *Foundations of educational sociology.* New York: Macmillan.

Peters, C. C. (1930b). *Objectives and procedures in civic education.* New York: Longmans, Green.

Peterson, B. (2005). Teaching math across the curriculum. In E. Gutstein & B. Peterson (Eds.), *Rethinking mathematics: Teaching social justice by the numbers.* Milwaukee, WI: Rethinking Schools.

Phenix, P. H. (1962). The disciplines as curriculum content. In A. H. Passow (Ed.), *Curriculum crossroads.* New York: Teachers College Press.

Phenix, P. H. (1964). The architectonics of knowledge. In S. Elam (Ed.), *Education and the structure of knowledge.* Chicago: Rand McNally.

Phenix, P. H. (1966). Curriculum and the analysis of language. In J. B. MacDonald & R. R. Leeper (Eds.), *Language and meaning.* Washington, DC: Association for Supervision and Curriculum Development.

Piaget, J. (1973). *To understand is to invent.* New York: Grossman.

Plowden, B. (1967). *Children and their primary schools: A report of the central advisory council for education.* London: HMSO.

Posner, G. J. (1992). *Analyzing the curriculum.* New York: McGraw-Hill.

Postman, N., & Weingartner, C. (1969). *Teaching as a subversive activity.* New York: Delacorte Press.

Powell, A. B., & Frankenstein, M. (Eds.). (1997). *Ethnomathematics: Challenging eurocentrism in mathematics education.* Albany: State University of New York Press.

Prospect Center. (n.d.). [Web site]. Retrieved October 24, 2006, from http://www.prospectcenter .org

Quirk, B. (2005). *The anti-content mindset: The root cause of the "math wars."* Retrieved October 22, 2005, from http://www.wgquirk.com/content.html

Rathbone, C. H. (1971). The implicit rationale of the open education classroom. In C. H. Rathbone (Ed.), *Open education: The informal classroom.* New York: Citation Press.

Ravitch, D. (2000a). *Left back: A century of battles over school reform.* New York: Simon & Schuster.

Ravitch, D. (2000b). *The American reader.* New York: HarperCollins.

Ravitch, D., & Viteritti, J. (2001). *Making good citizens.* New Haven, CT: Yale University Press.

Resource Center for Redesigning Education. (1993). *Student directed learning: The Alpha Program.* Brandon, VT: Author.

Rousseau, J. J. (1979). *Emile* (A. Bloom, Trans.). New York: Basic Books. (Original work published 1762)

Rugg, H. O. (1927). The foundations and techniques of curriculum construction. In G. M. Whipple (Ed.), *Twelfth yearbook of the National Society for the Study of Education* (Pts. 1–2). Bloomington, IL: Public School Publishing Company.

Rugg, H. O. (1936–1938). *Man and his changing society* (Vols. 1–8). New York: Ginn.

Rugg, H. O., & Shumaker, A. (1928). *The child-centered school.* New York: World Book.

Ryle, G. (1949). *The concept of mind.* London: Hutchinson.

Schiro, M. (1978). *Curriculum for better schools: The great ideological debate.* Englewood Cliffs, NJ: Educational Technology.

Schiro, M. (1992). Educators' perceptions of the changes in their curriculum belief systems over time. *Journal of Curriculum and Supervision, 7*(3), 250–286.

Schiro, M. (2004). *Oral storytelling and teaching mathematics.* Thousand Oaks, CA: Sage.

Schoenfeld, A. (2004). The math wars. *Educational Policy, 18*(1), 253–286.

School Mathematics Study Group. (1962). *Mathematics for the elementary school, Grade 4: Student's text* (Pt. 2). New Haven: Yale University Press.

Schubert, W. H. (1986). *Curriculum: Perspective, paradigm, and possibility.* New York: Macmillan.

Schubert, W. H. (1987). Foundations of curriculum and program design. *Teaching Education, 1*(1), 88–91.

Schubert, W. H. (1996, Summer). Perspectives on four curriculum traditions. *Educational Horizons,* pp. 169–176.

Schultz, A. (2006, January). The reform movement: Was it good for you? *Techniques: Connecting Education and Careers,* pp. 44–45.

Schwab, J. J. (1958). On the corruption of education by psychology. *The School Review, 67,*169–184.

Schwab, J. J. (1962). The concept of the structure of a discipline. *The Educational Record, 43*(3), 197–205.

Schwab, J. J. (1964a). Problems, topics, and issues. In S. Elam (Ed.), *Education and the structure of knowledge.* Chicago: Rand McNally.

Schwab, J. J. (1964b). The structure of the natural sciences. In G.W. Ford & L. Pagno (Eds.), *The structure of knowledge and the curriculum.* Chicago: Rand McNally.

Sealey, L. G. W. (1966). Looking back on Leicestershire. In *ESS Quarterly Report, Spring-Summer.* Newton, MA: Education Development Center.

Secada, W. G., Fennema, E., & Adajian, L. B. (Eds.). (1995). *New direction for equity in mathematics education.* Cambridge, UK: Cambridge University Press.

Seguel, M. L. (1966). *The curriculum field: Its formative years.* New York: Teachers College Press.

Shulman, L. S. (1968). Psychological controversies in the teaching of science and mathematics. *The Science Teacher, 35*(6), 34–38, 89–90.

Silver, E, A., Smith, M. S., & Nelson, B. S. (1995). The QUASAR project: Equity concerns meet mathematics education reform in the middle school. In W. G. Secada, E. Fennema, & L. B. Adajian (Eds.), *New direction for equity in mathematics education.* Cambridge, UK: Cambridge University Press.

Sizer, T. R. (1964). *Secondary schools at the turn of the century.* New Haven, CT: Yale University Press.

St. Pierre, E. A. (2006). Scientifically based research in education: Epistemology and ethics. *Adult Education Quarterly, 56*(4), 239–266.

Sudbury Valley School. (n.d.-a). [Web site]. Retrieved October 22, 2006, from http://www.sudval.org

Sudbury Valley School. (n.d.-b). *Independence: Creating leaders.* Retrieved April 10, 2007, from http://www.sudval.org/01_abou_01.html

Sudbury Valley School. (n.d.-c). *Involvement: The day at Sudbury Valley.* Retrieved April 9, 2007, from http://www.sudval.org/01_abou_02.html

Sunburst Technology. (2001). *Type to learn 3* [Computer software]. Valhalla, NY: Author.

Tanner, D., & Tanner, L. (1989). *History of the school curriculum.* New York: Macmillan.

Taylor, F. W. (1911). *Principles of scientific management.* New York: Harper.

The Teaching Commission. (2004). *Teaching at risk: A call to action.* Retrieved March 14, 2007, from http://www.csl.usf.edu/teaching%20at%20risk.pdf

Tyler, R. W. (1949). *Basic principles of curriculum and instruction.* Chicago: University of Chicago Press.

Vygotsky, L. S. (1979). Consciousness as a problem in the psychology of behavior. *Soviet Psychology, 17*(4), 3–35.

Walberg, H. (1984). Improving the productivity of America's schools. *Educational Leadership, 41*(8), 19–27.

Walberg, H. J., & Thomas, S. C. (1971). *Characteristics of open education: Toward an operational definition.* Newton, MA: Educational Development Center.

Ward, L. F. (1883). *Dynamic sociology.* New York: Appleton.

Ward, L. F. (1893). *The psychic factors of civilization.* Boston: Ginn.

Watson, G. (1934). Education is the social frontier. *The Social Frontier, 1*(1), 22.

Weber, L. (1971). *The English infant school and informal education.* Englewood Cliffs, NJ: Prentice Hall.

Weiler, K. (2004, Spring). What can we learn from progressive education? *Radical Teacher.* Retrieved March 14, 2007, from http://www.findarticles.com/p/articles/mi_m0JVP/is_69/ai_n6146721

Whitefield, R. C. (Ed.). (1971). *Disciplines of the curriculum.* London: McGraw-Hill.

Who Is Francis W. Parker? (n.d.). Retrieved October 22, 2005, from http://www.parker.org/WhoAreWe/who_is_francis_w_parker.htm

Wikipedia. (n.d.). *Ideology.* Retrieved October 22, 2005, from http://en.wikipedia.org/wiki/Ideology#History_of_the_concept_of_ideology

Wilson, S. M. (2003). *California dreaming: Reforming mathematics education.* New Haven, CT: Yale University Press.

Yecke, C. (2003). *The war against excellence.* Westport, CT: Praeger.

Zeichner, K. M. (1993). Traditions of practice in U.S. preservice teacher education. *Teaching and Teacher Education, 9*(1), 1–13.

Index

About the Author ❖

Michael Stephen Schiro was born and raised in Washington, DC. He was a mathematics major at Tufts University, with minors in philosophy and English. He taught at the high school, middle school, and elementary school levels in Massachusetts, North Carolina, and Pennsylvania. He received his master's and doctorate from Harvard University in curriculum and instruction. He has taught courses on curriculum theory and mathematics education at Boston College for the last 30 years. He has published four books that explore ways of enriching the teaching of mathematics. His last book, also published by Sage Publications, is entitled *Oral Storytelling and Teaching Mathematics*. He resides in Newton, Massachusetts, and Mendocino, California. He has two children, Stephanie and Arthur. His current hobbies include writing children's novels, collecting puzzles that can be used in the teaching of mathematics, and walking in forests and next to the ocean.